WESTMAR COLLEGE

O9-ABG-879

The Center for South and Southeast Asia Studies of the University of California is the unifying organization for faculty members and students interested in South and Southeast Asia Studies, bringing together scholars from numerous disciplines. The Center's major aims are the development and support of research and the language study. As part of this program the Center sponsors a publication series of books concerned with South and Southeast Asia. Manuscripts are considered from all campuses of the University of California as well as from any other individuals and institutions doing research in these areas.

PUBLICATIONS OF THE CENTER FOR SOUTH AND SOUTHEAST ASIA STUDIES

Eugene F. Irschick
Politics and Social Conflict in South India: The Non-Brahman Movement and Tamil Separatism, 1916–1929 (1969)

Robert L. Hardgrave, Jr.
Nadars of Tamilnad: The Political Culture of a Community in Change (1969)

Briton Martin, Jr.
New India, 1885: British Official Policy and the Emergence of the Indian National Congress (1969)

James T. Siegel
The Rope of God (1969)

78519

OPPOSITION IN A DOMINANT-PARTY SYSTEM

THIS VOLUME IS SPONSORED BY THE
CENTER FOR SOUTH AND SOUTHEAST ASIA STUDIES,
UNIVERSITY OF CALIFORNIA, BERKELEY

OPPOSITION IN A DOMINANT-PARTY SYSTEM

A STUDY OF THE JAN SANGH,
THE PRAJA SOCIALIST PARTY,
AND THE SOCIALIST PARTY
IN UTTAR PRADESH, INDIA

Angela Sutherland Burger

UNIVERSITY OF CALIFORNIA PRESS

Berkeley and Los Angeles 1969

329.954
B954

JQ
299
.U83
B86

UNIVERSITY OF CALIFORNIA PRESS / BERKELEY AND LOS ANGELES, CALIFORNIA

UNIVERSITY OF CALIFORNIA PRESS, LTD. / LONDON, ENGLAND

COPYRIGHT © 1969, BY THE REGENTS OF THE UNIVERSITY OF CALIFORNIA

LIBRARY OF CONGRESS CATALOG CARD NUMBER: 77-76540

PRINTED IN THE UNITED STATES OF AMERICA

TO VIRGINIA AND HENRY C. HART

_____

PREFACE

VERY LITTLE has been written about the three political parties studied here. In the past there was scant reason to do so. They were small opposition parties in a system dominated by the Indian National Congress. The fourth general elections, in 1967, changed that. The Congress declined markedly in strength. In Uttar Pradesh—the locus of this study—the three parties allied with several others to form the Government. They are no longer opposition parties.

The changed situation does not reduce the value of this study, for two reasons. First, being concerned mainly with comparative rather than area politics, I made a considerable effort to identify factors, develop categories, and draw up hypotheses which would have general import. The hypotheses tested on these parties in Uttar Pradesh can be tested in other dominant-party systems.

Secondly, the changed political situation in Uttar Pradesh raises questions about the former minority parties and the causes for their rise in strength. In this respect I am able to offer analyses of the social, economic, and political forces utilized in party building, set forth problems of party maintenance, and provide background information on the state legislators elected in 1962.

This study was undertaken in 1963–1964. A large part of the data was obtained in interviews with politicians of Uttar Pradesh. State legislators, party organizational leaders, and activists in districts, towns, and villages gave their time freely to explain facets of Indian politics. Without their great hospitality and frankness, the study could not have been made. Among the members of various parties to whom I am particularly grateful are Nanajii Deshmukh, Rajendra Kumar, Babu Lal Srivastava, and Mukut Behari Lal, of the Jan Sangh; Triloki Singh, Riasat Hussain, Hori Lal Yadav, Satya Narain Pandey, Kamla Singh Yadav, and H. P. Misra, of the Praja Socialist Party; and Ugra Sen, Gaya

Prasad, and D. V. Vajpayee of the Socialist Party. In addition, Pitamber Das (of the Jan Sangh) and S. M. Joshi, Chandra Shekar, Genda Singh, and Mukut Behari Lal (of the Praja Socialist Party) granted interviews. Among many Congress leaders who provided assistance were C. B. Gupta, Mohan Lal Gautam, Charan Singh, Ram Narain Pandey, Jai Ram Verma, Munishwar Dutt Upadhyaya, and Jagat Pal Singh.

The study was made under a fellowship grant from the Foreign Area Fellowship Program, whose support I very much appreciate. The statements and interpretations, of course, are mine, and not necessarily those of the Fellowship Program.

I wish to extend thanks to Dhirendra K. Vajpeyi, who helped solve a host of multifarious problems during the course of the research, particularly in finding interpreters and interviewers. Vijai Prakash Sharma and K. L. Malkani undertook the arduous task of interpretation in the constituencies studied. Both interviewed a number of legislators in Lucknow, as did Badar-Uddin Siddiqui, Prem Narain Dixit, and Virendra Srivastava. Ralph C. Meyer made available his socioeconomic data on Uttar Pradesh legislators over the years, thus providing a needed supplement to my data. Prabir Pal drew the map. My thanks go also to Mrs. Evelyn Baumann and Mrs. Marge Sherlock, who typed the manuscript.

Dr. Marie Burger, my sister-in-law, lent a helping hand on many occasions; among other things, she punched I.B.M. cards and calculated hundreds of percentages. From steadily encouraging me to continue toward the doctorate to taking care of the babies so that I might type, my husband, Dr. Josef Burger, provided essential support. Dr. Austin Ranney read drafts of the manuscript and offered helpful suggestions and criticisms, which were much appreciated. Special recognition and gratitude go to my adviser, Dr. Henry C. Hart, who with infinite patience spent countless hours trying to turn a graduate student into something that would at least resemble a political scientist.

Angela Sutherland Burger

CONTENTS

Part One

AN OVERVIEW

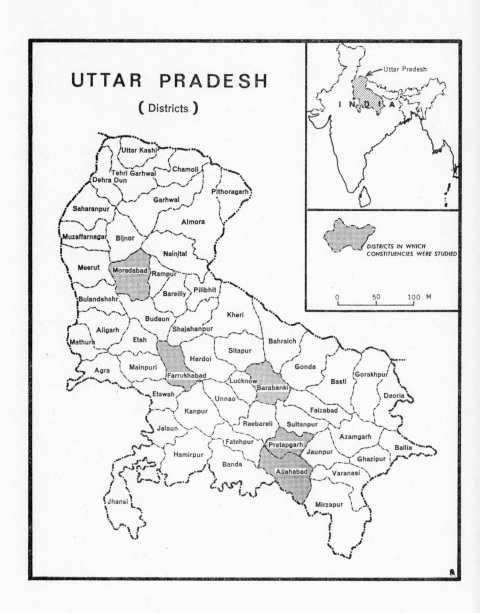

UTTAR PRADESH

(Districts)

Uttar Kashi

Tehri Garhwal Chamoli
Dehra Dun

Pithoragarh

Saharanpur Garhwal

Almora

Muzaffarnagar Bijnor

Nainital

Meerut Moradabad Rampur

Bulandshahr Bareilly Pilibhit

Budaun Kheri

Aligarh Shajahanpur

Mathura Etah Sitapur Bahraich

Agra Mainpuri Hardoi

Farrukhabad Lucknow Gonda Basti Gorakhpur

Etawah Barabanki Deoria

Unnao Faizabad

Kanpur Raebareli Sultanpur

Jalaun Azamgarh Ballia

Fatehpur Pratapgarh Jaunpur Ghazipur

Hamirpur Banda Allahabad Varanasi

Jhansi Mirzapur

Uttar Pradesh

I N D I A

DISTRICTS IN WHICH
CONSTITUENCIES WERE STUDIED

0   50   100 M

Chapter I

FRAMEWORK OF ANALYSIS

IN ANY POLITICAL SYSTEM there are agencies that link people and groups to government. Particularly important in representative forms of government are political parties, which not only provide a link, but whose members are often directly involved in governmental decision-making. In addition to representational, aggregative, articulative, and decisional roles in government itself, parties have a role, along with other organizations, in a variety of functions. These include the recruiting of new participants, the integrating of individuals and groups into society, the transmitting of political and social values from one generation to another, the harmonizing or containing of diverse interests and providing channels of communication within a society, and, in many cases, the furthering of the development of a nation-state.

Although studies of parties and party systems abound, no comprehensive theory of parties has been developed, and none is offered here. What is attempted is the development and testing of a few hypotheses about processes involved in building and maintaining opposition parties in underdeveloped countries where, under a parliamentary form of government, the political system is dominated by one party.

The building process focuses on the relationship between the party and the electorate; it encompasses the establishment of party units and their extension to winning status. Necessarily, parties can "win" only where there are directly elected positions to be won, and it is here that the party/electorate interaction is overt and critical. Although opposition parties are, by definition, "losing parties" on some levels of government (the national, the state), they can be "winning" on other levels (in some legislative constituencies, for example). When a party wins a directly elected position, the maintenance process begins. To remain victorious over successive elections involves keeping the support of those who previously voted for the party. The electoral supporters can be loosely considered party members.[1] Even though some effort may be placed on extending the party further within the electorate, it is the intraparty relationships that are the more important. On all levels where there are no directly elected positions to be won, the maintenance process is central. Lesser units must be kept within the party fold; defection and schisms within the party must be prevented. Here intraparty relationships—the focus of the maintenance process—are far more crucial than the party/electorate relationships of the building process.

Within political parties different kinds of membership and degrees of participation can be distinguished. The permanent members identify with the party, have a high degree of participation, and remain in the party over the years, performing managerial, communication, recruitment, and other functions. Among these members are the "pillars of the permanent party," who have more prominent roles and the highest degree of participation, and the "regulars," who are a source of continuing party strength although their roles and participation are more limited. In contrast, the electoral supporters are temporary members whose allegiance must be gained for each election. They may be active during a campaign, but their participation drops precipitously thereafter, and they do not personally identify with the party. Among the supporters are the "notables," important personages in a community to whom others look for guidance in voting behavior;[2] the "campaigners," who help staff the electoral organization but are basically sunshine soldiers aroused by the excitement of a campaign; and last, the voters who support the party in a particular election.

The building and maintenance of opposition parties is affected by several major factors and their interactions; and from the latter, hypotheses can be developed for testing. The factors, which comprise the setting in which parties operate, can be subsumed under four broad categories: the political structures, the political processes, the social groupings, and the social processes. While each

---

[1] See pp. 210–213 for discussion of party structure.

[2] F. G. Bailey applies the term "vote banks" to these persons. See his *Politics and Social Change: Orissa in 1959* (Berkeley and Los Angeles, 1963), pp. 109 ff.; hereafter cited as Bailey, *Politics and Social Change.*

particular setting will have unique features, some similarities can be found among many underdeveloped countries having a representative government. A brief analysis of the North Indian state of Uttar Pradesh, in which the hypotheses will be tested, will serve as illustration.

Independent India in 1947 inherited from British rule a functioning administrative system. The present republic, as established by the constitution of 1950, governs a federation of states and territories under a parliamentary system. Guarantees of civil rights and an independent judiciary place some restraints on the political process. Indians had limited experience with federalism and parliamentary government under the British, but before independence the franchise, although gradually extended over several decades, was restricted to about 15 percent of the adult population and the electorate was divided into separate voting groups on the basis of religion, race, education, and so forth. Independent India's establishment of universal adult suffrage was accompanied by the removal of voting divisions. The result was that many individuals and groups who were not politically conscious were given the right to vote.

From independence until the fourth general elections, in 1967, a multiparty system with one dominant party existed nationally in India and also in Uttar Pradesh. For this classification I use as criteria (a) the proportion of seats held by different parties in the lower house of the legislative branch, designating a system as one-party, two-party, or multiparty according to the number of parties whose seats in the lower house must be combined to reach 90 percent, and (b) the degree of competitiveness between parties, designating a multiparty system as one-party-dominant when one party obtains a majority of 56 percent, or more, of the seats.[3]

In the first three general elections to the Lok Sabha, the lower house of the Indian Parliament, the seats held by more than three parties or independent groups of legislators had to be combined to reach 90 percent, and the proportion of seats won by the Con-

[3] Other degrees of competitiveness for a multiparty system would be: highly competitive, when no party obtains a majority of the seats, and moderately competitive, when one party obtains a majority of 51 to 55 percent. In the 1967 elections the national government became moderately competitive and the state government of Uttar Pradesh became highly competitive.

gress, the dominant party, ranged from 73.1 to 75.1 percent. In those years no opposition party obtained as much as 6 percent of the seats. In Uttar Pradesh the Congress declined from a high of 90.7 percent of the seats in the first general elections to 66.5 percent in the second and 57.9 percent in the third. The largest opposition party won 11.4 percent of the seats in the third election, leaving the Congress still in a clearly dominant position.[4]

The kind of party system that exists has a bearing on the building and maintenance of opposition parties, but in a system with a dominant party the characteristics of that party are also important. The Indian National Congress would probably be termed a pragmatic-pluralist party.[5] A multiparty system with a dominant pragmatic-pluralist party naturally provides a context for the building and maintenance of opposition parties different from that of other types of systems and other types of dominant parties.[6] In India, the Congress Party is identified with the struggle for and gaining of independence; it is also associated with great charis-

---

[4] National election results are based on data in Election Commission, *Report on the First General Elections in India, 1951–52* (2 vols.; New Delhi, 1955), II, 7; Election Commission, *Report on the Second General Elections in India, 1957* (2 vols.; New Delhi,1959), II, 89; and Surindar Suri, *1962 Elections: A Political Analysis* (New Delhi, 1962), p. 48.

Uttar Pradesh elections results are from Office of the Chief Electoral Officer, Uttar Pradesh, *Results of Third General Elections (1962) to the Uttar Pradesh Legislative Assembly* (Allahabad, 1962), pp. v–vii.

[5] In a study of dominant and single parties, pragmatic-pluralist parties are distinguished from revolutionary-centralizing parties on the basis of differences in ideology, popular participation, and organization. See James S. Coleman and Carl G. Rosberg, Jr. (eds.), *Political Parties and National Integration in Tropical Africa* (Berkeley and Los Angeles: University of California Press, 1964), pp. 5 ff.

[6] For a few examples of the different classifications that have been made, limited to recent works, see the categories developed in Gabriel A. Almond and James S. Coleman (eds.), *The Politics of Developing Areas* (Princeton: Princeton University Press, 1960), by several authors; Sigmund Neuman (ed.), *Modern Political Parties* (Chicago: University of Chicago Press, 1956), pp. 395–421; Maurice Duverger, *Political Parties* (2d rev. ed.; New York: Wiley, 1959); Coleman and Rosberg (eds.), *op. cit.;* Ruth Schachter "Single-Party Systems in West Africa," and Martin C. Needler, "The Political Development of Mexico," in *American Political Science Review* LV, 2 (June, 1961), pp. 294–307, 308–312; David E. Apter, *Ghana in Transition* (rev. ed.; New York: Atheneum, 1963); Aristide R. Zolberg, *One-Party Government in the Ivory Coast* (Princeton: Princeton University Press, 1964); Douglas E. Ashford, *Political Change in Morocco* (Princeton: Princeton University Press, 1961); and Charles A. Micaud, Leon Carl Brown, and Clement Henry Moore, *Tunisia: The Politics of Modernization* (New York: Praeger, 1964).

matic leaders such as Mahatma Gandhi and Jawaharlal Nehru. Before independence, loyalty to Congress was loyalty to India. The aura surrounding it is thus a factor which has an impact on the efforts to build opposition parties. Under Congress a parliamentary form of government was set up and has been maintained, elections have been held that were termed fair, no party has been banned by the Government, no attempt has been made to rule without benefit of parliamentary bodies, and general civil liberties have been protected—all providing a favorable climate for the development of opposition parties. Probably both advantages and disadvantages for opposition parties follow from the Congress's not demanding a continuous or intense commitment and participation by the populace. Participation in the Congress is both direct and indirect; pluralism is tolerated within the party, limited attention is given to ideological matters, and the party has not monopolized other associations or fused them with itself.

Owing to the unamalgamated nature of Indian society, profound cultural differences have been preserved, which parties can reflect or exploit. There are a number of ways of characterizing different culture groups. One of the more common ways is to assign groups to positions somewhere in a traditional/modern continuum. The usual key indices are language of education, degree of education, occupation, place of residence, and class. In India, as in other former British colonies, the modern cultural group is likely to be described as having an English-language education and being highly educated, urbanized, professional, and "new middle class." Value indices such as secularism, equalitarianism, nationalism, and democracy are also sometimes used, without its being specified whether persons must hold to these values if they are to be deemed modern or whether such are simply held by a large proportion among the modern group.

One of the difficulties in utilizing these indices is that other culture-group distinctions which are highly significant may defy easy allocation along the traditional/modern continuum. For example, Myron Weiner identifies a "ruling culture" group in India which would include the former rajas, talukdars, zamindars, and the like, who were rulers and shared a "common attitude toward the dispersion and democratization of power."[7] Individ-

[7] *Political Change in South Asia* (Calcutta, 1963), pp. 32 ff.

uals in this category show wide variation as to education, place of residence, and present occupation, yet as a group they would doubtless be placed in a traditional category along with the peasantry, even though the differences between these two culture groups are immense. Weiner identifies also an "articulate lower middle class in the small towns," whose members fall between traditional and modern, having vernacular-language education and no great extent of it. Small-town shopkeepers, lawyers, ayurvedic doctors, and teachers, together with some wealthier peasants, would be placed in this group.[8] Here there is a question whether its members should be termed more or less traditional than those of the "ruling culture" group.

Certain groupings, more traditional than not, nevertheless present characteristics for which modern or traditional indices would be of little significance. For example, there are culture groups based on religion. Between the Muslim and Hindu cultures there has been interaction, but the Muslim and Hindu groups have remained distinct. Friction over the centuries and the effects of British policies of "divide and rule" were not mitigated by the rise of a Muslim nationalism and the call for a separate state of Pakistan, or by the Hindu nationalist elements in Gandhi's teachings and the establishment of India and Pakistan as separate countries. These and other religious groups in India are in opposition over languages, educational policies, and the definition of "secularity." Complicating the differences are the divisions within the major religious groups, such as the Sunni and Shi'a sects within Islam and the orthodox Sanatan Dharm and reformist Arya Samaj within Hinduism.

Yet another complication is provided by the distinct social structures based on castes, found within both the Hindu community and the Muslim. Castes are far more than extended kinship groups, being hierarchically arranged, endogamous social units, with prescribed interrelationships and differing ethics and customs. "Each caste is a social unit in itself,"[9] and as such can be regarded as a culture group.

In addition there are cross-cutting geographic social groupings, such as the village or village faction, the town, and the city. There

[8] *Ibid.,* p. 135.
[9] John Henry Hutton, *Caste in India* (London, 1963), p. 2.

are also occupational groupings. In the West, occupational and professional groups are usually based on achievement rather than ascriptive criteria. In India, a business organization or labor union may be composed of a single caste. Yet, whereas an individual is born into a caste, he is not born into a formal caste association; he must take positive action to join an association of his caste.[10] Further, while class differences abound in India, here again there is a striking contrast with the West, where economic indices play an important determining role. In India the hierarchic caste structure—not based on economic indices as such—is a vital factor in class ranking. For some individuals and groups the caste and economic ranks coincide; for others they do not.

One of the most important social processes taking place in India, as in many developing countries, is social mobilization. The development of a market economy, industry, and a modern transportation and communication system is accompanied by urbanization, education, and the growth of mass media, all of which increase an affected individual's mobility—geographic, psychic, and social. By this process, individuals and groups become part of a "participant society."[11]

Differential rates of mobilization in a society can refer either to lack of balance in the development of education, urbanization, industrialization, and the like, or to the mobilization of various specific groups at different rates. It is the latter sense that is utilized here. Social mobilization precedes or accompanies political mobilization—the awareness of, interest in, and participation in political activities. Cultural groups are politically mobilized at different rates also.

From the interaction of these several factors, tensions are produced which can energize the building of opposition parties in a

[10] Suzanne H. Rudolph and Lloyd I. Rudolph, "Caste Associations in Indian Politics," *Pacific Affairs*, XXXIII (January, 1960), pp. 1–22. The caste association is the formal organization of a particular caste, but only those who join are members.

[11] See Daniel Lerner, *The Passing of Traditional Society* (Glencoe, Ill.: Free Press, 1958), pp. 43–76. See also Robert E. Ward and Dankwart A. Rustow (eds.), *Political Modernization in Japan and Turkey* (Princeton: Princeton University Press, 1964), and Seymour Martin Lipset, "Political Cleavages in 'Developed' and 'Emerging' Politics," in Erik Allardt and Yrjo Littunen, (eds.), *Cleavages, Ideologies and Party Systems* (Transactions of the Westermarck Society, Vol. I; Helsinki, 1964), pp. 21–55.

one-party-dominant system. A primary type of tension follows from successive mobilization. Recently mobilized groups may discover that an established party has been preempted by social rivals who were mobilized earlier. Those in control of the party are likely to be reluctant to relinquish their position and may attempt to limit admittance of their rivals to leadership ranks.[12]

The Congress, as the oldest and the dominant party in India, can be expected to draw its leaders and members from groups that were mobilized before or by the time that India attained independence. The Congress is bound by its past identifications, as is any party with roots in a society. As such, the opposition parties with long-established ties in the society are similarly restricted, but they are probably less well organized at the state level and also in some districts. It should be easier for newly mobilized groups to enter and gain leadership positions in the opposition parties than in the Congress. These ideas can be put as hypotheses:

(a) A party of national independence (such as the Congress) tends to have its leadership frozen in those social groups which were mobilized by the time of independence

(b) Leaders of more recently mobilized groups will tend to seek recognition and position in opposition parties

In the concluding chapter of this book, these hypotheses and others advanced in the course of the next few pages are discussed in the light of the testing they received in field work.

A second source of tension arises from the threat to existing roles, functions, and social statuses posed by the processes of economic, social, and political change. If the threat is identified with the activities of a party, or with the activities of rival groups in society who are associated with a party, then the threatened group may try to utilize a modern weapon—namely, another party—to maintain its identity and position. This "defense mechanism" is not simply a reversal of the first tension. Talukdars and zamindars, many of whom were mobilized early, have tried in recent years to defend themselves in obsolescent roles. Many Muslims also were mobilized early, but now, following the establishment of and migration to Pakistan, those who remained in India find

[12] Lerner, *op. cit.*, p. 40.

themselves in a less favorable position vis-à-vis the Hindu community. Change erodes the position of some groups in society.

The Congress, as the ruling party, has instituted policies which have brought about or encouraged change. By establishing representative government, granting universal adult suffrage, and holding elections it has encouraged a democratization and dispersion of power, thereby increasing the rate of mobilization of various groups and changing their relative power positions. Numbers have become important. Change has been furthered also by various governmental policies, such as abolition of zamindari and restrictions on landholding. By offering special opportunities for education and for employment in government to members of less privileged groups, many of whom formerly were not politically conscious, Congress has encouraged the development of such a consciousness. To promote economic development, various agencies which are sources of funds have been established on local and district levels. Inasmuch as the obtaining of political office by a group member can give his group increased access to an agency and to the funds at the disposal of that agency, these institutions provide groups with incentive for political activity. This is not to say that the funds will be used for development purposes; their mere existence has a political impact. In a system with universal adult suffrage, large deprived groups can use the pressure of their numbers to obtain material benefits from government agencies. Groups which view such changes as a threat to their position or status are likely to view the ruling party as an antagonist. As a result, they may tend to identify with an opposition party. Formulation of a policy may alienate some groups. If the policy is not carried out as anticipated, those who might have benefited may turn to opposition parties for representation. Thus two further hypotheses may be advanced:

(a) Those who are threatened with loss of status, role, and function by reforms or policies instituted by the dominant party will seek representation in opposition parties

(b) If the dominant party does not carry out policies formulated or justified by its ideology, the unsatisfied beneficiaries of such policies will seek representation in opposition parties

There is clearly a psychological dimension to the factors and interactions just mentioned. In traditional societies, status was determined by ascriptive indices which were not necessarily congruent with economic position. Increased mobility—spatial, occupational, educational, and financial—and changes in reference groups and values have introduced achievement indices in status determination. Because of the lack of consensus on status-determining factors and on the weights to be given various factors, mobile individuals tend to suffer loss of defined status and role, and the nonmobile feel threatened in their status and role by the new indices. In either situation there is a corresponding need for reintegration into society. Parties can help to fill this need and thus perform a function of societal reidentification.[13]

Another functional role of parties, particularly opposition parties, is that of innovation.[14] This includes both the representation of new groups or interests and the adoption of new ways of organizing or mobilizing voters. The newly mobilized, the defensive, and the unsatisfied beneficiaries of reforms will probably be attracted to opposition parties, which on their part can be expected to try to draw on these groups, presenting themselves either as defenders of a traditional societal structure or as spokesmen for the demands of rising groups.

The hypotheses developed thus far apply to the building of opposition parties, centering on those party units organized to contest a directly elected position. In India the two key units are based on national Parliamentary and state Legislative Assembly constituencies.[15] For this study, the latter party units are the focal point. By winning constituencies a party can claim some of the fruits of victory and obtain some material advantages for its supporters. Victory gives prestige and status to local leaders and raises the self-esteem of groups represented by these leaders—psychological benefits which should not be underestimated. The ability

---

[13] Myron Weiner, *Party Politics in India* (Princeton, N.J., 1957), pp. 234–240.
[14] Theodore Lowi, "Toward Functionalism in Political Science: The Case of Innovation in Party Systems," *American Political Science Review*, LVII, No. 3 (September, 1963), 570–583.
[15] In Uttar Pradesh five state Assembly constituencies comprise one national Parliamentary constituency. Village and municipal councils are also directly elected, but the former are not contested by parties and the latter (contested by parties) are based on ward constituencies. Other elections are indirect.

of a party and its elected personnel to operate effectively and make maximum use of its victories is related to the existence of an experienced leadership echelon. "Experience" refers to knowledge of the system and how it operates, and the ability to maneuver within it. If an elected legislator is ignorant of the powers and procedures—formal and informal—of the various governmental bodies of which he is a member, it is doubtful that he will be able to make maximum use of his position. An individual can acquire knowledge and can learn about informal procedures either before or during a term of office. Efforts to acquire practical knowledge while holding office can be materially eased if there are experienced leaders who can provide guidance. To build an experienced leadership echelon which can serve to teach newly elected politicians to operate within the system, scattered and sporadic party victories are not sufficient. Maintenance of "winning" constituencies and continuity of leaders are important. Furthermore, differences between parties on this index would tend to affect the party's performance in the formal political arena. There are constitutional and extraconstitutional forms of behavior. A party lacking a pool of experienced leaders might be increasingly drawn to extraconstitutional behavior because of inability to operate effectively within the constitutional order. A party with such leadership might be much more inclined to work within the system. Maintenance is also important because one measure of the strength of a party is its entrenchment in society—which means its ability to continue victorious over long periods of time in the same geographic area.

Many of the problems of maintaining opposition parties are directly related to the factors which can be utilized to build a party. When an opposition party wins on the constituency level, another party remains dominant on the state and national level. The form of government, universal adult suffrage, and civil liberties continue. In a parliamentary system with disciplined parties, neither one opposition legislator nor all opposition legislators will be able to achieve their major policy goals.

Social mobilization, and particularly the tensions associated with successive mobilization, can help those trying to build opposition parties. The process continues to operate, at differential rates, after the victory of an opposition candidate. Over time, the party is likely to be identified more and more closely with one or more specific groups. These groups are likely to be those represented by the candidates or other top leaders on the local level. In the constituency, it is highly probable that the composition of the higher leadership echelon will tend to be fixed by or at the time when victory at the polls is achieved. Eldersveld points out that a fundamental problem of parties is that of reconciling the need for broad social representation with the need for internal cohesion and manageability.[16] Riker's "size principle" indicates the logical point at which a party might be expected to cease following an expansionist policy in favor of consolidation or even retrenchment. That point is reached when there is subjective certainty of winning.[17] By this reasoning, the following hypothesis and subhypothesis are suggested:

(a) On the constituency level, an opposition party tends to have its leadership frozen among those groups whose representatives have gained leadership positions by the time of victory at the polls

(b) Over time an opposition party on the constituency level tends to be identified with the groups represented by the leadership echelon on that or the district level

Under continuing social mobilization, new or different group identifications can become significant. The social changes can lead to disruption of the local leadership echelon of the party. The effect may be to narrow the number and kinds of groups identified with the party, and workers of other parties can be expected to try to take advantage of social changes which produce conflicts within the party in question. Another subhypothesis can be derived from these considerations:

(c) On the constituency level, leaders of groups mobilized after the victory at the polls of an opposition party will tend to seek recognition and position in other parties

The "other parties" could be the dominant party or other opposition parties. Following the Eldersveld and Riker reasoning, it

[16] Samuel J. Eldersveld, *Political Parties: A Behavioral Analysis* (Chicago: Rand McNally and Co., 1964), pp. 47 ff.

[17] William H. Riker, *Theory of Political Coalitions* (New Haven: Yale University Press, 1962), pp. 32 ff.

might be expected that dominant party activists, having lost in the constituency, would open the party to new groups. Whether such a policy would be followed would partly depend on resolving the conflict between the desire for victory and the strength of subgroup loyalties in favor of the former. An additional factor would be the interpretation by dominant party activists of their defeat. If they attributed defeat to intraparty factionalism, or to the momentary defection of former supporters (not necessarily to the victorious opposition party), then leaders of the dominant party might not think it necessary or desirable to try to attract new groups or to permit the entry of leaders of new groups to party leadership positions. Therefore, even if leaders of new groups should turn toward the dominant party for representation, they might find that party closed to them. In this situation, they might turn to other opposition parties. Some groups might not consider the dominant party at all, but turn directly to other opposition parties.

Victorious party leaders are likely to have difficulties in adapting to social change. In most locales, the elected legislator probably plays a key role in maintenance. A basic factor in maintenance is his pattern of communication with permanent party members, electoral supporters, and constituents generally. Since he has to be absent from his constituency for varying periods of time, and since the mass media are not highly developed in underdeveloped countries, he is likely to be unaware of some social changes. When he is in the constituency, he can either initiate contact with con-stituents or wait for them to take the initiative. If he waits, he is even less likely to be aware of changes in the environment, and the process of communication can hardly result in much extension of the permanent party.

In building an opposition party, leaders can make bargains with notables, offering side payments of various kinds in return for electoral support. Given the party's distance from power, an offer of future legislation would probably lack credibility. An offer of future support for the notable or his nominee in other elections would be more attractive. Pressure or influence upon administra-tive officials for obtaining specific material benefits could be offered, yet ability to secure the benefits would require the action, or at least the acquiescence, of political bodies likely to be controlled by the dominant party or of administrative officials ulti-mately responsible to the dominant party. Thus the relationship between leaders of the dominant and the opposition party be-comes crucial. The stronger the tensions between the two, the less likely it is that the opposition leaders will be able to obtain benefits. Then it is possible that a group of unsatisfied benefici-aries-to-be will arise among the notables. Failure of opposition party leaders to fulfill specific local promises is the basis of this group's existence. The unsatisfied beneficiaries could become apathetic or turn away from the party. In a multiparty system, apathy on the part of such former supporters of an opposition party can lead to its defeat at the polls. These ideas can be restated as an hypothesis and a subhypothesis:

(a) On the constituency level, the stronger the tensions between the leaders of a victorious opposition party and those of the dominant party, the less able are the opposition party lead-ers to obtain benefits for their supporters

(b) On the constituency level, if victorious opposition party leaders do not carry out pledges of specific actions made as side payments to notables in winning their electoral sup-port, the unsatisfied beneficiaries will tend to become apa-thetic toward or alienated from the party

Thus some of the same factors that can aid the building of an opposition party tend to operate to its disadvantage after it has become successful at the polls. The party might frequently lose in constituencies previously held, while winning in new con-stituencies.

Many of the problems of intraparty maintenance on the district and state level are related to factors previously mentioned. In addition to the different cultural and social groups and their mobilization at differential rates, a geographic variable must be introduced. Mobilization of specific groups is not necessarily uni-form throughout a state or even a district. A party which tries to base itself on a particular group or set of groups throughout the state, or even a district, is likely to be handicapped because of this feature. Not only is the party at a disadvantage in trying to build successful local parties, but also there are likely to be differences inside the party itself within a group whose members are at varying stages of mobilization. It is probable that leadership will reside in those segments that represent a higher stage of mobilization. Because these leaders are identified with specific geographic areas, friction is likely to arise on both a geographic and a stage-of-mobilization basis. If leaders of the more recently mobilized sectors are not systematically brought into higher leadership echelons with the party, they are likely to become disgruntled and be open to appeals made by other parties. If strongly challenged by more recently mobilized sectors, the established leaders are apt to feel threatened with the loss of position, role, and status in the party. The threat may be so severe that some of them will choose to leave the party rather than remain in a possibly subordinate status.

A party does not have to be based on the same group or groups over a district, section, or state. Party leaders and activists can try to take advantage of whatever tensions exist in various locales. The result is that a single party will contain many competitive cultural and social groups. Even so, it is difficult to take advantage of tensions on one level and try to resolve them on another. Not only will there be friction among the competitive cultural groups, but also between groups at various stages of mobilization. A time dimension must be recognized. A party does not emerge "full grown." It is established and extended in different areas over a period of time. Leadership is likely to rest in a "founding fathers" echelon comprising leaders of those groups mobilized at the time of party formation. Since these leaders are identified with certain groups, with geographic areas, and with a stage of mobilization, friction within the party, especially over the question of leadership, can arise from differences based on any, some, or all of these dimensions.

One reason conflicts between intraparty groups are hard to resolve appears to be related to the kinds of decisions made within a party. Decisions fall in four categories, as they pertain to broad ideological questions, to more specific public policy positions, to leadership questions, or to essentially procedural matters of action by party members (such as whether to cooperate with either the dominant party or other opposition parties in particular ways, whether to support one faction in the dominant party in a certain situation, whether to organize an agitation of some sort, and so on). The fact that these are small opposition parties operating in a parliamentary system, and therefore far removed from exercising governmental power, probably means that much debate on policy positions takes place in a vacuum, and that different positions become entangled with their proponents and the groups which they represent. Many groups are likely to be unconcerned with policy matters, given the distance from power, save in defense of the position and status of their own group's representatives. It is highly probable that different positions on broad ideological questions will be inextricably bound with their proponents and the groups which they represent. The selection of leadership will doubtless be one of the areas of greatest concern for members, and this question automatically brings into play a host of tensions. On procedural questions, such as cooperation with other parties or with factions in other parties, the fact that social and political situations differ from place to place makes formation of a general line of action difficult. In most areas of decision, group will be pitted against group in such a way that amelioration and compromise will be difficult to achieve. When policy and ideological positions boil down to questions of the status of competing groups and personalities, resolution or containment of conflict is not an easy task.

Another aspect of the leadership question is that concerning the set of leaders, organizational or legislative, which is to be dominant in particular areas of party activity. This question is likely to assume greater prominence in a party as its number of legislative seats increases and as legislators gain expertise in their roles. If the group composition of the two sets of leaders varies widely, it is highly probable that the friction will be heightened.

An important element of maintenance is morale within the party. Morale can be related to the party's electoral fortunes within the state, in other states, and nationally. Expansion in other states or nationally can bolster the morale of members in a state where the party is declining or holding its own. Increasing success within the state can serve as a spur to greater effort. The attitudes of nonmembers can be influenced by the seeming expansion, stagnation, or decline of party victories on the three levels. Yet the actual electoral results, viewed over time, are not solely important for morale. Prior expectations as compared with achievements must be considered also. Members and leaders of a party who have very high expectations regarding the victories to be won may be greatly disappointed in the results even though there has been expansion, and disillusionment can then pervade the party. Conversely, if party successes are greater than expected, morale will tend to rise. The psychological climate or morale within the party can be expected to have some influence on members, either in dampening enthusiasm or in providing incentives and encouragement, and also on individuals not in the party who may be considering supporting it.

The functions of opposition parties in government are well known: to offer an alternative government; to criticize the government and administration; to check or brake the use of governmental powers; to articulate and aggregate interests; to harness the interests of group loyalties to the nation. In the present case, the parties are so small that they cannot offer themselves as an alternative government. Their role is to be found in other functions. In performing these functions their legislators and party workers can participate in a variety of activities both in and outside the formal governmental bodies, some constitutional and some extraconstitutional. These activities are considered from the standpoint of building and maintaining opposition parties—not with respect to how opposition parties maintain the existing political order by preparing alternative government leadership or policies, how and to what degree the opposition participates in legislative and administrative policy decisions, or how they support or attack the existing constitutional order.

The focus in this study is the building and maintenance of opposition parties in a multiparty system with a dominant pragmatic-pluralist party. Key factors in the political and social system have been specified, and some hypotheses for testing have been developed from expected interactions. In investigating these questions, the inquiry is logically extended to include whether the interactions are such as to sustain opposition parties, whether they encourage centralization or decentralization in opposition parties, and whether they encourage fragmentation or unification of opposition parties. The functional relationship between the operations of opposition parties and the dominant party must also be considered. Does the existence and operation of minority parties have the effect of furthering the dominant party's functions of social integration and social reform? All these matters are related to the broader question of the party system and its stability. Is this a stable "multiparty with one party dominant" system, or does it contain seeds of either a more competitive multiparty system or a single-party system?

Chapter II

UTTAR PRADESH:
GENERAL BACKGROUND

UTTAR PRADESH DIFFERS from most states in India in a number of important ways. For almost a century it has been a political and administrative unit; its democratic experience before and after independence has been as one entity.[1] It is predominantly Hindi-speaking, and there have been no groups in post-independence years trying to break away and form a separate state. The virulent anti-Brahminism of South India, the Kamma-Reddi friction in Andhra, and the hill-versus-plains friction in Orissa present tensions which are almost negligible in Uttar Pradesh. In most other states, major issues concerning state boundaries and language have aroused emotions and polarized allegiances on which opposition parties have occasionally capitalized. An important question is whether in the near absence of cataclysmic issues, as in Uttar Pradesh, the factors and interactions postulated for opposition parties are to be found. If they appear in the politics of this state, it can be assumed that they are basic and likely to operate continuously.

The North Indian plain for centuries has been a broad avenue for invaders and a base for ambitious rulers who have established their sway over large parts of India. It has also been the oldest hearth for developing what there is of an "Indian culture." The Hindu culture was first firmly established here. Later came its interaction and competition with Buddhism—for Buddha was born here, and here he taught and died. Still later came the superimposition and partial Indianization of Islam. Then came the British with still another culture.

The state of Uttar Pradesh occupies a central place in this vast

[1] There were three small princely states within Uttar Pradesh during British times, but these became part of the state with no difficulty. After the 1956 States Reorganization Act only a few minor boundary adjustments were made.

area. Between its northern Himalayan slope and the southern hills lies the great Gangetic Plain. Cities such as Varanasi, Allahabad, and Hardwar attract Hindus from all parts of India, and Sarnath is a magnet for Buddhists from over the world. The complex of Agra–Fatehpur Sikri–Sikandra Rao and such cities as Rampur and Lucknow stand as political and cultural centers of former Muslim rule. Kanpur is the great industrial center in the state.

The largest of Indian states, Uttar Pradesh in 1961 had a population of more than 73,000,000 in an area about the size of Arizona. The eastern districts are among the most poverty-stricken in India and have a higher population density (more than 900 persons per square mile in several districts) and a higher proportion of persons engaged in agriculture, together with average rural landholdings of smaller size and a lower degree of urbanization, than the western districts.[2] The settlement pattern of villages also differs, with groupings of hamlets in the east, a cluster-and-hamlet pattern in the center, and compact villages in the west; in the north and south hill areas a dispersed settlement pattern is found.[3] The more industrialized and urbanized western districts are economically better off, although there is some general diversity, with certain districts undergoing development while others are stagnant and some are in decline. Among crops, rice is important in the east and wheat in the west. Although the population is predominantly Hindi-speaking, there are east-to-west language distinctions. Urdu is spoken in both areas, but Western Hindi and its subdialects are found in the west, and Eastern Hindi and the Avadhi dialect in the east-central districts; in the northeast Bhojpuri is spoken.

Not all differences can be ranged on east-west lines.[4] Sugar cane is an important crop in the northern half of the state, but not in the southern, and sugar mills, important for the economy, are found only in the north. Although in literacy the eastern districts have slightly lower rankings than the western, the main division

[2] *Census of India, 1951,* Vol. II: *Uttar Pradesh* (Allahabad, 1953), Parts A-E; *Census of India, 1961,* Vol. XV: *Uttar Pradesh* (Delhi, 1964), Part II-A, *General Population Tables.*

[3] Enayat Ahmad, "Rural Settlement Types in the Uttar Pradesh," *Annals of the Association of American Geographers,* XLII, 2 (June, 1952), 223–246.

[4] William Crooke, *The North-Western Provinces of India* (London, 1897), pp. 27 ff. Oskar H. K. Spate, *India and Pakistan* (New York, 1957), pp. 150 ff.

lies between the border districts on the west, south, and east as compared with the interior, which has the lowest rates.

Differences also exist based on the divisions of the state during British rule. The British established their control over a period of eighty-six years, moving from the southeastern districts both westward and northward around the Kingdom of Oudh, in the process reducing Oudh to some twelve districts. The outer areas were first called the North-West Provinces and later designated as Agra. (Inasmuch as there is a district of Agra, I use the older term.) British land-tenure policies in the North-West Provinces, which affected the social, economic, and political order, differed from those in Oudh. The British tried to establish landowning where ownership in the Occidental sense never existed, but as they learned of traditional practices, they modified initial policies. By the late 1850's there was land tenure by proprietors, permanent tenure holders and "fixed rate" tenants, occupancy tenants with some rights of succession in land but not the right of sale, and tenants-at-will. Ownership was vested in lineage groups within villages, thus strengthening these groups.[5]

In Oudh a different pattern was established, partly to obtain peace. Before the British annexed Oudh in 1856, the talukdars and zamindars did not own the land although they had considerable jurisdiction and control over it.[6] Upon learning that the British intended to reduce their power, the talukdars resorted to arms in the Mutiny of 1857, whereupon the British conferred landownership on them.[7] The result was that estates were much larger in Oudh than in the North-West Provinces, while rights of a subordinate nature were fewer.

By the latter years of the century, more than half of the cultivators in the North-West Provinces were either proprietors or

[5] This land tenure system is known as *mahalvari*.

[6] Talukdars were large-scale revenue farmers and semi-independent political chiefs whose authority was derived from the King of Oudh. Zamindars were small-scale revenue farmers and prominent local leaders whose authority was derived from Hindu rajas owing allegiance to the King of Oudh (a Muslim). Both exercised judicial powers. A Hindu raja could also be a talukdar.

[7] Talukdars, listed by name, had permanent, heritable, and transferable rights in the villages and lands of the estate; were protected from losing their land by indebtedness; and could not transfer the status of talukdar to those not entitled to the status. Those zamindars who had successfully kept their power were also recognized as landowners, but received no special treatment.

privileged tenants, as compared with only 12 percent in Oudh, where fully 88 percent were tenants-at-will.[8] During the 1920's the first peasant movements in Uttar Pradesh were begun in Oudh and were easily coupled with the nationalist movement because of the pro-British tendencies of many talukdars and zamindars. In some places the nationalist and peasant movements had a close relationship to caste divisions because of the caste composition of the talukdar and zamindar classes. The social, economic, and political tensions involved with the nationalist movement were more intense in Oudh than in the North-West Provinces. After taking power in Uttar Pradesh in 1937, the Congress Party passed legislation to abolish the zamindari system, but resigned from the Government before the reforms were implemented. In 1952 the Congress accomplished zamindari abolition,[9] and in 1959 a law to limit individual landholdings was passed, but the effect of these reforms was primarily psychological; there was no substantial shift in social, economic, or political power.

The most important element of the social structure is caste. Although some restrictions and regulations of social intercourse have crumbled over the years, particularly in urban areas, and although there has been legislation to end some of the severest forms of caste discrimination, traditional practices and attitudes persist. The Government has recognized caste in legislation designed to better the lot of specific castes. Among the various methods of describing the caste hierarchy, I have adopted here a threefold grouping based on divisions recognized by the Indian Government. Only in the highest grouping is the rank of specific castes indicated, for it is only with regard to this group that there appears to be general agreement; in the lower groupings the status of specific castes varies from place to place. Only those castes are mentioned which, at this time, have some political importance.

The lowest grouping consists of the scheduled castes—the former Untouchables—who are defined, protected, and given advantages in education and government employment by legislative fiat.

[8] Walter C. Neale, *Economic Change in Rural India* (New Haven, 1962), pp. 14 f., 36–40, 73–77, 99 f.

[9] A zamindari system is one in which there are intermediaries between the ruler and the cultivator. The intermediary collects the revenue. Both talukdars and zamindars are included within a zamindari system, and both positions were abolished.

Seats in elective bodies are reserved for the scheduled castes, and only members of these castes can seek election to them. The Chamars, the largest caste in Uttar Pradesh, are usually considered to have benefited most from scheduled caste legislation.[10] Most Reserved Seat legislators are Chamars and have been elected on the Congress ticket, although the small Republican Party, which has its greatest strength in the southwestern districts, is commonly referred to as the Chamar Party. The Chamars are widely distributed and generally poor. The Pasis, another scheduled caste of importance, are concentrated in the central and east-central districts, where their numbers put them among the largest castes. Since the late 1930's this caste has tried to raise its status by the process of Sanskritization, or adopting the customs of the upper castes. Unsuccessful efforts by the state Pasi Mahasabha and some of its district units in the early 1950's included appeal to the courts.[11] More recently this group has turned to electoral politics, possibly as an alternative method of raising its status.

A middle grouping consists of the backward castes, who are also defined by law and given some advantages through legislation. Their advantages are fewer than those given to the scheduled castes, and no elective seats are reserved for them. They are generally peasant castes such as were described in the *District Gazetteers* of British days as the "backbone of the cultivating community." The three most important are the Kurmi, Yadav, and Lodhi castes. The Kurmis have their main concentration in the eastern and north-central districts. For many years they have claimed to be in the higher Kshattriya or warrior caste category, as the name of their caste organization, the Kurmi Kshattriya Mahasabha, suggests. The *District Gazetteers* usually noted that, as a group, they were better off economically than other middle or low castes.

[10] The Chamars, who prefer to be called Jatavs, are here referred to under the older name to prevent confusion with Yadav caste.

[11] Accounts are given in D. P. Sinha, "Caste Dynamics," *Man in India,* XL (1960), 19–29; D. N. Majumdar, M. C. Pradhan, C. Sen, S. Misra, "Intercaste Relations in Gohanakallan, A Village Near Lucknow," in D. N. Majumdar (ed.), *Rural Profiles* (Lucknow, 1955), pp. 63–86. The Pasis tried to wear the sacred thread (a mark of high-caste status) and adopt various dietary and occuptional niceties of the upper castes. They were beaten, suffered social boycott, had land taken away from them, were fired from jobs, et cetera. "Mahasabha" means association or organization.

The Yadavs are a large, rather evenly distributed caste, with great strength in all districts except those of the western tier and the northwestern hills. Formerly in most reports the Yadavs were referred to as Ahirs and Ahars, the two groups being listed separately. The Ahirs were found in the eastern and central districts. The Ahars were concentrated in a few west-central districts at the turn of the century, but in the 1931 census sizable numbers appeared "out of nowhere" in some north-central districts, although in the districts between these areas there were none.[12] Today the two castes claim to be one and prefer to be called Yadavs. Intermarriage is the strongest test that can be used to determine whether one or two castes exist, and those who were formerly Ahirs and Ahars now claim that they intermarry freely, though to what extent is not known. While there are no Ahir or Ahar caste organizations, there is a Yadav Mahasabha and a Yadav Sangh; these organizations reportedly are not based on Ahir-Ahar differences; the Yadav Sangh is said to be the result of a revolt of younger Yadavs against the older generations.[13] The *District Gazetteers* do not describe the Yadavs in quite as glowing terms as the Kurmis. The Yadavs have openly called for merger, including intermarriage, with various castes in Uttar Pradesh. This kind of integration, however, runs counter to Indian history, and the Yadavs' attempt to merge with the Jats, Gujars, and several other castes does not appear to have borne fruit.

A third significant backward caste is the Lodhi, whose members prefer to be called Lodhi-Rajputs. This caste also has upward aspirations.[14] The economic and social status of this group varies

[12] William Crooke, *Tribes and Castes of the North-Western Provinces of Agra and Oudh* (Calcutta, 1906), Vol. I; *Census of India, 1931,* Vol. XVIII: *United Provinces of Agra and Oudh* (Allahabad, 1933), Part II, pp. 499–548.

[13] The friction between the two seems to have dissipated, and many Yadavs reported membership in both organizations. The Yadav Sangh is almost inactive, holding no meetings although publishing a journal. The Yadav Mahasabha does hold meetings in addition to publishing a journal and putting out other publications.

"Sangh," like Mahasabha, means association or organization.

[14] There is some suspicion that the Lodhi-Rajputs contain other formerly separate caste groups besides the Lodhi. The 1931 census lists Lodhas, Lodhs, Lodhis, and Kisans. In Farrukhabad in 1911 the Kisans were said to be similar to the Lodhas of other districts. *District Gazetteers of the United Provinces of Agra and Oudh*, IX: *Farrukhabad*, by E. R. Neave (Allahabad, 1911). Today, the Kisans of that district have successfully changed their names to Lodha and

considerably within Uttar Pradesh. In some districts, particularly in the south-central part, many Lodhi-Rajputs were and are large landowners; in others they are less well-off. The Lodhi-Rajputs have a caste organization, with an office in a south-central district.

Other backward castes, less prominent but of some importance in politics, include the Gujars, Gadariyas, Kachhis, Koeris, Muraos, Sainthwars, and Sainis. Most of these aspire to higher status. Some respondents stated that the Koeri and Kachhi castes had merged and become "Kushwaha" (a subcaste name common to both castes, which may explain why they chose it).

A number of backward castes maintain their own caste associations. Some participate in the Backward Classes Association and the Backward and Depressed Classes Association. At various times since independence other, more political organizations of these castes have been formed in Uttar Pradesh, such as the Shoshit Sangh in the eastern districts and AJGAR in the west; leaders of the Shoshit Sangh have tended to be either Kurmis or Yadavs; those of AJGAR have usually been Yadavs or Jats (the latter are cultivators, but are not listed as backward).[15]

In a third grouping are all castes not listed as either scheduled or backward. These are the "elite castes." Among these, the highest ritual and social status is held by the Brahmins, whose traditional caste occupation is that of priests. In Uttar Pradesh there are several Brahmin clans, including the Kanyakubja Brahmins —the highest in status—and the Sanadhia, Sarjuparia, and Gaur. Just below the Brahmins are the Rajputs, or Thakurs, the traditional ruling and warrior caste, divided into numerous clans and subcastes among whom there is often great rivalry. Next below are the Banias, a small but important caste, and the related Khattris, even smaller; these are the business, trading, and money-lending castes. They are followed by the Kayasths, the traditional

---

now are claiming to be Lodhi-Rajputs. It is not clear whether the Lodhs have tried to identify with the Lodhi-Rajputs. The movement of merger among backward castes is worthy of detailed study.

[15] S. V. Kogekar and Richard L. Park, *Reports on the Indian General Elections 1951–52* (Bombay, 1956), pp. 164–165. The caste composition of the leadership of these two organizations, not given in the book, was provided by respondents from several districts.

The name AJGAR is formed from the initial letters of five caste names: Ahir, Jat, Gujar, Ahar, and Rajput.

scribes and government servants. In the 1931 census, 70 percent of the male Kayasths were recorded as literate.[16] In rural areas the Kayasths often are the recorders of landholdings; in urban areas many are engaged in government service, teaching, the legal profession, or politics. The former Chief Minister of Uttar Pradesh, Dr. Sampurnanand, and the second Prime Minister of India, Lal Bahadur Shastri, were Kayasths. The next elite caste, the Jat, is the only peasant caste not listed as backward. Jats are concentrated in the western districts. The older ethnographies have given them a status midway between the Rajputs and the Ahirs, and many Jats consider themselves to be the leaders of the backward classes. An elite caste of somewhat ambivalent status is the Bhumihar, concentrated in a few northeastern districts. In status the Bhumihars are somewhere between Brahmins and Thakurs; many have been large landowners.

Members of these castes are usually Hindu in religion, but Muslims are also divided into castes ranging from high to low. Although there are Muslim Brahmins, Muslim Rajputs, and so on, the largest Muslim castes are peculiar to Islam. Listed from high to low, the more politically prominent ones are the Sayyid, Sheikh, Pathan, and Ansari or Julaha. Despite caste divisions, the Muslims appear to have developed a consciousness of themselves as Muslims.

In some states of India a "dominant" caste exists, or there may be two or more geographically separated dominant castes. Such is the case of the Kammas and Reddis of Andhra Pradesh, the Patidars of Gujarat, and the Nayars of Kerala, among others. According to M. N. Srinivas: "A caste may be said to be "dominant" when it preponderates numerically over the other castes, and when it also wields preponderant economic and political power. A large and powerful caste group can more easily be dominant if its position in the local caste hierarchy is not too low." [17] To be numerically preponderant, of course, a caste must be significantly larger than others. In Uttar Pradesh there is a dominant caste—the Thakurs—only in the sparsely populated

---

[16] *Census of India, 1931*, XVIII, Part II, 480.
[17] "The Social System of a Mysore Village," in McKim Marriott (ed.), *Village India* (Bombay, 1961), p. 18.

Himalayan hill districts. Elsewhere, according to the 1931 census, which was the last to record caste, there are no castes with more than 25 percent of a district's population, and only three castes, in five districts, have as much as 20 percent of the population (the Thakurs in two northwestern districts, the Chamars in two districts, and the Yadavs in one district).[18] Uttar Pradesh is a multi-caste state, having in most districts several castes of approximately the same size. Furthermore, the larger castes tend to be state-wide rather than regional in distribution—for instance, the Brahmins, Yadavs, Chamars, the Thakurs. Some other large castes, such as the Kurmis and the Pasis, are found throughout much of the state. A few castes loom in importance because of geographic concentration which puts them among the largest in certain districts. The Jats and Gujars in the western, the Kachhis in the south-central, and the Kewats and Koeris in a few northeastern districts fall in this category.

Muslims comprise 14 percent of the state's population. There is no district in which Muslims hold a majority over Hindus, but in 1951 in the district of Rampur (formerly a princely state) they comprised 49 percent of the population, and in seven other districts they represented 20 percent or more.[19]

District percentages give only one side of the coin, because within a district a particular caste may be concentrated in one part. Further, village settlement patterns vary. Thus diversity again characterizes the state. There are many multicaste or mixed villages: "Probably in no comparably large area of India are there as many castes per village, on the average, as in the plains of Central Uttar Pradesh. That the degree of fractionization of society has important political and social consequences should be fairly obvious." [20]In contrast, there are also some totally one-caste villages and predominantly one-caste villages.

When the socioeconomic indices are viewed together, it becomes obvious that boundaries do not accumulate. Language

[18] *Census of India, 1931,* XVIII, Part II, 499–548.
[19] Calculated from *Census of India, 1951,* V: *Uttar Pradesh* (Allahabad, 1953), Part II-C, *Age and Social Tables,* 560–575.
[20] Joseph E. Schwartzberg, "The Geography of Caste in the North Indian Plain," paper presented at the University of Chicago Conference on Social Structure and Social Change in India, June 3–5, 1965, p. 4 (mimeographed).

divisions are modified by caste distributions, a caste is divided by economic indices, and so forth. The cross-cutting diversities of the state make it an interesting choice for study.

Political History

Numerous shifting kingdoms and empires characterized the early political history of the region which is now the state of Uttar Pradesh. This basic pattern continued through the period of Muslim rule. Formal British control began in 1775 with the cession of Banaras Province. Acquisition of the region was completed in 1856 when the remainder of the Kingdom of Oudh was annexed. In 1877 Oudh and the adjoining North-West Provinces were placed under a combined administration.[21]

For a few decades after the Mutiny of 1857 Uttar Pradesh was relatively quiescent. The Indian National Congress was formed as a pressure group in 1885, but most of its leaders came from other areas of India; a notable exception was Madan Mohan Malaviya. After the First World War Uttar Pradesh became the political center of the nationalist movement, and Allahabad became the headquarters of the All-India Congress Committee. The state produced many of the eminent national leaders identified with the Congress, including Motilal Nehru, Jawaharlal Nehru, and P. D. Tandon, and has also provided several post-independence Congress leaders, among them Lal Bahadur Shastri, Mrs. Indira Gandhi, Pandit Govind Ballabh Pant, Rafi Ahmed Kidwai, K. D. Malaviya, and Hafiz Mohammed Ibrahim. Moreover, many prominent opposition party leaders, originally in the Congress, can be claimed for Uttar Pradesh through birth or later residence. Among these are two noted socialists, Acharya Narendra Dev and Achut Patwardhan. J. B. Kripalani, who was the Congress president before becoming the leader of the Praja Socialist Party, lives in Lucknow and holds a seat in the Lok Sabha from an Uttar Pradesh constituency. His wife was chief minister for the Congress Government in Uttar Pradesh from 1963 to 1967. Jaya Prakash Narayan and Dr. Ram Manohar Lohia have very close ties

---

[21] In 1902 the title was changed to the United Provinces of Agra and Oudh, and in 1937 it was shortened to the United Provinces. After independence the name was changed to Uttar Pradesh.

to the state from their years of organizational and agitational activity.[22]

Besides being an important center for the Congress and for several present-day opposition parties, Uttar Pradesh has contributed significantly to the Muslim League, producing such leaders as Liaquat Ali, Ghulam Mohammed, Khaliq uz Zaman, the Nawab of Chhatari, and Nawab Mohammed Ismail. Aligarh Muslim University has played an important role in the political socialization of Muslims, and many of its graduates were active participants in the movement for separating Pakistan from India.

The Congress had a dominant position in Uttar Pradesh politics until 1967, but it has not been without opposition. In the 1937 elections to the Provincial Assembly the chief opposition came from the Muslim League and the pro-British Nationalist Agricultural Party, composed of the landed aristocracy, which won 26 and 22 seats, respectively, while the Congress won 136 seats and thus held a majority. One Liberal and 43 Independents were also elected. In 1946 the Muslim League won 54 seats, while the Congress won 153. The only other successful party, the National Muslims, won seven seats.[23]

There were many political changes between 1946 and 1952. With the creation of Pakistan and the subsequent migration of prominent leaders of the Muslim League, this party disappeared as a political force in Uttar Pradesh. Many Hindus were upset by the Congress's acceptance of the partition plan. Some of these helped found, or later gave support to, a new opposition party, the Jan Sangh, in 1951.

The Congress was never a monolithic movement. It encompassed many groups with differing political orientations and ideologies. In its transition from movement to party, some groups were forced out. In 1947 it invited the Congress Socialist Party to disband or leave, and some who withdrew went on to form the Socialist Party. Under P. D. Tandon the Uttar Pradesh Congress adopted a distinctly rightist policy. In 1950 factional differences led to the departure of many of Rafi Ahmed Kidwai's followers, who formed the Jan Congress. In 1951, after his defeat in seeking the Congress presidency, J. B. Kripalani withdrew and with his

[22] Dr. Lohia died in 1967.
[23] Shri Ved Prakash Gupta, *Franchise in India* (Bombay, 1965), pp. 36, 40.

followers formed the Kisan Mazdoor Praja Party.[24] Despite these departures, the Congress remained pluralist. Factional rivalry persisted and became more intense as the years passed.[25]

In the first general elections to be held after independence the Congress reached the peak of its strength in Uttar Pradesh. Winning 390 of 430 Assembly seats and 81 of 86 Lok Sabha seats, it captured 47.9 percent of the popular vote for the state legislature, and 53 percent for the Lok Sabha, as compared with its national average of 45 percent.[26] Since then it has steadily declined. In 1957, when the Congress won 286 of 430 Assembly seats and 70 of 86 Lok Sabha seats, its share of the popular vote dropped to 42.4 percent in Uttar Pradesh although in the country as a whole it obtained 48 percent.[27] In 1962 the Congress won 249 Assembly seats and 62 Lok Sabha seats, with its share of the popular vote dropping to 36.3 percent against a national average of 45 percent.[28] By late 1966, by-elections and defections from other parties had increased its seats in the state legislature from 249 to 275.[29] The debacle came in the 1967 elections, when the Congress failed to win a majority in the legislature. After a brief, unsuccessful attempt to form a ministry with the support of Independents, one Congress faction resigned and joined with the opposition parties to form the Government.

The Congress is still the single largest party in Uttar Pradesh. In 1962 the Jan Sangh, the largest opposition party, had less than one-fifth the strength of Congress in the legislature. In 1967 the Jan Sangh still had less than half the strength of Congress. Even so, the period of Congress dominance had apparently ended.

---

[24] These events are taken up in greater detail in discussing the history of the opposition parties later in this chapter.

[25] The history of Congress factions is covered extensively in Paul R. Brass, *Factional Politics in an Indian State: The Congress Party in Uttar Pradesh* (Berkeley and Los Angeles, 1965); hereafter cited as Brass, *Factional Politics in an Indian State.*

[26] India Election Commission, *Report on the First General Elections in India, 1951–52* (2 vols.; New Delhi, 1955), II, 7.

[27] India Election Commission, *Report on the Second General Elections in India, 1957* (2 vols.; New Delhi, 1959), II, 7.

[28] Office of the Chief Electoral Officer, Uttar Pradesh, *Results of the Third General Elections (1962) to the Uttar Pradesh Legislative Assembly* (Allahabad, 1962), pp. v–vii; Surindar Suri, *1962 Elections* (New Delhi, 1962), pp. 147–154.

[29] *National Herald* (Lucknow), November 16, 1966.

Opposition Parties

Opposition strength is fairly well distributed throughout Uttar Pradesh except in the northwestern districts. The Independents tend to be strong in the western districts. In general, opposition parties have their greatest strength in the eastern, central, and southwestern districts.

Opposed to the Congress in 1962 were seven opposition parties and Independents (Table 1). On the left were the Communist

TABLE 1

ABSTRACT OF ELECTION RESULTS, UTTAR PRADESH, 1952–1962

Party	Number of seats won in general elections for the State Assembly		
	1952	1957	1962
Congress	390	286	249
Jan Sangh	2	17	49
Praja Socialist	20 [a]	44	38
Lohia Socialist	—	24	24
Communist	—	9	14
Swatantra	—	—	15
Republican	—	—	8
Hindu Mahasabha	1	—	2
Other	3	—	—
Independents	14	50	31
Total	430	430	430

SOURCE: *Results of the Third General Elections (1962) to the Uttar Pradesh Legislative Assembly* (Allahabad, 1962), pp. v–vii.

[a] The Praja Socialist Party did not exist in 1952. The figure combines the nineteen seats won by the Socialist Party (former Congress Socialist Party) and the one seat held by the Kisan Mazdoor Praja Party.

Party, the Socialist Party, and the Praja Socialist Party. On the right were the Jan Sangh, the Republican Party (often called the "Chamar Party"), the communal Hindu Mahasabha, and the Swatantra Party (composed of former landed aristocrats). The Independents varied widely in their ideological orientation, socio-economic composition, and career backgrounds. While it would have been desirable to study the building and maintenance of each opposition party, time limitations made it necessary to restrict the number to be studied. The Jan Sangh, the Praja Socialist Party, and the Socialist Party were chosen because they were the largest and most prominent opposition parties in the state, and because they differed in ideology and history.[30] Presumably these parties would appeal to different segments of society and, as such, would have different problems of building and maintenance.

The Jan Sangh (JS), formed in 1951, is a relatively new party. It stems, however, from a militant but nonpolitical Hindu organization which was founded in 1925, the Rashtriya Swayamsevak Sangh (RSS).[31] During the 1940's the RSS showed a considerable increase in its membership and activities. It opposed the partition of India and Pakistan and is said to have been active in the Hindu-Muslim riots. In 1948 Gandhi was assassinated by a man who was a member of the Hindu Mahasabha and formerly of the RSS. Within a few days both organizations were banned by the Government and their leaders on national, state, and local levels were arrested. A year and a half later the ban was removed. Apparently, many RSS leaders judged that the Government would not have banned their organization, or would have lifted the ban on it sooner, if it had been represented in political bodies. In 1951 some RSS leaders and others, in particular Shyama Prasad Mookerjee (who had been a member of Nehru's cabinet), founded the Bharatiya Jan Sangh as a political party. Ostensibly, the Jan Sangh was to be entirely separate from the RSS. It was to be open to Muslims as well as Hindus, and although opposed to "appeasement of Muslims" it has, from its inception, called for "Akhand Bharat," or the union of India and Pakistan.

[30] Originally only the Jan Sangh and the Praja Socialist Party were selected for study. The Socialist Party was added near the end of the study when it became likely that the Praja Socialist Party would split, with one group joining the Congress and the other merging with the Socialists. In 1964, after my return from India, the split occurred, in the manner indicated. The Samyukta Socialist Party was formed from the Socialist Party and the rump of the Praja Socialist Party. Reports of grave dissension within the new party were given substance when some former Praja Socialists withdrew to reestablish the old party.

[31] The Jan Sangh's antecedents and manner of founding are studied in Myron Weiner, *Party Politics in India* (Princeton, 1957).

Jan Sangh means "People's Party." The name of the RSS translates as "National Self-Help Society."

The Jan Sangh program puts emphasis on the rebuilding of India as a "modern, progressive, and strong State on the basis of Bharatiya culture and true Bharatiya nationalism,"[32] and on foreign policy. Pakistan has been a matter of continuing concern, to which Communist China has been added in recent years. In economic matters the Jan Sangh accepts state ownership of basic industries, but favors increased scope for private enterprise under state regulation and is against the "concentration of economic power . . . through nationalization of all means of production."[33] It recommends special encouragement of small-scale units of production. Although "socialism" is not mentioned in connection with economic policy and appears to be regarded as an imported, alien doctrine, the policy set forth is little different from that practiced by the Congress or espoused by the socialist parties. Economic concerns, however, figure far less in Jan Sangh pronouncements than do social and cultural issues. To further national unity, a unitary government is favored, with power to be divided between a strong national establishment and small local bodies. The Jan Sangh calls for both the adoption of Hindi as the national language and the full development of other regional languages except Urdu, which is specifically excluded because bolstering of Urdu would amount to appeasement of Muslims.

The charge most often made against the Jan Sangh is that it is "communal"—that it represents the narrow, selfish, and aggressive attitudes within the Hindu religious community. Party leaders have repeatedly denied the charge and stressed that the Jan Sangh is a national organization open to persons of all religious beliefs. Yet the relationship with the RSS, a communal organization, cannot be overlooked. While a few Muslims are members, it is apparent that the party mainly attracts Hindus, and it is

[32] *Bharatiya Jana Sangh: A Brief Introduction,* (Delhi, n.d.,), p. 1. See also the party publications *Manifesto and Programme of the Bharatiya Jana Sangh* (Delhi, 1956); *Election Manifesto, 1957* (Delhi, n.d.,); *Election Manifesto, 1962* (Delhi, n.d.); Dr. Shyama Prasad Mookerjee, *Presidential Address* (Lucknow, 1951); *Important Economic Resolutions 1952–57* (Delhi, n.d.); *Resolutions of the Bharatiya Pratinidhi Sabha* (Delhi, 1963); Acharya Deva Prasad Ghosh, *Presidential Address* (Delhi, 1963); and A. Ramarao, *Presidential Address* (Lucknow, 1960).

[33] *Bharatiya Jana Sangh: A Brief Introduction,* p. 3. See also *Important Economic Resolutions 1952–57,* and the *Election Manifestoes* of 1957 and 1962.

known that on occasion the party has tried to win votes by calling on Hindu unity.[34]

Jan Sangh strength is found notably among small Hindu shopkeepers and businessmen and in the smaller towns.[35] In the course of the three general elections the party's strength in the state legislature has risen from two seats to 17 and then to 49 (Table 1). This is a remarkable and steady increase. There have been neither major splits within the party nor mergers with other parties. The Jan Sangh is reportedly a highly centralized and highly disciplined party.

The second largest opposition party in 1962 was the Praja Socialist Party (PSP). Its history, more complex than that of the Jan Sangh, goes back to 1934, when a group known as the Congress Socialist Party (CSP) was formed within the Congress.[36] This group did not put up candidates in the 1937 elections or in the Constituent Assembly elections of the 1940's, but it attained some prominence in 1942 when it led the "Quit India" movement. In 1947 the Congress adopted a rule that no organized groups should exist within itself. Some CSP members, including Acharya Narendra Dev, Jaya Prakash Narayan, Ashok Mehta, Dr. Ram Manohar Lohia, S. M. Joshi, and Achut Patwardhan, then decided to withdraw and form the Socialist Party.

In Uttar Pradesh the CSP was very strong, controlling much of the Congress organization on the state and district levels. Most of the CSP members stayed in the Congress, and several have had prominent roles in the Government, among them the former Chief Ministers Sampurnanand and C. B. Gupta. Other ministers, and many organizational and district leaders, have had CSP ties. Those who left the Congress did so in many cases owing to the personal influence of Narendra Dev, Jaya Prakash Narayan, and Dr. Lohia as well as to ideological commitments. Thirteen who were members of the legislature resigned their seats on the grounds

---

[34] Donald E. Smith, *India as a Secular State* (Princeton, 1963), pp. 469–479.

[35] Phillips Talbot, "The Second General Elections: Voting in the States," *American Universities Field Staff Report*, April 28, 1957, pp. 62–68 (mimeographed); Paul R. Brass, "An Industrial Labor Constituency: Kanpur," *Economic Weekly*, special number, July, 1962, pp. 1111–18.

[36] See Hari Kishore Singh, *A History of the Praja Socialist Party* (Lucknow, 1959), and Weiner, *Party Politics in India*, Pt. II.

Praja, in the party name, means "Peoples'."

that they had been elected as Congressmen. When by-elections were held, in which these ran as Socialists, none was elected. In the general elections of 1951–1952 the Socialists won 19 seats in the Assembly.

There was another current within the Uttar Pradesh Congress during the mid-1940's and until after the first general elections. As independence drew near and many leaders from the state (Nehru and Tandon, among others) were expected to serve the national government, various individuals and groups attempted to gain control of the state and district parties. A key figure was Pandit Govind Ballabh Pant, the chief minister in 1937–1939 and 1946–1954. Pant was a parliamentary leader, lacking an organizational base. Rafi Ahmed Kidwai, his political manager, had talents in organization. Beginning in 1946, Pant moved to reduce Kidwai's power and increase his own, with the result that Kidwai's supporters, who were dramatically pushed out of organizational offices, found themselves unable to share in the distribution of patronage. Reports of illegalities and corruption in these maneuvers are widespread even today. C. B. Gupta, one of Pant's several lieutenants, had been in the CSP, but Pant's scheme did not appear to be a movement of socialists. Rather, many of those who took over the Congress organization were newcomers, often with more education and money than the long-time stalwarts. Recognizing that the Congress would soon be the ruling power, they were delighted to accept the support of Pant's lieutenants in order to gain control of the party in their districts. To this day Kidwai's followers bitterly resent the treatment they received; most of them regard C. B. Gupta as their sworn enemy.

In 1950 a group of twenty-two members of the Legislative Assembly (MLA's) and two members of the Legislative Council (MLC's), followers of Kidwai who had been pushed to the background in the Congress, formed an opposition party known as the Jan Congress. It was purely a provincial party. Triloki Singh, S. K. D. Paliwal, and Gopal Narain Saxsena were the foremost leaders. As months passed, other Rafiats (as followers of Kidwai are known) joined.

Later in that year there was a contest in the national Congress between P. D. Tandon and Acharya J. B. Kripalani for the party presidency. Kripalani was defeated and then was not included on the Working Committee. Thereupon he left the Congress and formed the Kisan Mazdoor Praja Party (KMPP), a group often described as "Gandhian." The KMPP was intended to be a national party, and in Uttar Pradesh the Jan Congress promptly merged with it and took its name. A few other supporters of Kripalani joined in. Shortly before the 1951–1952 elections Rafi Ahmed Kidwai himself joined the KMPP, bringing many followers with him. A few weeks before the deadline for nomination for the elections Kidwai returned to the Congress with some of his followers, the others remaining in the KMPP. In the elections, however, only one KMPP candidate won a seat in the Assembly.[37]

Shortly before the elections there were rumors about a merger of the Socialist Party and the KMPP, but nothing materialized at that time. Afterward their leaders held talks, and in 1952 the two parties merged to form the Praja Socialist Party. The course of the new party did not run smoothly. Within the former Socialist Party there had always been differences over personalities and issues. One issue dating from 1947 was the relationship of the party to the Congress. Many national leaders were more in favor of some kind of cooperation with the Congress than were the militants. In 1953 the question erupted in various forms. First, talks between Jaya Prakash Narayan and Nehru concerning possible cooperation by the two parties aroused rumors of a merger. The militants, led by Dr. Ram Manohar Lohia, protested vigorously the holding of the talks and at the PSP convention that year sought assurance from the Party's national leaders that no overtures should be made to or accepted from the Congress. This assurance the leaders absolutely refused to give, insisting that they should not be forced into positions which they did not personally approve.[38] (The leaders were reelected, with the opposing faction leading the move, as seems to be a common practice in India.)

[37] Kidwai was a Minister in Nehru's Cabinet from 1946 to 1954, and according to Michael Brecher was one of Nehru's most trusted advisers (*Nehru: A Political Biography* [abridged ed.; London, 1961], p. 173). As a Minister he was in a position to bestow benefits upon his followers in the state, regardless of their party affiliation of the moment. There are reports that he felt some responsibility for his follower's loss of Congress positions and that he gave direct financial support to some of them for many years.

    The name Kisan Mazdoor Praja Party, or KMPP, means Farmer-Labor People's Party.

[38] *Report of the Special Convention of the Praja Socialist Party, Betul, June 14–18, 1953* (Bombay, 1953), pp. 8–87.

Later that year another incident further divided the two groups. In Kerala the Praja Socialists formed a minority Government with the support of the Congress. After a few months the police fired on a mob in Kerala. Dr. Lohia, the general secretary of the PSP, who was in jail at the time, ordered the Kerala PSP to resign from the Government. This action was taken without consultation of any kind with other PSP leaders. The question of cooperation with the Congress was again involved, along with the moral question of the police firing. Since other leaders did not agree with Dr. Lohia's instructions, friction at the top level quickly went from bad to worse. A final incident came when Madhu Limaye, a member of the Bombay City PSP, made accusations in the press that other local members, notably Ashok Mehta, were planning to join the Congress. This was denied, but Limaye refused to offer an apology. After a bitter dispute the Bombay City party suspended him. The National Executive Committee of the PSP reviewed the situation and, despite repeated requests from many state units for an investigation, decided that they had no power to take any action. The Uttar Pradesh branch of the party, whose leaders were members of Dr. Lohia's group, invited the suspended Limaye to inaugurate the state party convention. Unable to order or persuade the branch to withdraw the invitation, the National Executive suspended the entire State Executive and set up an *ad hoc* committee. Dr. Lohia and his group then left the PSP and formed the Lohia Socialist Party.[39] Two parties thus existed: the Praja Socialists and the Lohia Socialists. The split in Uttar Pradesh was not, strictly speaking, between the former KMPP and the former CSP. Although a few KMPP members left with Dr. Lohia, the split was basically within the former CSP group. The bulk of the former CSP and KMPP members stayed in the Praja Socialist Party.

In subsequent years the PSP suffered leadership losses. Acharya

---

[39] For various accounts of the split see Lok Nath Joshi, *The Farce of Discipline* (Lucknow, 1955); Dan Singh, *An Appeal to the Chairman and All Members of the Praja Socialist Party* (Naini Tal, Uttar Pradesh, [1955]); *Facts on Lohia's Attempts at Disrupting the PSP* (Delhi, 1955); and Hari Kishore Singh, *A History of the Praja Socialist Party*, pp. 168–216.

The party formed by Dr. Lohia and his associates took the name "Socialist Party." I refer to it by this name generally, but to distinguish it from the Socialist Party of 1947–1952 I refer to it in some passages as the Lohia Socialist Party.

Narenda Dev died in 1956. After the 1957 elections Jaya Prakash Narayan formally retired from politics and from the party, although he could be counted on to take an ex officio role in PSP affairs.

Despite the split and the loss of leaders, the Praja Socialists made substantial gains in the 1957 elections, winning 44 seats in the State Assembly. (The Lohia Socialists won 25.) There was frequent speculation as to how many seats might have been won by a united party. There was occasional talk of merger of the two parties, but nothing came of it.

In 1962 the Praja Socialists declined in strength, winning only 38 Assembly seats. Within a few months after the election, five of the MLA's who had joined the party just before the election left and joined the Congress, thus reducing PSP strength to 33 seats. The Lohia Socialist Party held its own, winning 24 seats.

During the 1957–1962 interval the Praja Socialists suffered no major splits; they were, however, plagued by a gradual drifting away of district and local leaders. Just after the 1962 election, moreover, Acharya Kripalani left the party to become an Independent. A struggle for power took place between Ashok Mehta and S. M. Joshi, with the issue of relationship to the Congress again a key feature. Joshi, with a policy of determined opposition, was the victor. A split came in 1964 after Ashok Mehta accepted the Government's offer of a position in the Planning Commission, refused to resign, and left the party with his group to join the Congress.

The PSP could be termed either an old-fashioned liberal party or a democratic socialist party. Its ideology is a poorly blended mixture of Marxism, Gandhianism, and social democracy. In contrast with the Jan Sangh, it puts great emphasis on economic policies and principles. Its program calls for nationalization of industries, splitting up of large state corporations so as to provide competition, decentralization of industries, and encouragement of small-scale units of production, with the Government providing the market for the output of small-scale units. The party is against all class distinctions whether based on economic, social, or cultural considerations. It favors rapid social change, economic equality, and an expansion of freedoms. Minorities are to be granted full self-expression in all areas—especially in regard to the practice of religion and the promotion of their language, script, and literature; institutions set up by minorities are to be entitled to state aid. In foreign policy nonalignment and anticolonialism are key features; the stand on Kashmir is the same as that of the Jan Sangh—namely, that Kashmir should be fully integrated with India. Most policy statements of the party exhibit a broad, vague humanitarianism together with concern over specific measures.[40]

The background of the Lohia Socialist Party (SP), established in 1955, has already been noted. Cohesion and discipline within the party appear to be greater than in the PSP and have led to charges of its being a dictatorial, one-man party. In 1959 a dissident but disunited group broke away. Some dissidents joined the Congress, some went to the PSP or to the Communists, some became Independents, and others retired from politics.

The Lohia SP is very much anti-Congress and was violently anti-Nehru. Its policy as regards cooperation with other opposition parties has fluctuated. At times Dr. Lohia has sought close cooperation with the Jan Sangh and the Communists, and at times has fervently opposed it. He has usually opposed cooperation with the Praja Socialists. In 1957 a move for merger with the PSP failed. After the 1962 elections legislative backbenchers of the two parties in Uttar Pradesh, manuevering secretly, established a "United Socialist Party" within the Assembly. Dr. Lohia opposed the action and was able to thwart the merger within a few weeks.

The great claim of the Lohia Socialists is that they are "militant." In practice this appears to mean unremitting involvement in agitations, civil disobedience movements, walkout from the Assembly, and noisy demonstrations on the Assembly floor. Compared with the PSP, the Socialists put less emphasis on economic policy and more emphasis on two related matters, language and backward castes.[41] They urge that English be abolished forthwith and regional languages utilized solely, except for Hindi as the

---

[40] Weiner, *Party Politics in India*, pp. 25–116; Hari Kishore Singh, *A History of the Praja Socialist Party;* and the following PSP publications: *Policy Statement* (Delhi, 1956), *Election Manifesto, 1957* (Delhi, n.d.), *Election Manifesto, 1962* (Delhi, n.d.), *Facing the Challenge* (Delhi, n.d.), *Bangalore Resolutions* (Bombay, 1956), *Economic Situation in 1957* (Delhi, 1957), *PSP General Council Meeting* (Delhi, n.d.), Political Perspective (Delhi, 1957), *Praja Socialist Party in Parliament* (New Delhi, 1962).

[41] *Socialist Party Statement of Principles* (Hyderabad, 1956); *Statement of Principles and Programmes* (Hyderabad, 1956); *Election Manifesto, 1962* (Hyderabad, 1962); *Lohia's Letters* (Bangalore, n.d.); *National Committee Resolutions* (Hyderabad, 1956).

link language, and that 60 percent of all government jobs and political seats be reserved for members of the backward and scheduled castes and for women. The Lohia Socialists take the position that the basic need of India today is to further unity, which requires participation in governing and a feeling that the government is of the people. Among the backward and scheduled castes, and among women, loyalty to India is minimal, say the Lohia Socialists, since these people have never participated in governing, and the basic reason for that is language: for centuries the language of the government has been different from that of the masses. It follows, then, that the government is "alien" and can be made democratic and "of the people" only by making its language the same as that of the people, whereupon those who failed to participate in the past will be able to do so. Just changing the language, however, is seen as insufficient, since jobs are often given on a caste basis, with the result that the upper castes dominate the government. Thus the party maintains that backward and scheduled castes and women, comprising more than 60 percent of the population, ought to hold at least 60 percent of jobs and political seats if they are to have "equal" opportunity to participate, arguing that no sense of nationalism can develop within these groups so long as they are excluded. The Lohia SP also stands for ending economic disparities, tearing down British statues, and abolishing the caste system. Its appeal is directed toward the rural areas and the lower castes.

Part Two

THE MIDDLE-LEVEL LEADERS

STATE LEGISLATORS, defeated Assembly candidates, and political figures in the districts and constituencies form the middle-level leadership in Indian political parties. Students of Indian politics have encouraged study of this group in order to probe the relationships between "modern" and "traditional" sectors of society and the modifications of each by the other. These leaders are the "gap-closers" [1] or, in another formulation, the "brokers" who function within a small-scale parochial population while simultaneously transcending it and taking on broader state or national roles.[2] There is no one accepted term in political science for this particular group. Perhaps the most serviceable term is "middlemen," signifying an elite cadre which performs managerial, planning, coordinating, and research functions as well as the recruitment and training of new members, but which is larger than the elite nucleus.[3]

There are a number of important questions which can be asked about the middlemen. Biographical data can show what kinds of people become active in politics and in the different political parties, suggest the individual dimension of social tensions in a changing society, and permit the classifying of individuals as representatives of particular groups and social movements. If a party has appeal for particular cultural or social groups, or is trying to gain

[1] W. H. Morris-Jones, "India's Political Idioms," in C. H. Philips (ed.), *Politics and Society in India* (London, 1963), p. 150.

[2] Bailey, *Politics and Social Change*. Bailey defines the "broker" both as an individual who links the village and the administration (pp. 60 ff., 100 ff.), which is the sense used here, and as a "man of substance, furthering his business interests by making contacts and recruiting followers for politicians" (p. 149). In this latter definition Bailey has mixed the function performed with the characteristics and motives of those taking on this role. For my purposes the concept has greater usefulness if the two aspects are separated.

[3] Dwaine Marvick, "The Middlemen of Politics," paper read before the 1962 Annual Meeting of the American Political Science Association, Washington, D.C., September 5–8, 1962, pp. 5–6 (mimeographed).

their support, indications of this are likely to be reflected in its middlemen.

Members of the Legislative Assembly, or lower house of the state legislature, usually called MLA's in India, form an easily identifiable and readily accessible category of middlemen. Many of these are also district or constituency leaders in their parties. It cannot be claimed that the MLA's are a representative sample of the total formal party membership, or of the total voting support garnered by a party. A sample survey taken from an accurate membership roll would be needed for the one, and a sample survey of the general adult populace for the other. Inasmuch as it is sometimes necessary for a party to put up a candidate of a certain group in order to gain the support of that group, there is likely to be some correspondence between the characteristics of (a) a party's MLA's (and MLA candidates) and (b) the permanent party and electoral supporters.

In the chapter which follows I offer an analysis of the socioeconomic characteristics of Uttar Pradesh MLA's elected in 1962 as indicative of the middlemen of the three opposition parties, the Jan Sangh, the Praja Socialist Party, and the Lohia Socialist Party. In chapter iv the backgrounds of their political careers are treated similarly. The data were gathered in interviews with those who were MLA's of the parties in question as of late 1963. There were interviews with 46 Jan Sangh MLA's (out of 48 elected in 1962), 33 Praja Socialist MLA's (out of 38 elected, five who joined the party just before the election and resigned from it afterward to join the Congress, have been eliminated from my analysis), and 22 Lohia Socialist MLA's (two of the 24 elected, having left the party, were eliminated). Some data collected in separate research by Ralph Meyer has been incorporated, with his permission; also, comparison with Congress Party MLA's has been made possible on some indices through the use of data collected and made available by him.[4] I collected information as to caste, directly or in-

---

[4] Ralph Meyer, of Lafayette College, Easton, Pennsylvania, collected data on the social origins of all MLA's from Uttar Pradesh from 1952 to 1962. Because of basic differences in asking certain questions, not all of his data could be utilized. For example, I asked MLA's for their present primary and secondary occupations. Meyer collected data on the pre-MLA greatest-source-of-income occupation. Also, the Meyer data is based on party membership as of the 1962 election, while mine is as of late 1963 membership. My data was

directly, on all MLA candidates in the 1962 election, but only the castes of Congress, Jan Sangh, Praja Socialist and Lohia Socialist candidates are noted.

---

collected directly, while Meyer's was collected directly and indirectly. Occasionally there was variance in the data, as when there would be a one- or two-year difference in age for some respondents, which became important if it resulted in their placement in different age groupings. These are minor discrepancies and there were few of them. In comparing the MLA's of the three parties with the Congress, the Meyer data on all the MLA's were tabulated and used. Any differences between his figures on the opposition parties and my own are noted.

Comparison with the Meyer data was facilitated through a common pattern of classification, jointly drawn up. The Meyer data are identified as such in the text with no further citation.

Chapter III

SOCIOECONOMIC BACKGROUNDS

THERE ARE SIGNIFICANT DIFFERENCES in the geographical distribution of strength of the Jan Sangh, Praja Socialist, and Lohia Socialist parties in Uttar Pradesh. Table 2 groups the districts of the

TABLE 2

GEOGRAPHICAL AREA GROUPINGS OF JAN SANGH, PRAJA SOCIALIST, AND SOCIALIST MLA's

(by percent and number of party MLA's)

Area	Jan Sangh		Praja Socialist		Socialist	
Oudh	50.0	(24)	—	—	40.9	(9)
Eastern districts	16.7	(8)	45.5	(15)	31.8	(7)
Southwestern and southern districts	18.7	(9)	45.4	(15)	27.3	(6)
Western districts	14.6	(7)	9.1	(3)	—	—
Total	100.0	(48)	100.0	(33)	100.0	(22)

state into four broad areas. The twelve districts in the former Kingdom of Oudh, with its historical identity, comprise one area. The Jan Sangh and Socialists have their greatest strength here, where the PSP won no seats in the 1962 elections. East of Oudh are nine districts of the Middle Ganges Plain which are among the poorest in India. In this eastern area the PSP is very strong, followed by the SP. Three former revenue divisions, differing in physical characteristics, are combined as a southern and southwestern area. The five southern districts are a hill and plateau region in which none of the parties has notable strength. In the adjacent southwestern region are ten districts of the Ganges-Jumna doab (Allahabad and Agra divisions), in which the PSP has considerable strength, followed by the Socialists and then the Jan Sangh.[1] All three parties are weak in the sixteen districts of the western area. For that reason these districts have been grouped together; they comprise the former revenue divisions of Meerut, Rohilkhand, and the Himalayan division of Kumaon.

Comparing the parties as to rural-urban constituency character-istics, it is clear that all have a rural base. Only two Jan Sangh seats and one PSP seat could be termed urban in 1962.

There is little difference in age among MLA's of the three parties. The median age of Jan Sangh MLA's is forty years; So-cialists, forty-two; and Praja Socialists, forty-three (Table 3).

TABLE 3

AGE OF JAN SANGH, PRAJA SOCIALIST, AND SOCIALIST MLA's, 1962
(by percent and number of party MLA's)

Age	Jan Sangh		Praja Socialist		Socialist	
32 and under	18.7	(9)	6.1	(2)	4.5	(1)
33–42	39.6	(19)	42.4	(14)	45.5	(10)
43–52	25.0	(12)	36.4	(12)	31.8	(7)
53 and over	16.7	(8)	15.1	(5)	18.2	(4)
Total	100.0	(48)	100.0	(33)	100.0	(22)

Meyer's data indicate that the Congress MLA's are slightly older, their median age being between forty-six and forty-seven years.

Most of the respondents are village born (Table 4). The Jan Sangh have more MLA's born in small towns than the other par-ties, and the Praja Socialists have a few MLA's born in cities. By birthplace the Socialists appear to be the most village-based party. Meyer's data indicate that almost 30 percent of the Congress MLA's were born in urban areas and 70 percent in villages. Taken together, the two socialist parties have more village-born MLA's than either the Congress or the Jan Sangh.

The rural or urban character of MLA's is better indicated by present residence than by birthplace. The Jan Sangh MLA's still

[1] The southern and southwestern area group could be logically subdivided into two or three more homogeneous units. With many categories and a small *N*, however, analysis would become meaningless.

TABLE 4

BIRTHPLACE OF JAN SANGH, PRAJA SOCIALIST, AND SOCIALIST MLA's
(by percent and number of party MLA's)

Birthplace [a]	Jan Sangh		Praja Socialist		Socialist	
Village	68.7	(33)	81.8	(27)	90.9	(20)
Small town	20.8	(10)	3.0	(1)	4.5	(1)
Medium to large town...	6.3	(3)	—	—	—	—
City	4.2	(2)	15.2	(5)	4.5	(1)
Total	100.0	(48)	100.0	(33)	100.0	(22)

[a] The village is taken as having fewer than 5,000 inhabitants, the small town from 5,000 to 20,000, the medium to large town from 20,000 to 100,000, and the city more than 100,000. Sizes were determined for birth date of respective respondents, to nearest census.

appear to be the least village-based. The Socialist Party MLA's show the greatest proportionate shift to urban residence. The MLA's of the Praja Socialist Party emerge as the most village-based, but, again, a few reside in large cities, primarily Allahabad (Table 5). Comparison of birthplace and present residence reveals that 55 to 60 percent of the MLA's reside now in the place of birth.

Contrasting mobile modern society with static traditional society, Daniel Lerner states that physical or spatial mobility, by

TABLE 5
PRESENT RESIDENCE OF JAN SANGH, PRAJA SOCIALIST,
AND SOCIALIST MLA's
(by percent and number of party MLA's)

Present Residence [a]	Jan Sangh		Praja Socialist		Socialist	
Village	35.4	(17)	63.6	(21)	54.6	(12)
Small town	18.8	(9)	9.1	(3)	13.6	(3)
Medium to large town...	27.1	(13)	9.1	(3)	18.2	(4)
City	18.7	(9)	16.2	(6)	13.6	(3)
Total	100.0	(48)	100.0	(33)	100.0	(22)

[a] Size of place of residence determined by 1961 census.

encouraging the development of individuals' psychic mobility, has an initial key role in the modernization of societies.[2] The difference between birthplace and present residence is one indication of spatial mobility. For my purposes a better measure would have been provided by data on all places where the respondents had resided. Efforts to obtain this information were dropped because of the time consumed,[3] but some movements of the MLA's could be traced from answers to other questions. A tentative spatial mobility score was drawn up, which, although based on incomplete data for some respondents, raises points for speculation. Responses indicating residence only in the place of birth ranged from 21 percent (Jan Sangh) to 27 percent (Lohia SP). The figures might well have been lower if full information had been obtained. Between 20 percent (Jan Sangh) and 30 percent (PSP) indicated change of residence four or more times. About half had moved from one to three times. Analysis of previous residence by size categories showed that few of the village-born had lived in villages other than the birthplace; most had moved to towns or cities, or both.[4] Some had lived in other parts of India, and a few had traveled abroad.

Even though incomplete, the data indicate exposure of most respondents to new situations, differing values, and different kinds of people through residence in urban environments. A few of these are settled permanently in the largest of the places in which they have resided. Most, however, are settled in a place somewhat smaller than the largest. This pattern suggests that one factor involved in political mobilization might be the experience of having lived in a setting more urbanized than the permanent place of residence. It may be that the less urban environment appears restrictive or stultifying, and that participation in political parties provides an outlet. It may also be that through spatial mobility these men perceived the opportunity to play a "broker" role.

Myron Weiner has suggested that many individuals who become politically active have broken away from the traditional joint

[2] *The Passing of Traditional Society* (Glencoe, Ill.: Free Press, 1958), pp. 47–52.

[3] Approximately two-thirds of the respondents were asked for all changes of residence. All were asked for place of birth and present residence.

[4] The mobility does not fully indicate the exposure to urban ways of life. Some who had never changed residence were city dwellers.

family and found a substitute for it in the party.[5] Very few of our respondents have such a background.[6] As Table 6 indicates, the proportion of those who have broken from the joint family is highest among the Lohia Socialists, being slightly more than a

TABLE 6

JOINT-FAMILY MEMBERSHIP OF JAN SANGH, PRAJA SOCIALIST, AND SOCIALIST MLA's

(by percent and number of party MLA's)

Joint Family Membership	Jan Sangh		Praja Socialist		Socialist	
Is member	75.0	(36)	84.9	(28)	72.7	(16)
Is not member	16.7	(8)	12.1	(4)	27.3	(6)
Not ascertained	8.3	(4)	3.0	(1)	—	—
Total	100.0	(48)	100.0	(33)	100.0	(22)

fourth. The fact that the Praja Socialists appear to be the most "traditional" in this respect is surprising, as the Jan Sangh might be expected to be highest.

In caste background, both the Jan Sangh and the Praja Socialists in 1962 elected far greater numbers of MLA's of elite castes than of lower castes. The Praja Socialists, however, elected many MLA's of backward castes and only a few of scheduled castes, whereas in the Jan Sangh there was a near balance between the two groups. The Socialist Party, whose MLA's were equally divided between elite and non-elite, had more backward- than scheduled-caste MLA's (Table 7). According to the Meyer data, fully 63 percent of the Congress MLA's were of elite castes; its Muslim MLA's (8.5 percent of the total) were mostly elite also, and if these should be added to the Hindu elite there would be

[5] Party Politics in India (Princeton, 1957), pp. 234–235.
[6] The criterion used was common residence of married sons with parents (lineal-joint ties). For a discussion and typology of what is meant by "joint family" see Pauline M. Kolonda, "Caste and Family Structure: A Comparative Study of the Hindu 'Joint' Family" (paper prepared for a conference on "Social Structure and Social Change in India: Methods and Results," Center for Continuing Education, University of Chicago, June 3–5, 1965 (mimeographed).

TABLE 7

CASTE DISTRIBUTION OF JAN SANGH, PRAJA SOCIALIST,
AND SOCIALIST MLA's

(by percent and number of party MLA's)

Caste	Jan Sangh		Praja Socialist		Socialist	
Elite castes:						
Brahmins	16.6	(8)	15.2	(5)	18.2	(4)
Thakur	27.1	(13)	18.2	(6)	27.3	(6)
Vaishya, Bania	12.5	(6)	6.1	(2)	—	—
Muslim [a]	—	—	6.1	(2)	—	—
Kayasth	4.2	(2)	9.0	(3)	4.5	(1)
Bhumihar	2.1	(1)	6.0	(2)	—	—
	62.5	(30)	60.6	(20)	50.0	(11)
Backward castes:						
Kurmi	4.2	(2)	3.0	(1)	9.1	(2)
Yadav (Ahir, Ahar) ...	6.2	(3)	21.2	(7)	13.6	(3)
Lodhi	4.2	(2)	3.0	(1)	—	—
Other	4.2	(2)	3.1	(1)	4.6	(1)
	18.8	(9)	30.3	(10)	27.3	(6)
Scheduled castes:						
Chamar (Jatav)	6.3	(3)	9.1	(3)	—	—
Pasi	10.4	(5)	—	—	18.2	(4)
Other	2.0	(1)	—	—	4.5	(1)
	18.7	(9)	9.1	(3)	22.7	(5)
Grand Total	100.0	(48)	100.0	(33)	100.0	(22)

[a] The two Muslim MLA's were of the Sheikh and Pathan castes. The Pathans are considered to be comparable to the Hindu Thakurs; the Sheikhs are rated slightly higher.

an even higher proportion. Backward-caste Congress MLA's comprised only 6.8 percent of the party total, a far lower proportion than in the Jan Sangh, PSP, or SP. Twenty percent of the Congress MLA's were of scheduled castes, comparable to the proportions in the Jan Sangh and the SP.

Several significant features appear in a specific caste analysis of the MLA's. In the three opposition parties there is a relative bal-

TABLE 8

General-Seat Candidates of the Congress, Jan Sangh, Praja
Socialist, and Socialist Parties in 1962, by Caste
(by percent and number offered by the parties)

Caste	Congress		Jan Sangh		Praja Socialist		Lohia Socialist	
Brahmin	31.5	(107)	27.3	(82)	18.4	(43)	17.1	(37)
Thakur	21.2	(72)	26.3	(79)	23.6	(55)	17.6	(38)
Bania	12.9	(44)	13.0	(39)	5.6	(13)	7.4	(16)
Kayasth	5.9	(20)	6.7	(20)	6.4	(15)	3.2	(7)
Other elite (Jat, Bhumihar, et al.)	6.5	(22)	5.0	(15)	7.3	(17)	2.8	(6)
Total elite	78.0	(265)	78.3	(235)	61.3	(143)	48.1	(104)
Kurmi	2.1	(7)	2.3	(7)	5.2	(12)	8.8	(19)
Yadav	3.5	(12)	6.3	(19)	12.5	(29)	13.9	(30)
Lodhi-Rajput	.9	(3)	3.3	(10)	2.6	(6)	1.4	(3)
Other backward	1.5	(5)	3.0	(9)	2.6	(6)	6.9	(15)
Total backward	8.0	(27)	14.9	(45)	22.9	(53)	31.0	(67)
Muslims	13.1	(45)	—	—	9.4	(22)	9.7	(21)
Scheduled castes in general seats	.3	(1)	2.7	(8)	3.4	(8)	7.9	(17)
Not ascertained	.6	(2)	4.1	(12)	3.0	(7)	3.3	(7)
Grand Total	100.0	(340)	100.0	(300)	100.0	(233)	100.0	(216)

ance between Brahmins and Thakurs. This is in contrast to the
Congress Party. In the first general elections Brahmins comprised
28 percent and Thakurs 13 percent of the Congress MLA's, and
in 1962 the Brahmins still had the largest caste representation,
with 30 percent to the Thakurs' 19 percent.[7] The distribution of
the castes of the candidates put forward by the various parties is
similar (Table 8), although the percentages, calculated on the basis

[7] Caste composition of Congress MLA's in the two elections is taken from
data collected by Meyer.

of general seats (all nonreserved seats), are not directly comparable.[8] Many respondents emphasized the importance of Brahmin-versus-Thakur rivalry in Uttar Pradesh politics, and the proportions of the two castes in the opposition parties seems significant of an effort to draw on the group which was less well represented in the Congress.

The Jan Sangh is reputed to have some attraction for the Banias (traders, moneylenders, or bankers) and small businessmen. Of the three opposition parties, it is the only one to have more than minimal representation of the Bania caste. No Banias were elected on the Socialist ticket. Banias comprise a slightly larger proportion of the Jan Sangh than of the Congress MLA's.

All three opposition parties, and the Congress also, have a small number of Kayasths among their MLA's and among the candidates. There are no Jat MLA's in the Jan Sangh, PSP, or SP, but there are a few in the Congress. Bhumihar MLA's are lacking in the SP and are only minimally present in the other two opposition parties and the Congress. The Praja Socialists were the only opposition party under study to elect Muslim legislators. They and the SP put up about the same proportion of Muslim candidates, while the Jan Sangh put up none. The Congress put up and elected a greater percentage of Muslim candidates than any opposition party.

Whereas Brahmins are the largest single caste among the Congress MLA's, among the Praja Socialist MLA's the Yadavs, a backward caste, are the largest. A feature distinguishing the three opposition parties is the predominance of Yadav MLA's in the PSP, the near balance between Kurmis and Yadavs in the SP, and the nearly equal proportions of several backward castes in the Jan Sangh (Table 7). The most striking difference, however, is the small proportion of backward-caste MLA's and candidates in the Congress as compared with the much larger proportions in the three opposition parties, with the Lohia Socialists having the largest percentage. The Yadavs apparently are the most important politically of all the backward castes.

As was noted in chapter ii, the Chamars appear to have bene-

---

[8] Both Brahmins and Thakurs are overrepresented in comparison with their proportions in the population. In 1931 the Brahmins comprised 9.2 percent of the total state population as compared with 7.6 percent Rajput. *Census of India, 1931* (Allahabad, 1933), XVIII, Pt. 2, 499–548.

fited more than any scheduled caste from legislative reforms. Chamars comprise all of the PSP scheduled-caste MLA's and almost three-fourths of those in the Congress. The Pasis, who have a history of trying to advance their status through nonpolitical activities, now predominate among scheduled-caste MLA's in the Socialist Party, which has no Chamar MLA's, and also in the Jan Sangh.

TABLE 9

EDUCATION OF JAN SANGH, PRAJA SOCIALIST, AND SOCIALIST MLA's
(by percent and number of party MLA's)

Education	Jan Sangh		Praja Socialist		Socialist	
Low:						
Literate-primary (5)[a]...	10.4	(5)	6.1	(2)	27.3	(6)
Junior high (8)[a].......	14.6	(7)	27.3	(9)	31.8	(7)
Total low	25.0	(12)	33.3	(11)	59.1	(13)
Medium:						
High school (10)[a]......	16.7	(8)	24.2	(8)	9.1	(2)
Intermediate college						
(12)[a]	8.3	(4)	12.1	(4)	13.6	(3)
Total medium	25.0	(12)	39.4	(12)	22.7	(5)
High:						
University degree (14)[a].	12.5	(6)	9.1	(3)	9.1	(2)
Graduate degree	14.6	(7)	9.1	(3)	9.1	(2)
Law degree	22.9	(11)	12.1	(4)	—	—
Total high	50.0	(24)	30.3	(10)	18.2	(4)
Grand Total	100.0	(48)	100.0	(33)	100.0	(22)

[a] Numbers indicate classes. Primary connotes completion of 5th class; high school, 10th class; and so on.

None of the respondents is illiterate, although a few have minimal schooling. The Jan Sanghiis are the most highly educated; fully half of their MLA's have a university or postgraduate degree. The Socialists are the least educated and have no MLA's with a background of legal training. The educational level of the Praja Socialists lies between the two [9] (see Table 9). According to

[9] These differences were shown to be significant at the .05 level in a chi-square test.

the Meyer data, a few Congress MLA's are illiterate, but otherwise
the educational level is fairly high and comparable to that of the
Jan Sanghiis.[10] These differences are another indication that the
various parties are drawing on different, though partly overlapping, strata of society for middle-level leadership positions.

Respondents were asked about the father's level of education
in order to investigate the extent and degree of intergenerational
mobility. Most of the respondents had reached higher educational
levels than their fathers; only one had less education. A scale was
constructed, with low mobility denoting that the father and son
were either on the same educational level or that the son had
advanced only one group higher (for example, father of junior
high with son of high school). Medium mobility signifies that the
son has risen two or three educational levels above the father (for
example, father of primary with son of high school or intermediate). High mobility covers cases in which the son has obtained an
educational level four or more groups higher than his father (for
example, father of primary with son having university degree). As
can be seen in Table 10, the large percentage of unknown educa-

TABLE 10

INTERGENERATIONAL EDUCATIONAL MOBILITY OF JAN SANGH,
PRAJA SOCIALIST, AND SOCIALIST MLA's

(by percent and number of party MLA's)

Mobility	Jan Sangh		Praja Socialist		Socialist	
High	31.3	(15)	36.4	(12)	27.3	(6)
Medium	33.3	(16)	42.4	(14)	40.9	(9)
Low	18.7	(9)	15.1	(5)	31.8	(7)
Not ascertained	16.7	(8)	6.1	(2)	—	—
Total	100.0	(48)	100.0	(33)	100.0	(22)

tional mobility among Jan Sangh MLA's quite possibly affected
the distribution. Among the three parties, the Praja Socialists appear to have the highest proportion of high and medium mobile
MLA's, and the Socialists a higher proportion than the other two
parties in the low-mobility group.

[10] When the four parties' MLA's were compared in a chi-square test using
the Meyer data, the differences again were significant at the .05 level.

Knowledge of various languages is partly related to education. The Socialist Party has more than twice the proportion speaking no English of the other two parties. About two-thirds of the Jan Sanghiis and Praja Socialists speak English as well as Hindi-Urdu. It is surprising to find even four of the 22 Socialists speaking other Indian languages (Table 11).

TABLE 11

LANGUAGES SPOKEN BY JAN SANGH, PRAJA SOCIALIST,
AND SOCIALIST MLA's
(*by percent and number of party MLA's*)

Language	Jan Sangh		Praja Socialist		Socialist	
Hindi-Urdu only	33.3	(16)	33.3	(11)	68.2	(15)
Hindi-Urdu and other indigenous languages..	4.2	(2)	—	—	—	—
Hindi-Urdu and English.	58.3	(28)	60.6	(20)	13.6	(3)
Hindi-Urdu, other indigenous languages, and English	4.2	(2)	6.1	(2)	18.2	(4)
Total	100.0	(48)	100.0	(33)	100.0	(22)

Knowledge of various languages, like exposure to different environments and education, can introduce new ideas and values. Another influence somewhat related to education and language is the reading of newspapers and magazines. Respondents were asked to name those regularly read. The results were categorized by language, place of publication, and party or nonparty character. With regard to reading nonparty periodicals, the Praja Socialists have the highest proportion reporting that they read English dailies, followed by the Jan Sangh and then the Socialists (Table 12). As to Hindi papers, most MLA's reported reading one or two; the Praja Socialists have the highest percentage reporting the reading of three or four regularly. The greatest proportion of nonreaders of Hindi papers is found among the Jan Sanghiis, reflecting a tendency to rely on the party organs.

With regard to place of publication, Praja Socialist MLA's represent proportionately the largest number reading Delhi papers,

TABLE 12
MEDIA EXPOSURE OF JAN SANGH, PRAJA SOCIALIST, AND SOCIALIST MLA'S
(by percent and number of party MLA's)

Reading Material	Jan Sangh		Praja Socialist		Socialist	
English dailies:						
None	54.2	(26)	45.4	(15)	81.8	(18)
One-two	27.1	(13)	36.4	(12)	13.6	(3)
Three or more	4.2	(2)	15.2	(5)	4.6	(1)
Not ascertained	14.5	(7)	3.0	(1)	—	—
Total	100.0	(48)	100.0	(33)	100.0	(22)
Hindi dailies: [a]						
None	18.8	(9)	15.2	(5)	4.5	(1)
One-two	56.2	(27)	63.6	(21)	90.9	(20)
Three or more	10.4	(5)	18.2	(6)	4.6	(1)
Not ascertained	14.6	(7)	3.0	(1)	—	—
Total	100.0	(48)	100.0	(33)	100.0	(22)
Delhi newspapers:						
None	62.5	(30)	66.7	(22)	81.8	(18)
One or more	22.9	(11)	30.3	(10)	18.2	(4)
Not ascertained	14.6	(7)	3.0	(1)	—	—
Total	100.0	(48)	100.0	(33)	100.0	(22)
Lucknow newspapers: [a]						
None	27.1	(13)	21.2	(7)	22.7	(5)
One	29.2	(14)	27.3	(9)	50.0	(11)
Two or more	29.2	(14)	48.5	(16)	27.3	(6)
Not ascertained	14.6	(7)	3.0	(1)	—	—
Total	100.0	(48)	100.0	(33)	100.0	(22)
Other major state newspapers: [b]						
None	66.7	(32)	45.4	(15)	68.2	(15)
One or more	18.7	(9)	51.5	(17)	31.8	(7)
Not ascertained	14.6	(7)	3.1	(1)	—	—
Total	100.0	(48)	100.0	(33)	100.0	(22)
Other periodicals:						
Minor local papers	4.2	(2)	3.0	(1)	13.6	(3)
Foreign publications	8.3	(4)	—	—	—	—
Weeklies, monthlies	4.2	(2)	21.2	(7)	—	—

[a] Hindi dailies and Lucknow dailies do not include party organs which might otherwise fall into these categories.

[b] The other major state newspapers are from Varanasi, Allahabad, and Kanpur.

with the Jan Sanghiis ranking quite close. Delhi papers are believed to give slightly more attention to national and international news than state papers. Reading a paper regularly does not mean reading the entire paper; moreover, no measure of selectivity of news read was attempted. Five dailies are published in Lucknow.[11] A greater proportion of Praja Socialist MLA's reported reading Lucknow papers than did those of other parties. Reading of newspapers of other cities in Uttar Pradesh appears to be related to residence in those cities or in nearby districts. Very few respondents reported reading small-town or local papers. A few Jan Sanghiis reported reading papers or magazines from other countries. Very few respondents reported reading weeklies or monthlies published in India.

Reading of a party organ can be a broadening influence insofar as new ideas are introduced and events beyond the individual's personal sphere of knowledge are brought to his attention. On the other hand, a party organ functions to reinforce specific ideas and interpretations, and limits exposure to dissenting views. Party organs can cement the tie of an individual to a party. Interpretation is biased to buttress the official party attitude toward events, policies, problems, and solutions. Thus the extent to which members read their party's organs may provide a crude measure of party cohesion. The Jan Sangh has three party organs; the PSP, one; and the Lohia SP, two.[12] Only one respondent read a party organ other than that of his own party. The two most striking features of Table 13 are how many Jan Sanghiis and how few Praja Socialists read their respective party organs. Eighty-five percent of the Jan Sanghiis read some Jan Sangh organ, and nearly half read two or more of the party's periodicals. One of the Praja

---

[11] These can be divided into two groups: the *National Herald, Nau Jiwan,* and *Quami Awaz* are really one paper in English, Hindi, and Urdu versions respectively, and the *Pioneer* and *Swatantra Bharat* are one paper in English and Hindi versions.

[12] Jan Sangh organs are *Tarun Bharat,* a Hindi daily published in Lucknow; *Panch Janya,* a Hindi weekly published in Lucknow; and *Organizer,* an English weekly published in Delhi. Curran identified the latter two weeklies as organs of the Rashtriya Swayamsevak Sangh. Both give much attention to Jan Sangh activities and personalities, and there is some question today as to whose organ it is. J. A. Curran, Jr., *Militant Hinduism in Indian Politics* (New York, 1951) p. 79. The one PSP organ is the English weekly *Janata,* published in Bombay. The Lohia SP organs are *Chaukhambha,* a Hindi weekly, and *Mankind,* in English, both published in Hyderabad, Andhra Pradesh.

TABLE 13

PARTY ORGANS READ BY JAN SANGH, PRAJA SOCIALIST,
AND SOCIALIST MLA'S

(by percent and number of party MLA's)

Organs Read	Jan Sangh		Praja Socialist		Socialist	
Jan Sangh organs:						
None	12.5	(6)	97.0	(32)	95.5	(21)
One	27.1	(13)	—	—	4.5	(1)
Two or more	45.8	(22)	—	—	—	—
Not ascertained	14.6	(7)	3.0	(1)	—	—
Total	100.0	(48)	100.0	(33)	100.0	(22)
Tarun Bharat [a]	56.3	(27)	—	—	—	—
Panch Janya [b]	50.0	(24)	—	—	4.5	(1)
Organizer [c]	25.0	(12)	—	—	—	—
Praja Socialist organs:						
None	85.4	(41)	97.0	(32)	100.0	(22)
Janata	—	—	—	—	—	—
Not ascertained	14.6	(7)	3.0	(1)	—	—
Total	100.0	(48)	100.0	(33)	100.0	(22)
Socialist organs:						
None	85.4	(41)	97.0	(32)	31.8	(7)
Chaukhambha,						
Mankind, or both [d]	—	—	—	—	68.2	(15)
Not ascertained	14.6	(7)	3.0	(1)	—	—
Total	100.0	(48)	100.0	(33)	100.0	(22)

[a] Hindi daily. [b] Hindi weekly. [c] English weekly. [d] There was only one respondent reading *Mankind,* and he also read *Chaukhambha.*

Socialists reported reading their party's *Janata.*[13] In contrast, two-thirds of the Socialists reported reading an SP organ. These read-

[13] Probes were made with many Praja Socialists just in case there was misunderstanding about party organs' being included in the question. Only one person replied in the affirmative, and in such a manner that it appeared highly doubtful that he did in fact read the organ: *"Janata?"* (Looking disturbed.) "Oh, sure. I sometimes see it. It comes here to the office, doesn't it?" (Looking at other MLA's in the party office for some confirmation.)

Had probes been made with all Praja Socialists it is possible that some affirmative replies might have resulted. It should be noted that no probes were given Jan Sanghiis or Socialists in regard to party organs.

ing patterns would tend to suggest greater cohesion within the Jan Sangh and the Socialist Party than within the Praja Socialist Party. Lack of reading of PSP organs cannot be attributed to lack of education or lack of knowledge of English: it will be remembered that the PSP respondents had the greater proportion reading newspapers other than party organs.

As Lerner has put it, the mass media are "mobility multipliers," in that they increase the exposure to a larger universe through vicarious experience. Such exposure aids the development of psychic mobility.[14] Although the mass media include radio, cinema, and television as well as newspapers and magazines, data were collected for this study only on the two latter media. The data indicate (Table 14) that very few respondents are not attuned to the

TABLE 14

PATTERN OF EXPOSURE TO MASS MEDIA OF JAN SANGH,
PRAJA SOCIALIST, AND SOCIALIST MLA'S
(by percent and number of party MLA's)

Exposure	Jan Sangh		Praja Socialist		Socialist	
Not exposed	2.1	(1)	—	—	—	—
Single channel:						
Party media	8.3	(4)	—	—	—	—
One nonparty medium.	2.1	(1)	12.1	(4)	18.2	(4)
Multi-channel:						
Party and nonparty media	66.6	(32)	—	—	68.2	(15)
Various nonparty media	6.3	(3)	84.9	(28)	13.6	(3)
Not ascertained	14.6	(7)	3.0	(1)	—	—
Total	100.0	(48)	100.0	(33)	100.0	(22)

mass media, as represented by newspapers and magazines. There are two possible directions of attunement: single channel and multi-channel. Single channel comprises exposure solely to party media, regardless of the number, or to only one nonparty medium.

[14] *The Passing of Traditional Society,* pp. 52–64.

Multi-channel indicates exposure to both party and nonparty media, or to a number of nonparty media. As the table demonstrates, most respondents fall into the multi-channel category, with the Praja Socialists having the greater proportion reading a variety of nonparty media.

Economic Background

When respondents were asked their primary and secondary occupations, the question was put in the present tense to find out how many thought of themselves as "politicians." The past tense would have emphasized a prepolitical occupation. Table 15 shows

TABLE 15

PRIMARY OCCUPATION OF JAN SANGH, PRAJA SOCIALIST,
AND SOCIALIST MLA's

(by percent and number of party MLA's)

Field of Principal Occupation	Jan Sangh		Praja Socialist		Socialist	
Agriculture	20.8	(10)	24.2	(8)	36.4	(8)
Zamindar	35.4	(17)	36.4	(12)	22.7	(5)
Law	16.7	(8)	3.0	(1)	—	—
Politics or social service	—	—	21.2	(7)	27.3	(6)
Business	8.3	(4)	3.0	(1)	4.5	(1)
Medicine	6.3	(3)	—	—	—	—
Education	6.2	(3)	3.0	(1)	9.1	(2)
Labor	—	—	3.0	(1)	—	—
Other	4.2	(2)	3.0	(1)	—	—
Not ascertained	2.1	(1)	3.0	(1)	—	—
Total	100.0	(48)	100.0	(33)	100.0	(22)

the field of primary occupation of the respondents. More than 50 percent of the MLA's in each party listed either agriculture or zamindari as their primary occupation, with the Praja Socialist members reporting the largest proportion. In Myron Weiner's study of party personnel in West Bengal the proportion of those in agriculture was much less.[15] For the majority in each party

[15] *Political Change in South Asia* (Calcutta, 1963), pp. 176–227. His study included state organizational party leaders, Members of Parliament, members of the Council (upper house in the state) as well as MLA's; also he included

whose primary occupation was agriculture or zamindari, the most numerous secondary occupations were business and politics or social service.

Few of the MLA's considered themselves to be educators. Only one gave his primary occupation as labor. Most of those in business and all of those in medicine are found in the Jan Sangh. The medical category is very close to business, for only one of the "medicine" respondents had formal training; the other two, who had picked up some knowledge on their own, conducted a pharmacy-type shop. The Jan Sangh is also the only party to have any lawyers to speak of. The Socialists have none, and although four Praja Socialists have law degrees, only one is a practicing lawyer.

One of the very interesting categories is that of politics or social service.[16] The Socialist Party has the greater proportion of MLA's reporting politics or social service as the primary occupation, followed closely by the Praja Socialists. No Jan Sangh MLA' reported this category in the primary position, although 10 percent gave it as the secondary occupation, far behind the Praja Socialists' 30 percent and a little above the Socialists' 9 percent. When primary and secondary occupations are combined, more than half the Praja Socialists identify themselves with politics or social service. The low percentage of Jan Sangh responses in this category probably reflects the official effort within the party to downgrade the importance of the popularly elected members and to increase that of organization workers.

---

five parties: the Congress, the Communists, two Marxist Left Parties, and a small PSP. Given these differences, his data is not really comparable to the group in Uttar Pradesh under study. There were only 11.9 percent in agriculture in his group. In another breakdown of rural MLA's (criteria for classification of rural constituencies was not reported), almost one-third were in the field of agriculture, which is still lower than the figure for the three opposition parties in Uttar Pradesh.

[16] Comparable figures are not available for West Bengal. Weiner evidently recorded few instances of dual occupations. He reports that some 41 percent of his respondents were political workers. If this figure is compared to the 15 percent in the politics and social-service category of the combined three parties, it appears that the state of Uttar Pradesh and West Bengal are quite different. A slightly different interpretation occurs when primary and secondary occupations are combined. Furthermore, inasmuch as the West Bengal group contained state organizational leaders, a higher proportion reporting themselves to be political workers is to be expected. *Ibid.*, p. 212.

All those reporting agriculture as either the primary or secondary occupation were queried as to zamindar background, and, where there was such background, on the size of the zamindari as indicated by the number of villages included. Because the system was abolished in 1952, the size of the father's zamindari was substituted for those who were minors at that time. Table 16 presents

TABLE 16

ZAMINDAR OR OTHER BACKGROUND OF JAN SANGH,
PRAJA SOCIALIST, AND SOCIALIST MLA's
(*by percent and number of party MLA's*)

Background	Jan Sangh		Praja Socialist		Socialist	
Large zamindar or talukdar [a]	14.6	(7)	9.1	(3)	—	—
Medium zamindar [a]	—	—	3.0	(1)	9.1	(2)
Small zamindar [a]	22.9	(11)	27.3	(9)	18.2	(4)
Zamindar of unreported size	12.5	(6)	—	—	—	—
Kisan	29.2	(14)	51.5	(17)	59.1	(13)
Tenant	6.2	(3)	3.0	(1)	13.6	(3)
Nonagricultural	14.6	(7)	6.1	(2)	—	—
Total	100.0	(48)	100.0	(33)	100.0	(22)

[a] The large zamindars "owned" twenty-five or more villages; medium zamindars, ten to twenty-four; and small zamindars, fewer than ten. In the latter category are some who "owned" only a few shares in one or two villages, or only a part of one village.

the size of former zamindari, together with proportions and numbers of MLA's of other agricultural classes and the nonagricultural remainder; for this table, primary and secondary occupations were combined.[17] The Socialist Party has no large zamindars among its MLA's. Within the Jan Sangh the small zamindars outnumber the large, though in comparison with the Praja Socialists the Jan Sangh has a greater proportion of large zamindars. The Socialist Party (followed by the PSP) has far greater numbers of kisans and tenants than the Jan Sangh. The data thus indicate that the Jan Sangh draws on greater numbers with high rural status; yet it also

[17] A kisan is an owner of land or holder of perpetual tenure. He may or may not personally cultivate the land.

has far more MLA's of totally nonagricultural occupations than the other two parties.

According to the Meyer data, 9 percent of the Congress MLA's were large zamindars, 7 percent were medium zamindars, 9 percent were small zamindars, and 7 percent were zamindars of unknown size. There is a greater proportion of zamindars within both the Jan Sangh and the Praja Socialist Party than within the Congress; only the Socialist Party has less. In all three opposition parties small zamindars outnumber the large, in contrast with the Congress's balance among the different sizes. Various Congress land reform policies have directly diminished the status and fortunes of zamindars. It appears that the opposition parties have been successful in mobilizing members of this group.[18]

TABLE 17

SIZE OF LANDHOLDINGS OF SAN SANGH, PRAJA SOCIALIST, AND SOCIALIST MLA'S

(by percent and number of party MLA's)

Size of Landholdings	Jan Sangh		Praja Socialist		Socialist	
None	8.3	(4)	12.1	(4)	22.7	(5)
5 acres or less	14.6	(7)	9.1	(3)	22.7	(5)
6–15 acres	16.7	(8)	21.2	(7)	13.6	(3)
16–30 acres	16.7	(8)	24.3	(8)	13.6	(3)
31–50 acres	8.3	(4)	12.1	(4)	4.6	(1)
51–90 acres	12.5	(6)	9.1	(3)	9.1	(2)
91 acres or more	12.5	(6)	9.1	(3)	9.1	(2)
Not ascertained	10.4	(5)	3.0	(1)	4.6	(1)
Total	100.0	(48)	100.0	(33)	100.0	(22)

Another highly significant indicator of both status and wealth is the amount of land owned (Table 17). It was not easy to ascertain the landholdings of the MLA's. Personal, not joint-family, holdings were asked for. This was done for the sake of comparability, both as between MLA's still living in joint families and others,

----

[18] I have spoken of zamindars in the present tense for the sake of convenience and in line with Indian habit. It is to be understood that legally this category is nonexistent.

and between members of large and small joint families. Even so, three problems emerged. (1) Family holdings may have determined rural standing, especially in the case of younger MLA's. In three cases young men reported no land of their own, but gave amounts owned by their fathers. They were coded as owning no land. (2) Another problem grew out of the land ceiling legislation of 1960 which set a limit of 40 acres. (The limit was not absolute inasmuch as groves were exempt and the quality of land was taken into consideration. Legally it is still possible for one person to own several hundred acres.) Land whose title was transferred to a spouse or child to comply with the ceiling was not covered by responses. (3) In spite of care taken to find out personal holdings, some responses must have been in terms of family holdings. This would explain discrepancies between responses on holdings and on incomes. It must be understood, further, that the respondents' information was accepted without a check of land records. About 5 percent of the replies are extremely suspect.

In the categories of Table 17 there are some benchmarks. The grouping of 31–50 acres denotes the acreage about the basic maximum holding of 40 acres. Five acres or less signifies a very small holding. Among the Socialist MLA's, large percentages—almost half—own no land or very little, and there is a steady decline in proportions owning larger acreages. Among the PSP legislators, on the other hand, nearly half own between 6 and 30 acres. The Jan Sanghiis have a much more even distribution. In interparty comparison there is a slightly greater percentage reporting larger landholdings, but also slightly more owning no land or very little (as compared with the Praja Socialists). The balanced distribution, however, could be seriously affected by the 10 percent which were not ascertained (two of the five were wealthy zamindars and may have owned many acres).

There is another way of analyzing occupational backgrounds. An attempt was made to construct a status scale of occupations with the purpose of designating the ranking of occupations as to general esteem, respect, and "standing" (rather than the skills involved or the monetary rewards).[19] Both primary and secondary

[19] No studies were found which provided such a ranking for India. Joseph Elder, a professor of sociology at the University of Wisconsin, at Madison, who has studied in Uttar Pradesh, was consulted in drawing up the scale. I am very grateful for Professor Elder's advice.

occupations were taken into consideration, as were the occupational "peculiarities" among the respondents.[20] Those recorded as engaged in agriculture or as zamindars were scaled in accordance with the amount of land owned at the time.[21] Kisan-zamindar categories were disregarded because the zamindari system had been abolished and because there were big kisans and very small, insignificant zamindars. Seven categories were established, from low to high, and were divided into low, medium, and high status.[22] Although the rankings were impressionistic and the order of some of the seven categories can be easily questioned, owing to such problems as having to meld rural and urban status rankings, the threefold division is probably fairly accurate.

In interparty comparison, the Jan Sangh has the largest proportion of MLA's in occupations of high status, the PSP in those of medium status, and the Socialist Party in those ranked low (Table 18). All the parties have their greatest numbers in occupations of medium-status groups. The differences indicate that the parties are attracting slightly different strata of society.

Leaving status aside, respondents were also asked about their fathers' primary and secondary occupations for the purpose of

[20] For example, the businessmen in the parties under study were not big industrialists. By and large they were small shopkeepers, moneylenders, brick-kiln owners, small flour-mill owners, and the like. There was one timber contractor who operated on a slightly larger scale. Most of these had their business in small towns and rural areas. In ranking business, these kinds of businesses were the specific referent. There was no ranking of administrative or executive positions, because there were no MLA's falling into this category. In the coding, the untrained medical doctors were separated from the trained; similarly, teachers in the lower grades were classified as white-collar workers while Ph.D's teaching in universities were classified as professional persons. This scale was drawn up for this particular group, and it may not be applicable to the general society.

[21] Large farmers, 51 acres or more; medium farmers, 16–50 acres; small farmers, 15 acres or less.

[22] The seven categories, from low to high, were:
1. Laborers or small farmers (less than 15 acres owned)
2. Politics or social service as occupation
3. Medium farmers (16–50 acres)
4. White-collar or clerical: teachers below university level; government clerks
5. Business: businessmen, untrained medical doctors operating shops
6. Professional: lawyers; trained medical doctors; university teachers
7. Big farmers (51 acres or more); priests

In the threefold division as to status, categories 1–2 were treated as low (however, the combination of 2 and 2 was moved to medium because of the nature of the work), 3–5 as medium, and 6–7 as high.

TABLE 18

OCCUPATIONAL STATUS SCALE OF JAN SANGH, PRAJA SOCIALIST,
AND SOCIALIST MLA's

(by percent and number of party MLA's)

Occupational Rankings	Jan Sangh		Praja Socialist		Socialist	
High status	37.5	(18)	24.2	(8)	22.7	(5)
Medium status	43.8	(21)	57.6	(19)	50.0	(11)
Low occupations	10.4	(5)	18.2	(6)	27.3	(6)
Not ascertained	8.3	(4)ª	—	—	—	—
Total	100.0	(48)	100.0	(33)	100.0	(22)

ª Three of these are probably "high"; all data are known except the amount of land owned. They are former large zamindars, quite wealthy, and most likely own more than 51 acres of land. If these were to be included, the proportion of high-status occupations among Jan Sanghiis would rise to 43.8 percent.

learning about intergenerational occupational mobility, which here would be found in a shift from agricultural to nonagricultural occupations. A scale of such mobility was drawn up, comparing the primary and secondary occupations of both the father and the respondent against the range of possible shifts.[23] On this scale of mobility, the Jan Sanghiis have the largest proportion of MLA's in the low group, the Praja Socialists in the medium, and the Socialists in the high (Table 19). Overall, the Praja Socialists

[23] The following distribution shows the possibilities of occupational mobility and the divisions utilized to form the high, medium, and low mobility groups:

Father's primary (P) and secondary (S) occupations

MLA's primary (P) and secondary (S) occupations	P & S Agric.	P Agric. S Nonagric.	P Nonagric. S Agric.	P & S Nonagric.
P & S Agric.	Low	Low	Low	Low
P Agric. S Nonagric.	Medium	Low	Low	Low
P Nonagric. S. Agric.	High	Medium	Low	Low
P & S Nonagric.	High	High	Medium	Low

TABLE 19

INTERGENERATIONAL AGRICULTURAL TO NONAGRICULTURAL OCCUPATIONAL
MOBILITY OF JAN SANGH, PRAJA SOCIALIST, AND SOCIALIST MLA's
(*by percent and number of party MLA's*)

Mobility	Jan Sangh		Praja Socialist		Socialist	
High	16.7	(8)	15.2	(5)	31.8	(7)
Medium	18.7	(9)	36.4	(12)	13.6	(3)
Low	56.3	(27)	45.4	(15)	54.6	(12)
Not ascertained	8.3	(4)	3.0	(1)	—	—
Total	100.0	(48)	100.0	(33)	100.0	(22)

have fewer following the father's occupation and more showing some mobility than the other two parties (low mobility as opposed to combined high-medium mobility). Even though the largest groups in all three parties show low mobility, a surprising number of MLA's registered some change from agricultural to nonagricultural pursuits in comparison with their fathers. The scale did not measure any MLA's change from the father's nonagricultural occupation to another nonagricultural occupation. If these were added, the proportion showing some mobility would be slightly higher. It is doubtful that figures of occupational mobility among the populace at large would be of this magnitude. Possibly there is a general "political recruitment stratum" comprising those who have ventured into occupations progressively more urbanized than those of their fathers.

Respondents were also asked to place themselves in one of four monthly income groups: Rs. 299 or less, Rs. 300–599, Rs. 600–999, and Rs. 1,000 or more.[24] A few comments are necessary regarding the accuracy of the responses. (1) The most suspect category is the lowest, in which most respondents placed themselves. It is possible that the interview situation was a factor biasing the replies, for there was often lack of privacy. This category is suspect also because the legislative salary is Rs. 200 per month, plus Rs. 10 per

[24] None refused to reply, but some were interviewed in places or situations in which it was inappropriate to ask the question. Some of these respondents were later queried, but others were not. This explains the large number in the not ascertained category.

day for attending the session. Months in which the Assembly is in session for ten days would thus give the MLA Rs. 300. Although the Assembly is not in session often enough to provide Rs. 300 a month regularly, almost any outside income would tend to raise a legislator above the Rs. 300 level. (2) Between income and amount of land owned there is a rough correlation, but there are some startling exceptions which raise the question whether the income reported was inaccurate or the joint-family landholding was reported, as in the case of one MLA who reported owning 90 acres of land (in addition to his income as an MLA) and yet put his total monthly income below Rs. 300. (3) Another complicating factor is that the level of lowest income taxation begins with Rs. 3,600 per year (or Rs. 300 per month). There are some pressures to avoid reporting a higher income. Also, most of the respondents live in joint families and many derive their nonpolitical income from agriculture; during a respondent's term of office it is likely that other family members take over his responsibilities in this area. Under these conditions, actual income could easily be "hidden" and made difficult to determine.

TABLE 20

REPORTED MONTHLY INCOME OF JAN SANGH, PRAJA SOCIALIST,
AND SOCIALIST MLA's

(by percent and number of party MLA's)

Income	Jan Sangh		Praja Socialist		Socialist	
Rs. 299 or less	29.2	(14)	63.6	(21)	54.5	(12)
Rs. 300–599	27.1	(13)	24.2	(8)	36.5	(8)
Rs. 600 or more	31.2	(15)	6.1	(2)	4.5	(1)
Not ascertained	12.5	(6)	6.1	(2)	4.5	(1)
Total	100.0	(48)	100.0	(33)	100.0	(22)

The reported figures (Table 20) indicate that proportionately the Praja Socialists have the lowest incomes, with the Socialists having slightly higher. The Jan Sanghiis are fairly well distributed through the income groups. The very small Rs. 600–999 group was combined with the largest for a chi-square test of differences among the three parties, which was significant at the .05 level.

A last economic index measured the sense of financial mobility as compared with parents.[25] There are striking differences among the MLA's of the three parties (Table 21). Most Praja Socialists

TABLE 21

SENSE OF INTERGENERATIONAL FINANCIAL MOBILITY OF JAN SANGH, PRAJA SOCIALIST, AND SOCIALIST MLA's
(by percent and number of party MLA's)

Sense of Financial Mobility	Jan Sangh		Praja Socialist		Socialist	
Better off than parents...	35.4	(17)	15.2	(5)	54.6	(12)
Same as parents	16.7	(8)	24.2	(8)	9.1	(2)
Worse off than parents...	29.2	(14)	51.5	(17)	31.8	(7)
Not ascertained	18.7	(9)	9.1	(3)	4.5	(1)
Total	100.0	(48)	100.0	(33)	100.0	(22)

claim to be worse off; extremely few report upward mobility. This is in contrast with the Socialists, more than half of whom report themselves as being better off. The Jan Sanghiis also have larger proportions better off than worse off. In a chi-square test these differences are significant at the .05 level. A high proportion of those with a zamindar background claim to be worse off than their parents. Most of the kisans report themselves as better off, with the exception of those in the Praja Socialist Party.

Financial mobility is an interesting index for trying to learn what kinds of people are attracted to various parties. From the data discussed so far, it will be recalled that the Socialists tend to have more of lower castes, lower educational levels, and lower-ranked occupations; yet most consider themselves financially better off than their parents. A slightly higher percentage report themselves in the medium-income groups and fewer in the low-income group, compared with the Praja Socialists. In contrast, the Praja Socialists have higher proportions in the elite castes, upper educational levels, and medium-ranked occupations, while large numbers claim to be in the lowest income group and report themselves

[25] The question was "Would you say that financially you are better off, the same, or worse off than your parents?"

worse off than their parents. These differences bring to mind a rather curious "broken" dialogue between two leaders of the state PSP. One leader declared that the Praja Socialists had the greatest numbers of highly educated, professional, highly qualified legislators and MLA candidates. A few weeks later, evidently having heard about his colleague's statement, another leader volunteered information on this point. He said that although there appeared to be large numbers of educated and professionally trained persons in the PSP, these were not successful in their fields: active district leaders might well be lawyers, but not top lawyers; persons who were not doing very well or were failing in their occupations tended to come to the PSP. This judgment seems to be supported by the reported income levels and the responses on the sense of financial mobility.

Furthermore, responses to this latter, subjective economic query seem to bespeak a lack of self-confidence among the PSP respondents. Since practically no Praja Socialist MLA reported reading the party organ (Table 13), it is possible that confidence in the party is lacking also. This may explain why, when a merger of the two socialist parties is proposed, it usually appears that the PSP (although larger in size) is the supplicant, while the Socialist Party leaders tend to set up preconditions and try to dictate the terms of merger, and perhaps why generally the PSP gives the impression of being "on the defensive" and the SP of being "on the offensive."

Up to this point, financial, educational, and occupational mobility have been separately introduced. To obtain a better conception of the relationships of these three indices, an overall social-mobility scale was constructed.[26] Obviously, two of the measures were objective, while the other was subjective. One difficulty in comparing financial mobility with the other two indices was resolved by taking the direction of movement into consideration. "Better off" was equated with high mobility, "same" with medium mobility, and "worse off" with low mobility. Three categories of high, medium, and low mobility were formed.[27] As Table 22 indicates, the Socialists have the greatest proportion in the high mobility

---

[26] The spatial mobility index was excluded because of the limitations on deductions.

[27] Criteria for classification were: (a) High (upward) mobility: 3 high indices; or 2 high and 1 medium. (b) Medium mobility: 2 high and 1 low; 3 medium; 2 medium and 1 high; or 1 high, 1 medium, and 1 low. (c) Low mobility: 3 low; 2 low and 1 medium; 2 low and 1 high; or 2 medium and 1 low.

TABLE 22

GENERAL SOCIAL MOBILITY SCORE OF JAN SANGH,
PRAJA SOCIALIST, AND SOCIALIST MLA's
(*by percent and number of party MLA's*)

Mobility	Jan Sangh		Praja Socialist		Socialist	
High	12.5	(6)	9.1	(3)	18.2	(4)
Medium	33.3	(16)	33.3	(11)	36.4	(8)
Low	33.3	(16)	48.5	(16)	40.9	(9)
Not ascertained	20.8	(10)	9.1	(3)	4.5	(1)
Total	100.0	(48)	100.0	(33)	100.0	(22)

ª The social mobility scores were obtained by compiling scores in inter-generational mobility on the basis of educational, occupational, and financial factors. The score takes into consideration the consistency from factor to factor as well as whether such mobility was high or low.

group, and the Praja Socialists in the low. In all the parties about a third of the MLA's fall in the medium-mobility category. Within the Jan Sangh there appears to be a balance between those of low and medium mobility, although this is a hazardous statement, given the 21 percent comprising the "not ascertained" category. A chi-square test was run on collapsed categories of high-medium versus low, which was necessary in order to obtain cells of sufficient size, but the variation was shown to be insignificant. There is greater variation within the separate indices.

If social mobility is not a measure distinguishing those in various types of parties, perhaps some combined indices on social status will provide a clue. In a study of social status in the United States, Gerhard Lenski points out that the social status of an individual is made up of several factors, and that an individual can have a different ranking for each factor. Particularly concerned with the concept of "status crystallization," or consistency in status among factors, Lenski hypothesizes that individuals with consistent ranking behave differently in politics from those whose ranking varies widely from one factor to another, and, further, that status crystallization is more important than status position.[28]

Lenski selected education, occupation, income, and ethnic

[28] "Status Crystallization," *American Sociological Review*, XIX (1954), 405–413.

group as indices. It may be interesting, using the data obtained from the MLA respondents in Uttar Pradesh and substituting caste for ethnic group, to test two alternative hypotheses: (*a*) that individuals with a high degree of status *crystallization* will tend to have a different party affiliation from those with a low degree, and (*b*) that individuals with a high status *ranking* will tend to have a different party affiliation from those with a low ranking. The first is, of course, Lenski's hypothesis, while the second is the reverse of it.[29] These will be tested in null form.

The results of status crystallization scores are given in Table 23.

TABLE 23

STATUS CRYSTALLIZATION OF JAN SANGH, PRAJA SOCIALIST, AND SOCIALIST MLA's

(*by percent and number of party MLA's*)

Crystallization	Jan Sangh		Praja Socialist		Socialist	
High	56.2	(27)	54.5	(18)	50.0	(11)
Low	31.3	(15)	39.4	(13)	45.5	(10)
Not ascertained	12.5	(6)	6.1	(2)	4.5	(1)
Total	100.0	(48)	100.0	(33)	100.0	(22)

[29] There were several steps in the methodology. Lenski's methodology was utilized, with one revision. The first step was to make comparable scores for each of the factors. This was done by making for each factor a cumulative percentile range of the *N* in each frequency group of the factor. The midpoint of the percentile range of each group was the score to be given any individual falling in that group.

Second, a combined score was constructed by taking, for each individual, the square root of the sum of the squared deviations from the mean of the four hierarchy scores and subtracting the resulting figure from 100.

Third, these scores were then divided into high and low crystallization categories at what appeared to be natural breaking point. (Cf., *ibid.*, pp. 405 ff.)

This method was applied to the Uttar Pradesh data, but the scores were not comparable. There was a 40-point variation among respondents who were medium in three factors and high in one factor—depending on which particular factor was high. The reason for this discrepancy might lie in the number of frequency groups within the categories. For example, in Lenski's study there were eleven income groups; in this study there were three. Further, to make computation somewhat easier, collapsed categories had been used for all four factors (three groups in each factor). To remedy this deficiency, arbitrary scores were established for high, medium, and low groups in each factor (30 for high, 20 for medium, and 10 for low). Then the composite score for each individual was constructed, following Lenski's directions.

There is not much difference among the respondents in regard to party affiliation. The Jan Sanghiis have a slightly larger proportion in the high crystallization group, and the Socialists in the low. A chi-square test shows these differences to be insignificant at the .05 level. The null hypothesis that there is no relationship between status crystallization and party affiliation is accepted. The possibility that differences might be reflected between Congress Party and opposition-party members could not be tested because of lack of data on incomes of Congress Party members. Another possibility, also untestable in this study, is that most middle-level leaders tend to fall into a high crystallization category.

To test the second hypothesis, that status ranking is more relevant to party affiliation than crystallization, a status score was constructed, giving three points for membership in each high group, two for medium, and one for low, on each of the four factors (education, occupation, income, caste). The range was from 4 to 12 points and was divided into three groups (high, 10–12; medium, 7–9; low, 4–6). The results are given in Table 24. In com-

TABLE 24

STATUS SCALE OF JAN SANGH, PRAJA SOCIALIST, AND SOCIALIST MLA'S
(by percent and number of party MLA's)

Score	Jan Sangh		Praja Socialist		Socialist	
High	33.3	(16)	21.2	(7)	9.1	(2)
Medium	39.6	(19)	48.5	(16)	54.5	(12)
Low	14.6	(7)	24.2	(8)	31.8	(7)
Not ascertained	12.5	(6)	6.1	(2)	4.5	(1)
Total	100.0	(48)	100.0	(33)	100.0	(22)

parison with the other parties, the Jan Sanghiis have the greater proportion of high-status MLA's and the Socialists the greater proportion in both the medium and the low categories. The Praja Socialists fall between, with the largest intraparty group in the medium category. A chi-square test shows these differences to be significant at the .05 level. The null hypothesis of "no difference" is thus rejected. Status ranking seems to be related to party affiliation. This is an indication that the three parties tend to attract different segments of society.

Patterns of Participation

In addition to the questions on socioeconomic background, respondents were asked two series of questions regarding participation in nonparty activities. One series inquired about past positions in governmental capacities, the other about general organizational memberships (Tables 25, 26).

TABLE 25

LOCAL-GOVERNMENT EXPERIENCE OF JAN SANGH,
PRAJA SOCIALIST, AND SOCIALIST MLA's
(*by percent and number of party MLA's*)

Type of office	Jan Sangh		Praja Socialist		Socialist	
Rural	18.8	(9)	42.4	(14)	36.4	(8)
Urban	10.4	(5)	18.2	(6)	9.1	(2)
None reported	70.8	(34)	39.4	(13)	54.5	(12)
Total	100.0	(48)	100.0	(33)	100.0	(22)

The two most prominent governmental offices at the village level are those of pradhan of the panchayat and sarpanch of the rural court.[30] The few Jan Sanghiis who have held rural positions have largely been on the court. Some Praja Socialists and Socialists have held the pradhan office. Few big or medium zamindars have held village positions. Perhaps they are "too big" to take part on such a minor level. Small zamindars and kisans have provided this type of rural leadership. Nearly all the small kisans of the Jan Sangh and the Socialist Party have participated in village government. In contrast, it is the large and medium kisans in the PSP who have such a background. With respect to caste, Jan Sangh MLA's of the backward and scheduled castes have a much higher record of rural participation than those of the elite castes. In the PSP, rural positions were held by Thakurs, by members of backward and scheduled castes, and by Muslims. It would appear that the Jan Sangh, besides attracting some big zamindars (who, although having a rural base of strength, are not a product devel-

[30] A pradhan is the chief executive officer of the panchayat (or village council), a sarpanch is the chief judge of the rural court.

TABLE 26

ORGANIZATIONAL MEMBERSHIPS OF JAN SANGH,
PRAJA SOCIALIST, AND SOCIALIST MLA's
(*by percent and number of party MLA's*)

Membership	Jan Sangh		Praja Socialist		Socialist	
Number of organizations:						
None	10.4	(5)	15.1	(5)	18.2	(4)
One	20.8	(10)	27.3	(9)	18.2	(4)
Two	20.8	(10)	33.3	(11)	18.2	(4)
Three	14.6	(7)	6.2	(3)	27.3	(6)
Four or more	25.0	(12)	12.1	(4)	18.1	(4)
Not ascertained	8.4	(4)	3.0	(1)	—	—
Total	100.0	(48)	100.0	(33)	100.0	(22)
Type of organization:						
Professional	27.1	(13)	6.1	(2)	13.6	(3)
Business	6.2	(3)	3.0	(1)	—	—
Labor unions	12.5	(6)	6.1	(2)	22.7	(5)
Kisan organization	6.2	(3)	30.3	(10)	50.0	(11)
Social service	6.2	(3)	12.1	(4)	—	—
Caste association [a]	37.5	(18)	30.3	(10)	27.3	(6)
RSS	43.7	(21)	3.0	(1)	—	—
Arya Samaj	27.1	(13)	—	—	9.1	(2)
Other	25.0	(12)	18.2	(6)	4.5	(1)

[a] Included as caste association members are one Jan Sanghi, two Praja Socialists, and one Socialist who were identified with a specific caste association although they were not officially members of it. One has been an officer at the state level in an active caste association. The two Praja Socialists reported their unofficial membership as being due to a party prohibition against open or active membership.

oped within and thrown up by the rural society), is also attempting to draw on a different stratum of the rural society. This stratum seems to be primarily composed of small kisans of the lower-caste groups who have a record of participation in rural governmental institutions. It seems that the Socialist Party also attracts or is attempting to attract small kisans with experience in local government, but of more varied castes. The Praja Socialists seem to be drawing on those having larger landholdings, of varied castes, who have such a political background.

The considerably fewer Jan Sangh MLA's who have held governmental positions in urban areas tend to be of high castes and in business. Very few Socialists have a record of experience in urban government. In contrast, more than half of the Praja Socialists living in urban areas have had such experience; none of these were of the backward castes.

Politicians have been called inveterate "joiners." In Uttar Pradesh the opposition MLA's tend to belong to organizations rather than not, but the extent of participation varies (Table 26). A greater proportion of Jan Sanghiis report membership in four or more organizations than MLA's of the other two parties. More than half the Praja Socialists belong to only one or two associations. The Socialists are evenly divided among those with few and those with more numerous memberships.

The high proportion of Jan Sanghiis reporting membership in the RSS is to be expected, since it was the parent organization of the party. There are also many Jan Sanghiis who belong to the Arya Samaj, a religious reform organization. MLA's of the two socialist parties do not participate in these cultural and religious organizations in large numbers. In all three parties there are several MLA's belonging to various types of caste associations, with Jan Sanghiis having the greatest proportion and the Socialists the smallest. Fully half the Socialists reported membership in kisan organizations, as did many Praja Socialists. The Jan Sanghiis are not as interested in this occupationally-oriented rural group. Both the Jan Sanghiis and the socialists have a few MLA's working in labor unions. The type of union appears to vary according to the party, with the Jan Sanghiis tending to be active in nonindustrial "service" unions (of university employees, hotel employees, and the like), while the two socialist parties are more active in "blue-collar" unions (of railroad workers, sugar-mill workers, rickshaw operators, and the like). Professional groups include bar associations, teachers' organizations, and medical societies. The higher proportion of Jan Sanghiis reporting such membership is a reflection of the larger numbers of lawyers in the party. Surprisingly few MLA's belong to social service organizations, perhaps because most social service organizations are Congress-dominated and in some places appear almost to be Congress Party affiliates.

Among the various categories of organizations, one set which was separated from the rest includes economic organizations of a semiofficial nature: the District Cooperative Bank, District Cooperative Development Federation, and the Cane Union Cooperative. These tend to be dominated by the Congress Party and are one source of Congress strength. As Table 27 shows, the Praja

TABLE 27

MEMBERSHIP IN SEMIOFFICIAL ORGANIZATIONS OF JAN SANGH, PRAJA SOCIALIST, AND SOCIALIST MLA's

(by percent and number of party MLA's)

Membership	Jan Sangh		Praja Socialist		Socialist	
Number of organizations:						
None	81.3	(39)	42.5	(14)	59.1	(13)
One	10.4	(5)	42.4	(14)	31.8	(7)
Two or more	6.2	(3)	12.1	(4)	9.1	(2)
Not ascertained	2.1	(1)	3.0	(1)	—	—
Total	100.0	(48)	100.0	(33)	100.0	(22)
Specific organizations:						
District Cooperative Bank	10.4	(5)	24.2	(8)	13.6	(3)
District Cooperative Development Federation	8.3	(4)	30.3	(10)	22.7	(5)
Cane Union Cooperative	6.2	(3)	12.1	(4)	13.6	(3)

Socialists have the largest numbers reporting membership in these groups, followed by the Socialists. Very few of the Jan Sanghiis have taken part in these organizations.

Summary

Several important characteristics are shared by these middlemen of the three parties. In terms of modern/traditional attributes, they are transitional. Modern society is characterized by empathetic individuals; traditional society is not. Spatial mobility, urbanization, literacy, media participation, and political participation are all related to a characterological transformation. Mobile personalities are the end product.[31] Although the study did not test for empathy, through physical mobility or residence the Uttar Pradesh MLA's of the opposition parties have been exposed to urbanization. They are literate, and most are media participants. As party members and legislators they are political participants. The information on occupational and educational mobility shows that many have moved slightly away from the world of their parents. On the basis of these findings many of the respondents might be considered transitional. If they were not transitional before their election to the legislature, the new role which they then assumed would tend to encourage change. For example, those respondents who had always lived in a rural area or had never changed residence were, by becoming legislators, obliged to move to Lucknow for part of the year. Respondents residing in places where newspapers are not readily available are exposed to the mass media while in Lucknow. Most legislators live in the state-provided MLA quarters while in Lucknow. In addition to residence in multi-apartment quarters, the fact that MLA's have no separate legislative offices but share a party office (two adjoining rooms of varying size for each party) facilitates interaction. Such physical proximity to and interaction with other legislators is probably a factor furthering change from the traditional and encouraging the development of psychic mobility.

Each party has representatives from varied groups in society, but the mixture differs for each. In their competition, no stratum is left unsolicited. The Jan Sanghiis fall primarily into two groups: the "ruling culture" representatives and the urban semiprofessionals. Those of the ruling culture might well be considered discontented. There is a third, smaller Jan Sangh group of the rural discontented: smaller kisans with lower educational levels, tending to be of lower castes and to have lower incomes, and with a background of local-government participation. Perhaps a strong ideology is needed to hold these groups together.

The Praja Socialists have their largest numbers in the group of rural discontented just described. A few are from the ruling culture and urban semiprofessional categories. Proportionately more of their elite-caste members fall into the "rural discontented"

[31] The process is set forth in Lerner, *The Passing of Traditional Society*, pp. 43–75.

group than do those of the Jan Sangh. Some extrapolations from the data suggest that typically the Praja Socialists are persons who have not found absorbing economic vocations. This may be the cause or the effect of their interest in politics. Their backgrounds suggest a civic orientation.

The Socialists also have their largest numbers in the group of rural discontented, with even fewer in the other two categories than the other parties. Different groups within the rural discontented distinguish the Socialists from the Praja Socialists. On various indices (education, occupational status, landholding, caste, media participation) the Socialists tend to rank lower than the Praja Socialists. On a traditional-transitional-modern continuum, the Socialists would tend more to a lower transitional category than the Praja Socialists. On the other hand, the Socialists are better off in income and sense of financial mobility. Does this indicate that the Socialist Party is marked by "men on the make"? Possibly the strict ideology of the party provides sustenance for such a group, and also its more tightly knit organization. These characteristics are weak in the Praja Socialist Party. It is possible that such are not necessary for the more civic-minded and slightly "higher-transitional" PSP legislators; or it may well be that such are needed, but are not available within the party. The drifting away of members, the lack of identification with the party, and the almost constant reaching out toward merger with other parties suggest the latter interpretation. The fact that merger movements are directed toward the Socialists (with a strong ideology) or toward the Congress (with a weak ideology) suggests that different members of the PSP have different needs. The small opposition party with a weak ideology has little to offer in comparison with an opposition party having a strict ideology or a majority party having a weak ideology.

Chapter IV

POLITICAL CAREER BACKGROUNDS

THE SECOND MAJOR FIELD of inquiry about the MLA's concerned the career patterns followed in politics. The focus is on the process of political socialization: how did these individuals become interested in politics; how did they become attached to political parties, and to their particular parties? Through investigation of these matters, also, something may be learned about the party-building processes from the standpoint of the individual MLA's and of the groups that they represent. Factors involved in the socialization of these men can be expected to have applicability in the society at large. Yet it cannot be assumed that these factors are identical with the factors which the MLA's and others utilize to mobilize the populace politically. Active politicians can recognize and exploit various factors which may not have played a part in their own mobilization pattern. For example, many of the respondents were mobilized during and by the nationalist movement. After independence the nationalist cause, as a mobilizer, disappeared. Present-day mobilization patterns include a variety of processes which were less important or absent in earlier years.

In discussing patterns of political socialization, there is a problem in separating motivation and process. The question of motivation is important, but such a complex subject cannot be adequately covered through a few questions. Nevertheless, many MLA's expressed themselves in motivational terms in explaining how they became interested in politics and in various parties. They often specified events, situations, and conditions as the stimuli resulting in political interest and activity. On a few occasions ideology, principles, and policies appeared as the stimuli, and in such cases efforts were made to determine the specifics involved and the process by which these became known to and important to the respondent. Emphasis on process tended to deemphasize responses of ideology, principles, policies, "public purpose," and the like. That the investigation was not conceived as a study of motivations must be stressed; the basic concern was with process. A number of questions were asked to elicit meaningful and full responses, and probes which depended on the responses were utilized.[1]

Political Mobilization Patterns

For the time of arousal of interest in politics, India's attainment of independence marks a dividing line. More than three-fourths of the PSP and Lohia SP legislators reported that their interest in politics began before independence. In contrast, most of the Jan

TABLE 28

DATE OF AROUSAL OF INTEREST IN POLITICS FOR JAN SANGH, PRAJA SOCIALIST, AND SOCIALIST MLA's

(by percent and number of party MLA's)

Time	Jan Sangh		Praja Socialist		Socialist	
Before independence	35.4	(17)	75.8	(25)	81.8	(18)
After independence	58.3	(28)	18.2	(6)	18.2	(4)
Not known	6.2	(3)	6.0	(2)	—	—
Total	100.0	(48)	100.0	(33)	100.0	(22)

Sangh MLA's are recent recruits, with only one-third reporting interest before independence (Table 28). Given the similarity of ages in the three parties, it would appear that the two socialist parties have had difficulties in recruiting personnel since inde-

[1] Some of such questions were: How did you become interested in politics? What parties have you belonged to? How is it that you joined (each party)? How is it that you left (each party)? Was there any particular event, person, or issue that interested you in the party? In politics? Are any other members of your family interested in politics? What parties do they belong to? Who is your political guru?

The probes were tailored to individual response and are not susceptible of enumeration. In the coding of the data, replies on various related questions were combined in order to obtain the most complete picture. Since these were recall questions, it was somewhat common for respondents to become more voluble on subsequent questions.

pendence, or that upward mobility in the party has been limited by those who entered politics before independence.

Responses on how interest in politics was aroused were varied. These were classified under the headings of primary groups, political workers, events and conditions, participation (including education and membership in civic and political organizations), personal disposition, and ideology (Table 29).

TABLE 29

MAJOR SOURCES OF POLITICAL INTEREST OF JAN SANGH,
PRAJA SOCIALIST, AND SOCIALIST MLA's
(by percent and number of party MLA's)[a]

Source of Interest	Jan Sangh		Praja Socialist		Socialist	
Primary groups	18.8	(9)	21.2	(7)	9.0	(2)
Political workers	16.7	(8)	18.2	(6)	31.8	(7)
Events and conditions ...	39.6	(19)	57.6	(20)	68.2	(15)
Participation	56.3	(27)	42.4	(14)	45.4	(10)
Personal disposition	16.7	(8)	27.3	(9)	27.3	(6)
Ideology	4.2	(2)	—	—	—	—
Not interested	4.2	(2)	—	—	4.5	(1)
Not known	8.4	(4)	3.0	(1)	—	—

[a] Percentages were figured on the basis of total MLA's of the respective parties: 48 Jan Sangh, 33 PSP, and 22SP. The totals are more than 100 percent and more than the total number because of multiple responses.

Whereas in the United States primary groups tend to be important agencies of political socialization, these are less so in Uttar Pradesh. Among legislators of four American states, between 34 and 47 percent named primary groups as the source of interest in politics.[2] The highest percentage among the Uttar Pradesh legislators is 19 percent. The American state with the lowest proportion (34 percent) was California; this low figure was attributed to the "immigrant" background of the state, characterized by the lack of stable primary-group formation and the high mobility of the population.[3] Uttar Pradesh is not an "immigrant" state; few

[2] John C. Wahlke et al., The Legislative System (New York: 1962), p. 79. The same question concerning the source of political interest was used in the Wahlke study and in Uttar Pradesh.

[3] Ibid., p. 80.

TABLE 30

Primary Group Influence on Political Interest of Jan Sangh,
Praja Socialist, and Socialist MLA's

(by percent and number of party MLA's)

Primary Group	Jan Sangh		Praja Socialist		Socialist	
Family members	10.4	(5)	12.1	(4)	4.5	(1)
Friends	2.1	(1)	6.1	(2)	4.5	(1)
Ruling heritage	6.2	(3)	—	—	—	—
Total	18.7	(9)	18.2	(6)	9.0	(2)

residents have been born outside the state, and most, particularly males, live in the same districts in which they were born. With respect to the family as a primary group, it is probably much stronger and more stable in India than in the United States, and most of the MLA's reported joint-family membership, yet as a source of political interest it is weaker than the American primary groups. This is probably owing to differences in political history. Traditions and practices of representative government and political involvement of the citizen body are of long standing in the United States. Such traditions, including a civic tradition,[4] are lacking—or of recent origin—in India. Not until the 1920's did the nationalist movement begin to become a mass movement, and mobilization was usually through agitations and demonstrations. All of the respondents were born before independence (the youngest in 1938) and most were born in villages, but in very few cases were family members or friends interested or active in politics. What happened was that the nationalist movement aroused the impressionable children at the same time that it aroused their elder family members and friends. The main agencies of political socialization were thus the agitations and demonstrations of the nationalist movement rather than primary groups. More than half of those respondents who named family members or friends as sources of interest were among the small number born in urban areas.

Only three respondents related their interest in politics to the tradition of the ruling culture (Table 30). Two of these were

[4] Henry C. Hart, "Urban Politics in Bombay: The Meaning of Community," *Economic Weekly* (special number, June, 1960), pp. 983–988.

zamindars who pointed to their membership in ruling families as the basis for their interest and activity.[5] The third, who was not a zamindar, referred to his caste ethic: "I am a Rajput and it is my privilege to rule. We know how to die and how to live. It is our privilege to rule." It is significant that this lone expression of the caste "right to rule" should come from the oldest respondent among the MLA's. It is possible that some of the other zamindars who mentioned a member of the family as the source of political interest were indirectly referring to the ruling heritage.

A man drawn into politics by a political worker may, in the process, become personally close to him. Such enlistment would not be classed as due to a primary-group influence because there was no prior close relationship. The Socialists, with the lowest proportion interested in politics by primary-group members, have the highest proportion, comparatively, aroused by political workers (Table 29). This pattern would appear to be directly related to the high proportion of Socialist MLA's who were born in villages and were activated before independence. The Praja Socialists rank slightly lower than the Socialists in all these indices. The Jan Sanghiis, with the highest proportions born in urban areas, aroused after independence (Table 31), and citing primary groups as agents of political consciousness were the lowest in the proportion citing political workers as agents.

Among the American legislators of four states, particular events or conditions were noted as the agents of political mobilization for a low of 18 percent in one state to a high of 42 percent in another.[6] Among the Uttar Pradesh MLA respondents the pro-

---

[5] These two MLA's expressed different attitudes toward electoral activity. *Respondent A:* "My family is an old ruling family of zamindars. We are accustomed to ruling. When power and rule changed to government and to parties, we naturally turned to government and entered parties. I wanted to continue in power, so I entered into politics." *Respondent B:* "Having been a zamindar and having great lands, we have always been in politics in some manner or other; it used to be primarily with the administrative or management side. We had to be in politics." Asked, why electoral politics, he said: "People who were worth nothing were MLA's. Yet, I saw that when I went to see district officials I would be made to sit down and wait to be seen, while MLA's were bowed down to and got in to see the district officials at once. I saw where power was located and decided to enter. If I see my house is on fire and I keep sitting in it, no one will help me. I must get out and howl and shout."

[6] Wahlke *et al., op. cit.,* p. 79.

TABLE 31

EVENTS AND CONDITIONS AS SOURCES OF POLITICAL INTEREST FOR
JAN SANGH, PRAJA SOCIALIST, AND SOCIALIST MLA's
(by percent and number of party MLA's)

Events and Conditions	Jan Sangh		Praja Socialist		Socialist	
Nationist movement	20.8	(10)	36.4	(13)	45.5	(10)
Local situation	16.7	(8)	21.2	(7)	22.7	(5)
State-national situation. .	2.1	(1)	—	—	—	—
Total	39.6	(19)	57.6	(20)	68.2	(15)

portions are much greater (Table 31). The nationalist movement
provided the stimulus for many respondents. Key events included
the civil disobedience movement; the "Quit India" movement of
1942; speeches by Gandhi, Nehru, or other leaders; and various
demonstrations. Even so, no one event provided the stimulus for
more than a few respondents. For example, only three respondents,
one in each party, indicated the Quit India movement as the
stimulus of political interest.

Several respondents associated their youth with the great excitement of processions at the time of mobilization. "It was just
child psychology—I joined in," said one. The entertainment value
of such activities gradually led to awareness, reflection, and conviction. Older respondents were not immune to the emotions involved in mass action. Interest in politics was related to their
participation in agitations and "jail going." A few linked interest
in politics with participation in terrorist activities. Some simply
spoke of the desire for independence, the spirit of nationalism, the
teachings of Gandhi, and so on. As might be expected, the two
socialist parties have the highest proportions reporting the nationalist movement as the stimulus to interest.

A variety of local conditions and events were cited as a source
of interest. One subcategory pertained to the desire to change
socioeconomic conditions. Only Praja Socialist and Socialist
MLA's who became interested in politics before independence
made statements indicating this desire as a stimulus. In all cases
the individuals were relatively small kisans, and their foes in-

cluded zamindars, talukdars, moneylenders, and competitive caste groups (intra-elite and elite versus backward castes). The respondents were each personally involved in reported "oppression" by their enemies. For example: "Due to the treachery of zamindars, the police, and British administrators I was hurt, and so I decided to enter politics. My family was poor and the zamindars were forcing us to do their work without wages. . . . A zamindar Brahmin was very cruel to the poor. I am Rajput and the village is dominated by Brahmins, so they ill-treated our family." A few of these respondents gave replies indicating the amalgamation of a socioeconomic kisan movement with the nationalist-independence movement. The tale told by a backward-caste respondent living in a talukdari area is illustrative:

After the death of my father I got one bull buffalo and a debt of 10,000 rupees in succession. On the day of my father's death, the agent of the moneylender came and asked me to sell my land in his favor. Persons present scolded him. We made great efforts. The wage was only a half anna per day. Wheat was one rupee per maund, and there were no irrigation facilities. I came to know from my teacher that those on big farms get five rupees per day. So we also asked for that.

There was a lawyer, Babu Krishna Nath Khare, who was the founder of Congress in [our district]. He came to me one summer. He gave me a lecture. He told me the difference between Britain, India, and other countries—that we are slaves and can't get rid of it. He stayed with me that night. People came to meet him. About eight to ten people became one, and we sang the flag song, and from that time I was interested in politics.

In the morning police persons came and tortured us. So we became more angry. My older brother went into politics; I used to do the farming. My economic condition also became better and flourished.

A few respondents, all Jan Sanghiis and all aroused after independence, became interested in politics through a reverse process: they did not want and did not like socioeconomic change. A moneylender and former zamindar related his interest to dislike of zamindari abolition ("the loss of a nice relationship") and to "concern with poor people and their troubles." This concern was not sufficient to induce reduction of the 35 percent interest rate.

Another subcategory concerned relationships of the populace

with the police or with administrative officials. Observance or direct experience of "police harassment" or official misbehavior served as a prod for the political interest and activity of some respondents. In one case the norms learned in school by a scheduled-caste respondent were also involved: "When I read history and civics, I learned certain rules, and due to the difficulties of the people I was awakened: it was police torture." These few respondents, in all three parties, were nearly all mobilized before independence.

Local factions were an aspect of events and conditions that provided a source of political interest for some. Most of the responses in this subcategory were given by Jan Sanghiis, all mobilized after independence. The local factional alignment sometimes involved personal deprivation, as in the case of one respondent, a teacher, who was transferred to a school some ninety miles from his home because, according to him, he was friendly with a man of his village who belonged to the dissident Congress faction on the district level. The majority-faction leader who was responsible for the transfer was a district board chairman and MLA, and the respondent became interested in politics in order to try to defeat him. A personal affront was involved in a case where the government grant to an educational establishment was stopped "for political reasons." The head of the establishment "took up the challenge," resorting to political activity. In this district there was considerable Brahmin-Thakur rivalry. The opposing factional leader was a Thakur, and the Brahmin respondent, of a large-zamindar family, resented the affront to his position.

Other local conditions and events as sources of political interest were mentioned by a few respondents. Among these were the effects of natural disasters (floods, crop failure), dislike of certain Congress policies (primarily the partition of India and Pakistan cited by Jan Sangh respondents), dislike of Congress personnel, and desire to protect a religious group (only one respondent, a Praja Socialist, referred to "protection of the Hindu").

Participation in various activities also led to interest in politics. As was noted in the study of American legislators, participation in political as well as nonpolitical pursuits can be a mobilizing factor.[7] In that study, education was treated as such a category, with activity in school politics and classes in politics or civics as

[7] *Ibid.,* pp. 84–85.

subcategories.[8] For comparative purposes, education was put in the "participation" category of the Indian respondents although there were difficulties of conception involved. Before independence, student movements were part and parcel of the nationalist movement. Teachers, principals, and students were agents of political mobilization. Because of the few educational institutions of high school level or above in Indian rural areas, attendance at these levels usually meant that a village child was exposed to a more urban environment and one which was likely to be more highly politicized than his village. Without studying politics or civics or engaging in school politics, a child still might become interested in politics through meeting new people and learning new ideas as part of his experience of education.

Comparison of the legislators in the four American states with those of the three opposition parties in Uttar Pradesh reveals that the proportion interested in politics through education is far higher in the Indian case (Table 32).[9] This is, of course, to be expected. Some respondents reported the student movement or their roles as officers in student unions as the source of their interests. Several mentioned teachers who inspired them with stories of great Bengali revolutionaries and nationalist leaders, or who transmitted concern about the political and social conditions of India to their students. Some spoke generally of student days as providing a setting for the arousal of political interest, and in these cases it is likely that an important factor was the influence of the peer group, particularly when a boy was living apart from his immediate family. A few spoke of self-education. One respondent reported reading Tulsidas' *Ramayan* and then deciding that he, like Raam, would try to help others. The decision led him to social work and from there into political activity in order to be a more effective social worker.

Although in some instances education alone was sufficient to

[8] *Ibid.,* pp. 85–86.

[9] *Ibid.,* p. 85. Because the percentages in the Wahlke study were calculated on the basis of the N mentioning participation, it was not readily comparable to table 32. New percentages were drawn up for the three parties in Uttar Pradesh on that same base. The results: 44 percent of the Jan Sanghiis, 78 percent of the Praja Socialists, and 60 percent of the Socialists mentioned education as initiator of interest, as against 45 percent of the California legislators, 38 percent of those in Ohio, 21 percent in New Jersey, and 20 percent in Tennessee.

arouse interest in politics, many reported a combination of agents: education and contact with a political worker, education and family interest, or education and an organizational membership. In all the parties those mobilized before independence reported education as source of interest in a larger proportion than did those mobilized after independence.

A second subcategory reported political interest aroused through membership in religious, cultural, or ethnic organizations. The Arya Samaj, the RSS, and caste organizations fall under these headings. (No occupational or economic organizations were reported by respondents.) There is a difference between the two socialist parties and the Jan Sangh in regard to caste organizations (Table 32). The specific organizations reported by the socialists included the Arya Samaj and caste associations. The fourteen Jan Sangh respondents mentioned Arya Samaj or RSS membership, but none referred to caste associations.

TABLE 32

POLITICAL AND NONPOLITICAL PARTICIPATION AS SOURCES OF POLITICAL
INTEREST OF JAN SANGH, PRAJA SOCIALIST, AND SOCIALIST MLA's
(*by percent and number of MLA's*)

Type of Participation	Jan Sangh		Praja Socialist		Socialist	
Education	25.0	(12)	33.3	(11)	27.3	(6)
Religious, cultural, or ethnic organizations	29.2	(14)	3.0	(1)	9.1	(2)
Civic participation	6.3	(3)	9.1	(3)	9.1	(2)
Political or party work	2.1	(1)	9.1	(3)	4.5	(1)
Occupation	6.3	(3)	6.1	(2)	—	—
Social service work	4.2	(2)	6.1	(2)	—	—
Dual participation		(8)		(8)		(1)
Total *N* (and percentage based on *N*)[a]	56.3	(27)	42.4	(14)	45.4	(10)

[a] As is shown by the dual participation row, some respondents reported two types of activities as being the source of interest (for example, education and an organization). The total *N* rather than the total responses is given and the percentages are based on the *N*. Thus the columns do not add up to the totals given on the *N*.

Respondents of the three parties referring to the Arya Samaj sometimes noted as the basis for their interest and activity in politics the dictum of Arya Samaj leaders that religion and politics are not two different things, and mentioned being exhorted by them to engage in politics. Respondents citing the RSS as the agent of political mobilization pointed to no such ideological justification, although interest in politics and in a certain party (the Jan Sangh) came through RSS membership. Some of these respondents pointed to a similarity of principles and goals of the Jan Sangh and the RSS as the basis for their political interest. Quite a few said that they were either asked or ordered to join the Jan Sangh (many times as an Assembly candidate) by RSS leaders, while some were invited by Jan Sangh leaders. Many of the respondents in the RSS who were requested to participate in the Jan Sangh, and thus in politics, stressed the duty involved. "Duty" usually was indicated as obedience to such requests, although a few spoke of civic obligation. For several, political mobilization and party mobilization occurred simultaneously. Neither the Praja Socialist Party nor the Socialist Party has a "feeder" organization comparable to the RSS.

As Table 32 indicates, only a handful of respondents mentioned participation in civic groups (local government or broad public service organizations) as a source of political interest. Similarly, very few respondents cited specifically political work such as campaigns, meetings, or other party work as agents of political socialization. Even fewer reported that their jobs or occupations served to initiate interest. And only four mentioned social service activities as instrumental in their political awakening.

Comparison of the legislators in the four American states with the MLA's of these parties reveals that larger proportions of the MLA's reported education and membership in religious, cultural, and ethnic organizations as the agents of political socialization, compared with the American legislators. In contrast, none of the MLA's cited occupational or professional groups and some of the American legislators did, although in varying proportions. Very few of the MLA's recalled political or party activity as the source of political interest, whereas many of the American legislators did so. For both groups, political interest was aroused in comparable proportions by occupations and civic or community work,[10] yet if participation in the nationalist movement is combined with the categories of "political or party activity" or "civic activities," then the proportions of MLA's would be substantially greater than of the American legislators. Some of the disparities noted undoubtedly reflect the differences in development of various types of organizations in the two societies and the differences of political history in the two countries.

A few of the respondents (Table 29) referred to personal predispositions and characteristics as important factors in their political mobilization. Descriptions of self included such terms as "adventuresome," "risk-taking," and "I wanted to make my life in my own way." Ambition or desire for personal advancement was mentioned: "I was not interested in going into government service like my friends, and electoral politics was the only other way to advance." Responses included past failure in other spheres of activity as the prod to political interest, and a sense of obligation or civic duty.

The only Praja Socialist respondents to cite personality characteristics in relationship to their political interest were mobilized in the post-independence era. Considerably more than half of the PSP respondents who were activated after independence made such statements, and the remainder were aroused by political workers or by personal participation in local government-civic pursuits. These are highly individualistic and personalistic methods of interest development as opposed to local events and conditions (desire for socioeconomic change, local factions, and the like) or organizational memberships, both of which carry a group connotation. The few Jan Sanghiis who mentioned personality characteristics or personal ambition were almost wholly mobilized in the post-independence era also. Most of the post-independence Jan Sanghiis, however, cited group-related factors.

Two respondents reported only "ideology of Jan Sangh"; neither could be drawn into a discussion of the particulars of

[10] *Ibid.,* p. 85. For this analysis the percentages for the MLA's were recalculated on the same basis as those in the Wahlke study. It is realized that two different entities are being compared: MLA's of three parties in one state as opposed to all-party legislators in four states. A more meaningful comparison might have resulted from contrasting MLA's of specific parties with American legislators of specific parties in the various states. Unfortunately, no party breakdown was given in the Wahlke study.

ideology or of the process by which the ideology became known to them. Finally, three respondents reported emphatically that they were not at all interested in politics.

The process of party mobilization was frequently related to the patterns of political socialization. Further analysis of the factors involved will therefore be reserved until after discussion of the different party backgrounds of the MLA's and of the factors involved in affiliation or disaffiliation with respect to specific parties.

Party Affiliation Patterns

One of the difficulties encountered in analyzing party background is presented by the sheer variety of patterns reported by the respondents. Most respondents mobilized before independence

TABLE 33

FIRST PARTY JOINED BY JAN SANGH, PRAJA SOCIALIST,
AND SOCIALIST MLA's

(According to pre-independence or post-independence mobilization)

First Party Joined	Jan Sangh		Praja Socialist		Socialist	
	Pre-	Post-	Pre-	Post-	Pre-	Post-
Congress	11	4	22	3	18	—
Jan Sangh	5	21	—	—	—	—
Congress Socialist [a]	—	—	—	—	—	1
Praja Socialist	—	—	1	3	—	—
Lohia Socialist	—	3	1	—	—	3
Hindu Mahasabha	1	—	1	—	—	—
Independent [b]	—	1	1	—	—	—
Not ascertained	—	2	—	—	—	—
Total	17	31	26	6 [c]	18	4

[a] This party had formerly been a part of the Congress. The respondent joined the party after it disassociated itself from the Congress and before it merged with any other party. No respondents joined the Jan Congress or Kisan Mazdoor Praja Party as their first party.

[b] These two respondents had an active political record as independents, one having been an independent MLA. For both, the first party joined was the party of present affiliation.

[c] One of the 33 PSP respondents is omitted from the total because it was unknown whether this respondent was mobilized in the pre- or post-independence period.

were members initially of the Congress (Table 33). A few did not become affiliated with a party until after independence. The pattern differs for the post-independence group. Most of the present Jan Sanghiis joined the Jan Sangh directly and most of the present Socialists joined the Lohia Socialist Party directly; but of the respondents now members of the PSP who were mobilized after independence, half were first members of Congress and half joined the PSP initially. There was a scattering of respondents who were first affiliated with opposition parties other than those of which they were currently members.

Those who had first joined the Congress (both pre- and post-independence groups) were asked why. Most of the present Jan Sanghiis reported the nationalist movement and family members as the agents, while most of the present Praja Socialists and Socialists reported the nationalist movement and the influence of Congress political workers. A few cited education or desire to change the socioeconomic structure as stimuli.

Table 34 gives the dates when respondents who had belonged

TABLE 34

DATE OF LEAVING CONGRESS PARTY: JAN SANGH,
PRAJA SOCIALIST, AND SOCIALIST MLA'S

Date of Leaving	Jan Sangh	Praja Socialist	Socialist
Before 1947	3	1	1
1947–1951	8	20	13
1952 through 1957 election	2	1	3
After 1957 election to end of 1962	2	3	1
Not ascertained	2	1	—
Not applicable	31	7	4
Total	48	33	22

to the Congress left that party. The great period of upheaval and resignation is clearly between 1947 and 1951 when the Congress Socialist Party members as well as Jan Congress and KMPP members withdrew. This was also the time of the partition of India and the imprisonment of RSS leaders and members. The year 1951 saw the founding of the Jan Sangh.

TABLE 35

FACTORS INVOLVED IN LEAVING CONGRESS PARTY: JAN SANGH,
PRAJA SOCIALIST, AND SOCIALIST MLA's

Reasons Given	Jan Sangh	Praja Socialist	Socialist
Congress policies	7	4	4
Nasik Conference	—	11	5
Factions	4	7	2
Congress a party for the "big and rich"	1	2	6
Other	2	1	2
Not applicable and "don't know"	34	8	4
Total	48	33	23 [a]

[a] The total is given as 23 rather than 22 because one respondent mentioned two factors (factions and "big and rich").

Leaving the Congress was related to several factors (Table 35). Almost half of the Jan Sangh MLA's who were once in the Congress referred to Congress policies. Five of the seven mentioning policies cited partition: "I resigned over the question of partition in 1947. Congress had no mandate to do this." "I left Congress in 1947 over the issue of partition; I wrote to Nehru about the matter." A small group left the Congress because of local factions, as described in a typical response: "In early days I was in Congress along with my uncle. However, we had difficulty with the Gupta group [in the Congress] and they brought litigation [public, not legal] against us and tried to wash us out of Congress. Congress is divided down on the local level and they tried to destroy us. My uncle stayed in Congress and is still fighting them. I went out and into Jan Sangh."

The Praja Socialists tended to give divergent responses, depending on whether they were subsequently associated with the 1947 Socialist Party or with the Jan Congress–KMPP. Most who became members of the 1947 Socialist Party cited the Nasik Conference and attachment to leaders as the reason for leaving the Congress. (It was at the Nasik Conference that the Congress Socialist Party withdrew from the Congress.) Most who joined the

Jan Congress–KMPP cited Congress factions or attachment to leaders who were involved in factional struggles. Frequently the "prime mover" in the factional conflict on the district level was identified as C. B. Gupta and the respondents often identified themselves as Rafiats.[11] Great bitterness still exists concerning the conflict.[12] A few, of both subsequent SP and Jan Congress–KMPP affiliation, mentioned Congress policies (usually the absence of socialism). The few respondents who left the Congress after 1951 indicated local factions combined with policy differences as the reason.

Socialist Party MLA's tended to give one of three factors as reasons for leaving the Congress. The largest group cited a change in the party: "It had become the party of the big and the rich." "Congress was in favor of great people and not for the poor." "By 1947 Congress had risen so far that it had forgotten us. Capitalists captured Congress and there was no place for kisans." Such responses might be placed in the "local factions" category, for they indicate that changes were taking place in Congress leadership ranks and that the respondents were probably in the losing group. There were some obvious socioeconomic conflicts involved. One respondent, the president of his district's Yadav Mahasabha, in a district in which Yadavs are the largest nonscheduled caste (and are primarily farmers and villagers), reported that he left because the Congress parliamentary board refused in his district to select Congress candidates for the general elections solely from "farmers and village local people." This seems to contain a covert appeal for the selection of Yadavs as candidates. Most of the respondents who fell into this category of "Congress as the party of the big and rich" were kisan workers, frequently of backward and scheduled castes, many of whom had become interested in politics because of a desire for socioeconomic change. A second reason cited for leaving the Congress was the Nasik Conference or attachment to a leader. The third reason reported concerned policy differences, primarily "socialism," which they did not think the Congress supported.

The reasons for leaving the Congress and for joining the first

[11] Followers of Rafi Ahmed Kidwai. See chapter ii.
[12] See Brass, *Factional Politics in an Indian State*, pp. 35–44, for an account of the factional infighting.

significant "opposition" party were usually related. The Jan Sangh respondents reported that the Congress and Jan Sangh policy differences (for example, over partition) and local factions led them to the Jan Sangh. The reasoning of one respondent, involved in local factions, is illustrative: "Jan Sangh was the only alternative party. SP and PSP have no organization in my district, and Swatantra had not been formed. The RSS was well organized and Jan Sangh somewhat organized. Due to my influence and prestige as an ex-zamindar, I knew any party I went to would give me a ticket [i.e., nominate as a candidate] to fight Congress." In addition, contact with political workers and membership in RSS were reported as factors important in joining the Jan Sangh. Several mentioned state-level leaders by name, the chief among them being Nanajii Deshmukh. Others mentioned Ganga Bakht Singh, Raatiijii, or Pitamber Das. (See Table 36.)

TABLE 36

REASONS FOR JOINING AN OPPOSITION PARTY, MLA RESPONDENTS
FORMERLY MEMBERS OF CONGRESS PARTY

Reason for Joining an Opposition Party	Jan Sangh	Praja Socialist	Socialist
Political workers	7	20	13
Organization	5	—	—
Local conditions (factions)	6	11	9
Aims and objects of opposition party	7	3	5
Other (political entrance, primary groups, education) ...	3	1	1
Total [a]	28	35	28

[a] Some respondents gave more than one reason. Therefore the totals are larger than the number of MLA's formerly members of the Congress Party.

Praja Socialist respondents again divided, those with a subsequent Socialist Party history mentioning the Nasik Conference, attachment to leaders, or the efforts of political workers, and those with a subsequent Jan Congress–KMPP history mentioning local factions, attachment to leaders, or political workers as key factors.

Scattered responses mentioning political workers, local factions, and aims or objects of the party came from those who left the Congress and joined the Praja Socialist Party directly. The Socialist Party respondents also stated that the Nasik Conference, attachment to leaders, efforts of political workers, and local factions were key factors in their joining an opposition party.

Fourteen of the fifteen Jan Sangh MLA's with a Congress background transferred to the Jan Sangh directly and have never been affiliated with a third party. The situation is vastly different for former Congressmen now in the two socialist parties:

Praja Socialists		*Socialists*	
KMPP > PSP	6	KMPP > PSP > SP	1
1947 SP > PSP	14	1947 SP > PSP > SP	14
1947 SP > PSP > SP > PSP..	1	Direct to SP	2
Direct to PSP	4		17
	25		

Whereas almost all of those respondents with a KMPP background are now members of the Praja Socialist Party, the respondents with a 1947 Socialist Party background are equally divided between the two parties. This distribution tends to bear out the contention that the 1954 split of Dr. Lohia and his followers was primarily within the 1947 Socialist Party group.

When members of the Socialist Party were asked about leaving the PSP for the SP, almost all of the respondents cited their personal ties to Dr. Lohia (or to a local leader having close ties with Dr. Lohia) and the mass resignation of a local unit. Only two members referred to the dispute or the bases of the dispute between Dr. Lohia and the other leaders.

Among the opposition MLA's who had never been in the Congress the pattern of party membership varied (Table 37). Most of those now in the Jan Sangh joined it as their one and only party. (Five were in other opposition parties before becoming members of Jan Sangh.) Similarly, most of the present Socialists joined that party directly. About half the Praja Socialists joined the PSP directly, while the rest were first members of other opposition parties (though not either the Jan Congress–KMPP or the 1947 Socialist Party).

The respondents with sole Jan Sangh membership spoke of the

TABLE 37

PARTY HISTORY OF OPPOSITION MLA's NEVER IN THE CONGRESS PARTY

Past Party Affiliations	Jan Sangh	Praja Socialist	Socialist
Jan Sangh	26	—	—
1947 SP–PSP	—	—	1
PSP	—	4	—
Lohia SP	3	1	3
Hindu Mahasabha	1	1 [a]	—
Independent [b]	1	1	—
Not reported	2	1	—
Total	33	8	4

[a] One Praja Socialist was first a member of Hindu Mahasabha, then of the KMPP, and then of the PSP.

[b] These respondents had a record of electoral candidacy as Independents. The first actual parties they joined were those of present membership.

influence of political workers as a key factor. The Jan Sanghiis specifically referred to a few state-level leaders (Nanajii Deshmukh, Ganga Bakht Singh, Atal Behari Vajpayii, Deen Dayal Upadhyaya) and when mentioning district or local workers simultaneously linked their names with those of state leaders. The second factor cited by Jan Sangh respondents was their organizational tie with the RSS. The third was the ideology of Jan Sangh (opposing partition and favoring Bharat—that is, Indian —culture being the most frequent comments). The fourth concerned conditions (primarily local factions with the opponents being in Congress). Most respondents mentioned two or more of these factors (such as local factions and the influence of political workers, or the RSS, ideology, and political workers). A few spoke of joining the Jan Sangh because they considered it to be the "party of the future," an "up-and-coming party," and the like. None of the PSP or SP respondents mentioned such a consideration as being involved in their joining.

There are three respondents who first joined the Lohia Socialist Party and then joined the Jan Sangh. One left the SP and became an Independent, and then was asked by political workers to become a member of Jan Sangh. Two were zamindars (both

Thakurs). One of these joined the Jan Sangh because of family pressure. The other became interested in electoral politics upon realizing that this was the locus of power. He said that he joined the Socialist Party "to learn how to meet people . . . to learn how to be a politician." He got his "roughening and toughening" from the Socialists. "[Then] I had had my training. So I joined a more gentlemanly party." Also involved in the change was the lack of deference accorded him by SP leaders. He was a raja, and he realized that the "New Order" required activities and practices different from those of former times. Such an adjustment he was prepared to make—with the electorate. Within the party he expected to be paid the respect due a raja; when it was not forthcoming in the SP, and was "volunteered" by Jan Sangh leaders, he changed parties.

Those respondents who have had membership ties only with the Praja Socialist Party reported political workers or the offer of a party ticket as factors in their entry. Personal ambition was important for some, but local factions appear to have played a very insignificant role. The few who joined first the Lohia Socialist Party and then joined the PSP noted internal party friction as the key factor in leaving the SP. It is interesting that there were no individuals who had first joined the PSP and then shifted to the SP, or the Jan Sangh. Similarly there were none who joined the Jan Sangh and then became Socialists. The Lohia Socialists, in contrast, have lost members to both the Jan Sangh and the PSP.

Only four Socialist Party MLA's had no Congress background. Political workers played an important role in their mobilization; local factions and caste considerations were also mentioned.

The last question in this series concerned the date of entry into the party of present affiliation. As Table 38 shows, very few respondents joined the two socialist parties between 1958 and 1962, whereas during this period the Jan Sangh showed great growth.

Some distinctions appear in a comparison of the socioeconomic characteristics of the Jan Sangh MLA's who were mobilized before and after independence. (There were too few PSP and SP legislators in the group mobilized after independence to permit an analysis.) The characteristics of these two groups should indicate whether the Jan Sangh has tended to attract the same kinds of people as it has become stronger as it did originally, or whether

TABLE 38

DATE OF ENTRY INTO OPPOSITION PARTY OF JAN SANGH,
PRAJA SOCIALIST, AND SOCIALIST MLA's

Date of Entry	Jan Sangh	Praja Socialist	Socialist
1947–1951	15	22 [a]	14 [a]
1952–1957	11	5	5
1958–1962	18	5	3
Not reported	4	1	—
Total	48	33	22

[a] Those Praja Socialists who were in either the Congress Socialist Party or the Jan Congress–KMPP (which merged to become the PSP) were coded as having joined the present party in 1947–1951. Those Socialists who were in the Congress Socialist Party or the Jan Congress–KMPP and who left the PSP at the same time as did Dr. Lohia were coded as having joined their present party in 1947–1951. Those, regardless of past affiliations, who joined the SP after the period of mass resignations were coded according to the actual date of entry in the SP.

TABLE 39

SOCIOECONOMIC CHARACTERISTICS, JAN SANGH MLA's MOBILIZED
BEFORE AND AFTER INDEPENDENCE

(by percent and number of MLA's in group)

Socioeconomic Indices	Before Independence		After Independence		Not Ascertained
In years:					
32 and under	11.7	(2)	25.9	(7)	—
33–42	35.2	(6)	40.7	(11)	(2)
43–52	29.4	(5)	22.2	(6)	(1)
53 and above	23.5	(4)	11.1	(3)	(1)
Education:					
Low	29.4	(5)	25.9	(7)	—
Medium	17.6	(3)	29.6	(8)	(1)
High	52.9	(9)	44.4	(12)	(3)
Present residence:					
Village	23.5	(4)	51.9	(14)	—
Small town	29.4	(5)	11.1	(3)	(1)
Medium to large town	23.5	(4)	25.9	(7)	(2)
City	29.4	(5)	11.1	(3)	(1)

TABLE 39—*Continued*

Socioeconomic Indices	Before Independence		After Independence		Not Ascertained
Caste:					
Brahmin	11.7	(2)	14.8	(4)	(2)
Thakur	17.6	(3)	29.6	(8)	(2)
Other elite ....'.	41.2	(7)	11.1	(2)	—
Backward	17.6	(3)	22.2	(6)	—
Scheduled	11.7	(2)	25.9	(7)	—
Agricultural background:					
Large zamindar	11.7	(2)	18.5	(5)	—
Small zamindar	23.5	(4)	22.2	(6)	(1)
Zamindar, size not ascertained	11.7	(2)	11.1	(3)	(1)
Kisan	29.4	(5)	33.3	(9)	—
Tenant	—	—	11.1	(3)	—
Nonagricultural	23.5	(4)	3.7	(1)	(2)
Landholdings:					
None	17.6	(3)	3.7	(1)	—
Less than 5 acres	11.7	(2)	18.5	(5)	—
6–15 acres	5.8	(1)	25.9	(7)	—
16–30 acres	23.5	(4)	14.8	(4)	—
31–50 acres	11.7	(2)	7.4	(2)	—
51–90 acres	11.7	(2)	14.8	(4)	—
91 acres and above ..	11.7	(2)	14.8	(4)	—
Not ascertained	5.8	(1)	—	—	(4)
Reported monthly income:					
Less than Rs. 299 ...	11.7	(2)	44.4	(12)	—
Rs. 300–599	29.4	(5)	29.6	(8)	—
Rs. 600 and above...	52.9	(9)	22.2	(6)	—
Not ascertained	5.8	(1)	3.7	(1)	(4)

it has reached out to other segments of society. As Table 39 shows, the post-independence Jan Sanghiis are younger in age. There has been an increase in the proportion having a medium education. A really striking expansion of the party has taken place among those whose present residence is in the villages. There has been a small increase in Brahmins and backward-caste MLA's, and a sizable increase in Thakurs and members of scheduled castes. The "other elite" (primarily Bania) has shown a dramatic decline among the post-independence group, while the proportions of large zamindars and of kisans have risen and tenants, absent from the pre-independence group, are represented. The post-independence group shows an extremely sharp drop among those having totally nonagricultural occupations. Proportionately fewer own no land and more have small landholdings (1–15 acres); there is also a slight increase among those having large acreage. In reported monthly incomes, those mobilized before independence were clearly a wealthy group; those mobilized since are definitely a poorer group. In the sense of financial mobility (not given in the table) the post-independence group shows an increase in the proportions of those who consider their status to be the same as or better than that of their parents, and a decrease in the proportion considering themselves to be worse off. These indices indicate that the Jan Sangh has become "ruralized" and is tending to attract more of those in somewhat lower socioeconomic strata than it did formerly.

Among the varied responses on the questions of political socialization and mobilization into the Jan Sangh, two major patterns appear. A considerable proportion reported the role of political workers or of RSS membership as the agents. In analyzing the socioeconomic background of all those who became interested in politics or in the party through the RSS,[13] the caste index proved to be highly intriguing. As is evident in Table 40, during the period since independence the RSS has not served as an agent of activation for elite-caste respondents to the extent that it did before. Significantly, no Thakurs in this period referred to the RSS as a mobilizer. Among the backward-caste MLA's the situation is markedly different, with most being activated by the RSS. It is highly significant that all backward-caste respondents holding university degrees entered politics or the party through the RSS (one was mobilized before independence and four after), while only one of the remaining four backward-caste respondents having less education did so. The RSS thus appears as the mobilizer for

[13] These were often related, but in the coding were divided. For example, some became interested in politics through the RSS, but reported a Jan Sangh leader (i.e, political worker) as the party mobilizer. Others became interested in politics through local factions and entered the Jan Sangh through their RSS tie. To gain a comprehensive view of the role of the RSS as an agent of mobilization, the questions were combined.

TABLE 40

CASTE OF JAN SANGH MLA's MOBILIZED BEFORE AND AFTER
INDEPENDENCE, CITING RSS AS AN AGENT OF POLITICAL
SOCIALIZATION AND MOBILIZATION

Caste	Before Independence		After Independence		Not Ascertained
	RSS-Influenced	Not Influenced	RSS-Influenced	Not Influenced	
Elite:					
Brahmin	2	1	2	1	2
Thakur	3	1	—	8	2
Bania	3	—	1	2	—
Other elite	2	—	—	—	—
Subtotal	10	2	3	11	4
Backward	1	2	5	1	—
Scheduled	—	2	1	6	—
Total	11	6	9	18	4

the highly educated backward-class respondents. It is possible that
RSS–Jan Sangh membership is related to the process of Sanskritization. The RSS is an organization of militant Hinduism calling
for the revival of Indian culture and traditions, with "Indian"
usually defined as "Hindu." A regeneration of Hindu society is
desired; the Hindu race, religion, and culture are exalted. It
would be logical to expect that the more highly Sanskritized culture of the higher castes would be emphasized. The stress that the
RSS puts on the more highly Sanskritized form of the Hindi
language tends to buttress this interpretation. Since the Jan Sangh
also is concerned with the traditions and culture of Indian society
and in Uttar Pradesh there is a general movement among many of
the backward castes for higher status, it may be that as backward-
caste persons gain a university education they are drawn to the
RSS as part of the movement upward, related to their aspirations
for higher status. Further, Sanskritization extends to personal
habits, and it may be that those of backward castes who attend a

university find that they lack personal qualities to which they now aspire and tend to seek discipline in cleanliness, mental discipline, and self-control of several kinds through the RSS. This suggestion is only tentative, for the present study was not primarily sociological and no attention was given to determining why individuals joined the RSS, yet the relationship of RSS membership to the process of Sanskritization would seem a point worthy of investigation. Given the flow of RSS members to the Jan Sangh and the increasing levels of education among backward-caste persons, such a relationship between aspirations and RSS membership could portend future strength for the Jan Sangh among these groups.[14]

A considerable number of respondents mentioned specific present-day political workers in Uttar Pradesh as mobilizers, indicating that a handful of state leaders have played a prominent role. The radial pattern of mobilization in the Jan Sangh, with many individuals having ties to state leaders, differs from the hierarchic pattern in which individuals have ties to district leaders who have ties to state leaders. The radial pattern tends to strengthen the state leadership. The centralization of personal ties in the Jan Sangh stands in contrast to the pattern found in the Praja Socialist Party. Some Praja Socialist MLA's had ties to deceased or now inactive state leaders such as Acharya Narendra Dev, Rafi Ahmed Kidwai, and J. P. Narayan. The ties of others were to district leaders, many of whom are deceased. Another point is obvious: the Jan Sangh contains leaders who are willing and able to travel extensively about the state to recruit members. The party has sufficient financial means to support such travel and related expenses. The leaders of the two socialist parties, on both the state and the district level, bemoan their lack of funds. Yet not only ability but also willingness to recruit is involved. It appeared that the organizational and other state leaders of the PSP and SP were not eager to leave Lucknow (or their own homes) to engage personally in recruitment activities. Some district leaders of the PSP preferred not to leave the district town in order to build up the party and complained that the reason for the weakness of their party was the inability to pay someone else to do this work. The Jan Sangh has leaders on the state and district levels who are

[14] Henry C. Hart found that the RSS recruits select backward-caste youths for education. Interview, August 13, 1965.

willing to do the work themselves, and has financial resources to take care of their expenses and to pay a few other persons— organizers who are deputed to build up the party in specific areas.

The second major pattern of mobilization of the Jan Sangh respondents, particularly of those in the post-independence group, was related to various tensions: local factions, dislike of change in the socioeconomic structure, personal deprivation, dissatisfaction with the types of people who had become prominent in the local Congress, and so on. Personal ambition or desire for advancement was also reported. It appears that the Jan Sangh has been able to exploit such factors far more than the Praja Socialists or the Socialists. Such exploitation is, of course, related to having workers in the field to make use of the tensions.

The fact that there are so few MLA's mobilized after independence among the Praja Socialists and Socialists is, in one sense, a measure of their parties' weakness and decline. These two parties are evidently still drawing on the group mobilized before independence—a group which will be proportionately decreasing in size with every passing year—and on those individuals who were activated by great national and state (and sometimes district) leaders—leaders now deceased, inactive, or out of the party, whose places have not been filled. In the Socialist Party Dr. Lohia was a mobilizer, but he died in 1967. Today's district leaders are sometimes, like the MLA's, the former minor followers of previous leaders. With the disappearance of the great leaders has come a disappearance of recruitment efforts. There appears to have been little opening up of leadership positions to the few who are new recruits.

From 1957 through the end of this study, the two socialist parties in particular tended to rely upon agitations among the populace and the student community to build up their parties. Leaders perhaps hope to repeat the successes of pre-independence years, when many of them were mobilized in this manner. The choice of this approach is also related to the effort toward building rural support with very few active workers. Apparently it is easier to activate workers to organize a demonstration than it is to get workers to mobilize people on a door-to-door or village-to-village basis. Since villagers do tend to participate in large numbers in agitations, this tactic may well appear to be more rewarding than quieter methods. The results of the 1962 elections, however, raise questions about the long-term benefits of utilizing demonstrations to build a party.

Another handicap for the two socialist parties is that the Congress now attempts to maintain pluralism in the party. It no longer encourages dissident groups to leave, as it did from 1947 through 1951. The ability of Congress leaders to manage internal conflict has meant that the two socialist parties (and also the Jan Sangh) have not received periodic infusions of large numbers from the Congress ranks. Instead, a danger is posed for them by the attractiveness of the Congress Party for their own members.

Part Three

BUILDING AN OPPOSITION PARTY

SIX CONSTITUENCIES WERE CHOSEN for study to illustrate how opposition parties are built to winning status on the local level. Several considerations were involved in their selection. First, districts were chosen on the basis of three criteria: only districts in which an opposition party had won multiple victories in 1962 were considered, the assumption being that multiple victories might tend to indicate a party build-up rather than a purely "lone wolf" operation; to avoid duplication, districts studied by others in 1962 election analyses were excluded;[1] and because of the diversity within Uttar Pradesh, districts with contrasting characteristics were selected. For the Jan Sangh the districts of Pratapgarh (3 seats), Bara Banki (2), and Bareilly (2) were chosen. The Bareilly constituency was the only one in which field work had not been completed when the decision was made to include the Lohia Socialists in the study. There was not enough time to complete this case and study one for the Socialists.[2] Bara Banki (3 SP) was chosen for the Socialists, in part because the Lohia SP and the Jan Sangh have shown continuing strength in different parts of the district. For the Praja Socialist Party, Allahabad (6 seats), Farrukhabad (4) and Moradabad (3) were chosen.[3]

Second, various factors were taken into account in choosing the specific constituencies in these districts. Diverse yet comparable

[1] Paul R. Brass studied the districts of Deoria (5 PSP seats, 3 SP), Gonda (4 JS, 1 SP), Aligarh (1 SP), and Meerut and the city of Kanpur (where none of the parties under study won seats). See Brass, *Factional Politics in an Indian State*. Ralph Meyer studied the districts of Sitapur (5 JS, 1 SP), Basti (4 JS). Etah (4 JS, 1 PSP), Hardoi (4 JS), and Bijnor (2 JS). His study has not been completed.

[2] The Jan Sangh initially won the Bareilly constituency studied in 1962. A backward-caste Kurmi, a teacher with several graduate degrees, was the candidate. His opponents included three Kurmis and a Muslim.

[3] In 1962 three Praja Socialists were elected. Arrangements had already been made to study one constituency before it was learned that the other two MLA's had joined the Congress Party shortly after the election.

socioeconomic and political environments were desired. Because 100 predominantly rural seats had been won by these parties, as compared with only three urban constituencies, the more representative rural constituencies were selected. General seats were selected partly because so few reserved (scheduled caste) constituencies had been won in the districts selected, and partly because of the advantages in analyzing units with some common features. For each party a case illustrating an initial victory and a reelection in 1962 was desired. Party leaders were questioned as to which constituencies in the specific districts had good party organizations. While the constituencies chosen do not represent the most highly organized units of the three parties, they are the better organized parties in these districts.

The Jan Sangh initially won the Pratapgarh South constituency in 1962, and reelected an MLA in Rudauli (Bara Banki). The Socialists won Bhitauli (Bara Banki) in 1952 and in a 1956 by-election, lost in 1957, and won again in 1962. Karchana (Allahabad) and Moradabad Rural represent initial PSP victories in 1962, and Saurikh (Farrukhabad) the reelection of an incumbent MLA.

Third, while no two constituencies have identical socioeconomic and political environments, there are some points of similarity. (a) The talukdari heritage in Oudh provides a common setting for Pratapgarh South, Rudauli, and Bhitauli. The cases illustrate three methods of building parties in this environment. The mahalvari heritage provides a point of similarity for the remaining three. (b) The parties in Rudauli and Moradabad Rural operate in a setting of Hindu-Muslim friction, which is largely absent in the others. (c) The successful parties in Bhitauli and Saurikh are led by rural backward caste candidates, while in Pratapgarh South, Rudauli, and Karchana they are represented by elite-caste candidates living in urban areas, and in Moradabad Rural by a rural Muslim. (d) All the constituencies are rural. Moradabad Rural and Karchana, however, are adjacent to large cities, and Pratapgarh South, Rudauli, and Bhitauli contain small towns. Saurikh is totally rural and at some distance from any town. The number of villages in the constituencies ranged from 170 to nearly 300. The number is partly related to their population.

Transportation facilities varied in the rural constituencies. Moradabad Rural was served by five railway lines radiating from the city, Pratapgarh South by two, Saurikh by none, and others by one line. Moradabad Rural boasted four paved roads, Pratapgarh South had three, Rudauli, Karchana, and Saurikh each had two, and Bhitauli had one paved road cutting across a corner of the constituency. The number and placement of paved roads affects the ease of transportation in a constituency, as does the condition of unpaved roads. For example, the unpaved roads are fairly hard-packed in Pratapgarh South, while in Moradabad Rural the surface is a deep fine sand into which wheels and feet sink. In Rudauli and Saurikh the unpaved roads are deeply rutted and generally hazardous. In small towns cycle-rickshaws and horse-drawn vehicles are for public hire. These provide transportation into the rural areas, as do buses. Within the rural area, or from the rural to the urban, buses are basically the only means of public transportation. There are infrequent railway stations where trains stop to pick up or let off passengers. Inhabitants usually travel by bullock cart, cycle, or on foot. Travel within most rural constituencies is slow and difficult.

Public accommodations such as hotels and restaurants are practically nonexistent in the rural areas. A large market village might have a small tea stall or even a *dharmshalla* (rest house); most villages have neither. The towns in the constituencies studied had small restaurants, but no hotels or resthouses. The Public Works and Irrigation Departments operate Inspection Houses, which have electricity, for their officials.[4] There was minimal electrification in the towns and a handful of large villages.

Communication tends to be by word of mouth. A few radios can be found in the towns, but none or very few are come upon in the villages. Some pradhans obtain a radio for the village panchayat, but the radio frequently breaks down. Some newspapers are delivered to urban railway stations; some few villagers arrange to have commuters bring a newspaper to them. In rural areas mail is delivered not to homes, but to a few designated places (a school on a paved road or a market village "post office") and

[4] Inspection Houses are not open to the general public, but some Ministers, visiting dignitaries, and foreign research scholars can obtain permission to stay in them.

on a weekly basis. A few telephones exist in district towns and government offices, but not elsewhere.

With the difficulties of transportation and communication in rural areas, building a party is not easy.

The election studies were made over a period from eighteen to twenty-four months after the general elections of 1962. Information on the politics of each constituency was provided by respondents of different parties, administrative officials, village and town leaders, and other informants. Unfortunately, the newspapers published in Lucknow and Delhi pay very little attention to opposition parties in the districts, or to the interaction of opposition parties with the Congress in the districts. Most of the data could not be confirmed through accounts in the press. It had been hoped that polling-station electoral results could be compared with demographic data. The 1951 *Census of India* district handbooks and the 1891 *Census of Uttar Pradesh* give census data by village; but the handbooks provide no useful indices, and the 1891 records could not be obtained.

While the state Assembly elections are the focus of the study, there will be occasional reference to elections to the Lok Sabha, the lower house of the national Parliament. In Uttar Pradesh five state Assembly constituencies comprise one Lok Sabha constituency, from which is elected one Member of Parliament (MP). Both MP's and MLA's are directly elected at the same time; the Parliamentary contest often affects the Assembly contest. There is scant mention of the members of the upper houses of the state legislature (Legislative Council) and the national Parliament (Rajya Sabha) because they are indirectly elected. Members of the Rajya Sabha are also called "MP's," but in the following chapters the term will be reserved for the members of the Lok Sabha.

Villages are governed by an elected council called a panchayat, the chief of which is called a pradhan. Villages are grouped into Development Blocks, with the pradhans forming the Block Development Committee and electing a president. The block presidents and another representative from each block comprise the bulk of the District Board, and the board members elect a chairman.

Chapter V

THE RAJA RETURNS:
PRATAPGARH SOUTH
(JAN SANGH)

IN 1957 THE CONGRESS CANDIDATE, Bhagwati Prasad Shukla, a Brahmin, defeated his Jan Sanghi opponent, Babu Lal Srivastava, a Kayasth, in the Assembly constituency of Pratapgarh South. In 1962 the same two contested, and Babu Lal Srivastava emerged victorious. In addition to this seat, the Jan Sangh won two Assembly seats and one Parliamentary seat in Pratapgarh. This outcome marked the first penetration of the Jan Sangh in the district and the Congress Party's continuing decline in strength there.

Pratapgarh is a southeastern border district of the former province of Oudh. It contains eight Assembly and one and a half Parliamentary constituencies. In the first general elections, the Congress won all seats. In the second elections, the Congress won in the Parliamentary constituencies, but lost two Assembly seats to Socialists. In 1962 the Congress lost four Assembly seats (three to the Jan Sangh, one to the Socialists), and the "whole" Parliamentary seat.

To investigate the factors leading to the Jan Sangh victories, one constituency, Pratapgarh South, was chosen for detailed study. This roughly triangular-shaped constituency is in the south-central part of the district. In the northern tip is the district town of Bela Pratapgarh, with a population of 21,000. Save for this town, the constituency is rural. Pratapgarh South is one of the five Assembly constituencies in the Parliamentary constituency won by the Jan Sangh in 1962. The incumbent Congress MP who was defeated was Munishwar Dutt Upadhyaya, a Brahmin, and the "Iron Man" of the district Congress. The Jan Sangh victor was Ajit Pratap Singh, a Sombansi Rajput who is better known as the Raja of Pratapgarh.

The Jan Sangh had existed in Pratapgarh since 1951, but its

organization was limited to the town of Bela Pratapgarh and a few scattered units in the Pratapgarh South constituency. The party had been founded by Babu Lal Srivastava and a few others. The appointed organizing secretary, a Brahmin, left the district after the 1957 election and a new secretary, a Thakur, was appointed. Before the 1962 election, the town party consisted largely of businessmen and lawyers (primarily Banias, Mahwaris, and Kayasths). The seven rural Jan Sangh units tended to be dominated by a particular caste, depending on the locale: Banias in two, Thakurs in two, and Kurmis, Muslims, Noniyas, and scheduled castes in one each.

The Assembly contest in 1962 was basically fought between the Congress and Jan Sangh candidates, although there were three minor contestants (see Table 41). Their votes would not have changed the outcome, for the Jan Sangh polled an absolute majority. Both Bhagwati Prasad Shukla and Babu Lal Srivastava are

TABLE 41

CANDIDATES FOR ASSEMBLY IN PRATAPGARH SOUTH, 1962

Name	Caste	Party	Percent of Vote
Babu Lal Srivastava	Kayasth	JS	51.0
Bhagwati Prasad Shukla ...	Brahmin	Congress	32.0
Devi Saran Shukla [a]	Brahmin	Lohia SP	12.6
Vazir Ahmed [b]	Muslim	Independent	2.3
Surya Pal [c]	Kurmi	PSP	2.1

NOTE: Percentages calculated from *Results of the Third General Elections (1962) to the Uttar Pradesh Legislative Assembly* (Allahabad, 1962), p. 29.

[a] D. S. Shukla left the Congress Party in the late 1950's, reportedly because of personal friction and grievances against the "Iron Man" of Congress, Munishwar Dutt Upadhyaya.

[b] This Muslim is a former Jan Sangh district vice president and JS municipal board candidate, who rebelled when he was not given the MLA ticket by the party. This was confirmed by Congressmen of different castes, religions, and factions. He was not "put up" to take votes of Muslims away from Congress.

[c] This backward-class candidate was considered by several informants to have been put up and financially supported by the Jan Sangh in an effort to prevent some of the backward class votes from going to the Congress. The PSP has a paper existence in the district. That the "dummy" ran under a party label illustrates one method of "electoral agreement" among opposition parties.

lawyers living in the town of Bela Pratapgarh. The latter was born in a village of the constituency; his father was a clerk for a small Sombansi Rajput talukdar. He was an RSS organizer during the 1940's, was jailed after Gandhi's assassination, and was one of the most prominent leaders of the party in Pratapgarh. He was not, however, well known in the rural area. Bhagwati Prasad Shukla was from Madhya Pradesh and had been brought into Pratapgarh in the 1940's by Munishwar Dutt Upadhyaya.

To understand the 1962 election outcome, it is necessary to outline some of the socioeconomic and political movements of the past. The 1931 census reveals that the largest castes in the district of Pratapgarh were, in descending order, the Yadav (backward), Kurmi (backward), Brahmin (elite), Chamar (scheduled), Rajputs (elite), and Pasis (scheduled).[1] Although fifth largest in numbers, the Rajputs dominated the district economically and politically. In 1931 they owned 83 percent of the land. The talukdars, who owned more than half the land, were all Rajputs. They were of seven Rajput clans with clearly demarcated geographic spheres of influence. The constituency under study was a part of Pratapgarh pargana, which was Sombansi Rajput territory. The Sombansis owned about two-thirds of the villages in the pargana. The Raja of Pratapgarh's estate, the largest, included in 1931 slightly more than a third of the villages in the pargana. The large zamindar estates were held primarily by Sombansis, secondarily by other Thakurs.[2] The talukdars, mostly pro-British, dominated district politics.

Some of the talukdars actively promoted education in the district. One of these was the then Raja of Pratapgarh, who established Pratap Bahadur College in 1893. Although open to all, the school gave special privileges to Sombansi Rajputs.

Extension of education in Pratapgarh brought changes in the socioeconomic and political structure. The primary beneficiaries of education were the Thakurs, Brahmins, and Kayasths. As Brahmins became educated, they began to challenge the Thakurs.

[1] *Census of India,* 1931 (Allahabad, 1933), XVIII, Pt. 2, 499–548.

[2] *District Gazetteers of the United Provinces of Agra and Oudh,* XVIII: *Partapgarh,* by H. R. Nevill (Allahabad, 1904), xxxv and 78 ff. Also *Supplementary Notes and Statistics up to 1931–32,* XLII (D): Partapgarh (Allahabad: Superintendent, Printing and Stationery, 1935), xlii ff., 10 ff., and 30 ff. The pargana was an administrative subdivision of the district.

In the 1920's a few Brahmin lawyers in the town of Bela Pratapgarh invited a kisan worker, Babu Ram Chandra, to the district. He spearheaded a kisan movement against the Thakur talukdars and zamindars. The Brahmins became the leaders of this movement. Although highest in ritual status, they were lower than the Rajputs in other spheres; this was their chance to redress the balance. The socioeconomic kisan movement had definite caste overtones.

Partly because the talukdars tended to be pro-British, the kisan and nationalist movements were closely related. The leaders of the kisan movement became the leaders of Congress. Many were members of the Congress Socialist Party, but some belonged to other groups. In the 1930's the district Congress leadership appeared to be pluralist in regard to the factions and castes represented. There were, however, few Thakurs. The notable exceptions were two Thakur talukdars, both of whom had close ties to Jawaharlal Nehru.

In the 1940's the pattern of leadership in Congress changed. Part of one faction, primarily Brahmin, took control of the organization. This change occurred as Munishwar Dutt Upadhyaya, a Brahmin of the CSP, began his rise to power. His background illustrates some of the changes in the district, for he had been fed, clothed, housed, and provided an early education through the courtesy of the then Raja of Pratapgarh. After obtaining a law degree from the University of Allahabad, Munishwar Dutt Upadhyaya returned to the district in the 1920's. He is reported to have at that time organized a Brahmin caste organization. Later he became a leader of the kisan movement and gradually rose within the district Congress party. In the early 1940's, the usual date given being 1942 (the year of the Quit India movement, when many Congressmen were in jail), from his position as district secretary he moved to take control of the Congress. Upadhyaya brought young men, mostly Brahmin and all tied to him, into the party. As the need arose in succeeding years for educated leaders, these young Brahmins of his group were given higher and higher leadership positions. Backward-caste kisan leaders, also in the Congress Socialist Party, were swiftly pushed aside: they lacked education. Rafiats, whether Brahmin, Muslim, or of other castes, were also shunted aside with the aid of C. B.

Gupta and, reportedly, Pandit Pant. Munishwar Dutt Upadhyaya chose to stay in the Congress rather than leave with the CSP. The backward-caste leaders who had by then lost position in the district Congress left to form the Socialist Party. In the District Board elections of 1948, every member elected was of Upadhyaya's group. The Rafiats left the Congress with Rafi Ahmed Kidwai, but these soon returned as a small minority. They were unable to challenge Upadyaya's position successfully. The two Rajput talukdars were still in the Congress; neither could be removed because of their ties to Nehru. They were in effect "kicked upstairs" (one is now in the Central Ministry and the other is the lieutenant governor of a small state) and are reported to have little to do with district politics. By the late 1940's, and continuing into the 1950's, the district Congress was controlled by the powerful Munishwar Dutt Upadhyaya, and his faction was led almost exclusively by Brahmins.

In 1951–1952, six Brahmins of Upadhyaya's group were elected to Pratapgarh's six general seats in the Assembly. In 1957, all candidates were again of Upadhyaya's group. Of the four Brahmin candidates, three were elected. One Muslim and one Kayasth were put on the ticket by Upadhyaya, reportedly because of the composition of the Congress Parliamentary Board, and were elected. The District Board was dominated by Brahmins of Upadhyaya's group, as were other semiofficial institutions such as the District Cooperative Bank. By the mid 1950's, the district had been nicknamed "Shukalgarh." ("Shukla" is a well-known Brahmin subcaste and frequently is a Brahmin surname.)

During this period the Rajputs grumblingly acquiesced in the new situation of Brahmin dominance. Although not united, they tended to be anti-Congress. Some tried to salvage their position by associating with the Congress. A few tried to break into the higher echelons of the Congress district leadership, but were repulsed. One of these was the Raja of Pratapgarh. In 1958 he made a last attempt: he tried to get the Congress nomination for the Rajya Sabha. When this was refused, he joined the Jan Sangh and was elected to the Rajya Sabha. During this time there was animosity between Brahmins and Thakurs, but there was no concerted effort to dislodge either the Brahmins or the Congress from power.

In 1960 an incident occurred which drastically changed this situation. There was desire for a four-year degree college in the district. Two private intermediate colleges (two-year institutions) were put forward for recognition as degree colleges. One was Pratap Bahadur College, previously mentioned, which was the oldest in the district. Though the college gives special privileges to Sombansi Rajputs, it is open to all castes, teachers of various castes are employed, and scholarships are granted to all castes. The Raja and the Rajputs generally tend to look upon the school as peculiarly "theirs." The other college was established the year before by Munishwar Dutt Upadhyaya.[3] In this college, all teachers save one are Brahmin.

It was generally expected that the older Pratap Bahadur College would be granted recognition as a degree college. Instead recognition was accorded Upadhyaya's college. The decision was interpreted as having been made on political grounds. It was viewed as a direct slap at the Raja and as another case of the Brahmins humiliating the Thakurs. The incident set off a full-scale Thakur revolt. The intensity of feeling can be seen in the establishment of two literary societies and two bar associations: in each case, one is Brahmin and the other is Thakur.

The Jan Sangh, quick to recognize the possibilities of the situation, prevailed upon the Raja to accept nomination for the Lok Sabha in the coming election. The Raja had been a minor during most of the pre-independence years and had lived outside the district. Few had ever seen him. After the college decision he returned to Pratapgarh and began mobilizing his caste fellows. Politically, the Brahmin-dominated Congress was now opposed by the Thakurs supporting the Jan Sangh. It was reported that the Raja originally wanted a candidate other than Babu Lal Srivastava to contest the Pratapgarh South constituency, but that Jan Sangh state officials were opposed. They were probably not willing to hand over the entire district party to the Raja and his men. Babu Lal Srivastava had contested the seat in 1957, and his was the only constituency in which even a rudimentary organization existed.

---

[3] Upadhyaya has been active in promoting education. He owns some 22 schools. Since establishing schools is one method of bettering the condition of those persons who support him, this activity is regarded as part of the anti-Rajput movement.

The Raja then accepted Babu Lal as his running mate and the two worked closely during the campaign. It was reported, however, that a "split ticket" movement (Raja for MP, Congress for MLA) existed until a few days before the election. At that time, the Thakurs became worried lest voters should become confused in casting votes for a split ticket and might inadvertently defeat the Raja. A call went out to vote a straight Jan Sangh ticket, which appeared to be effective, in that the votes given the two candidates were very close in all polling stations. Babu Lal Srivastava was not a strong candidate on his own. Without the Raja's presence on the ticket and the college incident which aroused the Thakurs, the Jan Sangh would not have fared as well as it did.

As would be expected, the Thakurs rallied to the Jan Sangh standard in large numbers. Others did too: former employees of the Raja's talukdari and of other talukdari estates, and former tenants, many of backward castes. One factor present was the sentiment of "the Raja has come!" Many respondents pointed out that the Raja as an individual was unknown in the district. Surrounding him was an aura of glamor, excitement, and mystery. Some of the practices of the talukdars had been forgotten (or the memories mitigated), and the Raja himself was not identified with those practices because he had been a minor. The Raja toured the constituency three times before the Congress candidates were chosen, smoking the hookah with his fellow Rajputs, sitting on the charpoys of the lower castes and taking sweets from them, and, in doing this, exploiting the feeling of "the Raja has come!"

In the election there were several factors concerning the Congress Party and particularly the person of Munishwar Dutt Upadhyaya. In politics one makes enemies. Over the years Upadhyaya had made many: Thakurs, Rafiats, and displaced backward-caste leaders. Members of his own caste who were formerly of his faction had become disenchanted. As an MP and prominent state political figure, he had lost touch with his constituents and activists. He became a "new Raja" in his manner. His snobbery and discourtesy were reported to have alienated party workers and important supporters. Added to this was the reported phenomenal increase in his wealth. Many businesses and commercial agencies had been acquired in his son's name; there were recurrent stories of various governmental manipulations redounding to his or his son's financial benefit. For all to see was the construction of his third house. This grandiose "84-pillar house" was cited as "proof" of illegal personal aggrandizement. When this variable was combined with the many criticisms of Upadhyaya and with other factors in the election it carried an impact.[4]

Another factor was Congress factionalism on the state and local level. For many years Upadhyaya was a member of the state "Gupta group." He had been elected president of the Pradesh (state) Congress Committee. When Upadhyaya discovered that Gupta would not support him for reelection as state president, he switched to the Gautam-Tripathi group and was defeated in the party election. C. B. Gupta still controlled the state organization. For the first time there was a strong state leader interested in challenging the local power position of Upadhyaya. At the same time, not all of Upadhyaya's faction in the district had been willing to shift to the Gautam-Tripathi group. Bhagwati Prasad Shukla remained in the Gupta group and was appointed Deputy Minister in the state government. On the district level he became one of the leaders of the anti-Upadhyaya forces. One consequence was that in Pratapgarh South, the MP and MLA campaigns were not closely meshed. The MLA (an incumbent who was seeking reelection) was willing to sanction the split-ticket movement. Upadhyaya and others in his group insisted that Congress factions had no impact at all on the electoral outcome; however, some anti-Upadhyaya Congressmen did actively campaign against the "Iron Man." Given the total situation, factional in-fighting has to be regarded as an important factor.

Congressmen considered the party's procedure in selecting candidates as a factor important in the election. The decisions were made late and in Delhi; hopefuls had to spend much time in Delhi just prior to the nomination filing deadline either to get the ticket

---

[4] The Raja's wealth proved to be an advantage in the campaign. At the time of the study no respondent of any party or caste was able to conceive of the Raja's using his governmental position to benefit himself financially, or desiring to do so. Only one respondent suggested that Babu Lal Srivastava would use his official postion to benefit himself. These attitudes were in stark contrast with those expressed about most of the Congress leaders in the district.

or to ensure getting the ticket for a constituency in which they had worked. The difficulty was not so much in the lateness of the decision as it was in the uncertainty engendered by the process. Few had incentive to build, extend, or repair an organization until sure of the ticket. In contrast, the Jan Sangh candidates had known for well over a year that they would be contesting from specific constituencies. They spent their time campaigning in the field rather than in Delhi.

The Congress election campaign raised the old anti-talukdar, anti-Thakur issue. For decades this call had mobilized both Brahmins and lower castes; but in 1962 zamindari had been abolished for eleven years, and the Brahmin enemies of the Thakurs had administered the land reforms. Memories of landlord abuses were superseded by pin-pricks of the newer Brahmin elite. The anti-talukdar appeals had lost their old rallying power.

There were a few other issues: the Jan Sangh opposed cooperative farming, which was supported by Congress. The Hindi phrase for "cooperative farming" is pronounced "sah^{e}kaarii kheetii." This was corrupted to "sarkaarii kheetii" ("government farming") by the Jan Sangh, who campaigned that the Congress wanted to take ownership of land away from the kisans. This was said to be an important issue, but its significance can be questioned. The same issue was raised in identical form in many other constituencies where the Jan Sangh fared poorly at the polls.

Jan Sangh workers made promises which are not unfamiliar: to reduce taxes, to build one road and two bridges, to provide honest government. These were recalled by some villagers and party workers. Congress workers in the town appeared still perturbed about their use, considering them irresponsible. It is difficult to gauge the impact of such promises.

Another issue arose a few days before the election as the aftermath of a speech by Jawaharlal Nehru in the district town. As usual, Nehru spoke against the evils of casteism and communalism. He also derided the pandits and astrologers who were forecasting doom on the date of coincidence of seven planets. His comments were said to have been interpreted by many as antireligious. The Jan Sangh workers tried to exploit this reaction. Congress workers in the town considered the issue to have some impact, but more in the light of "everything tended to work against us."

These various issues and promises were probably not decisive factors. The general socioeconomic tensions appeared to be far more crucial, although the possible cumulative impact of all the factors and issues raised cannot be disregarded.

In field work it was learned that several other factors affected the voting decisions on lower levels—in specific villages or for small groups of people. Some Congressmen charged that Thakurs or their henchmen prevented pro-Congress scheduled-caste voters from going to the polls by strong-arm methods. Interviews turned up the allegation repeatedly, but no evidence to confirm it, at least as a decisive factor. Voter participation was not noticeably down in those polling stations where intimidation was reported. In fact, the turnout varied only by fractions of a percentage point —both up and down—as compared with neighboring areas where no force was reported. The defeated MLA himself claimed only that these practices heightened the Jan Sangh plurality in an election which they would have won in any event.

Local factors also important included village factional alignments and economic class distinctions. A "sentimental tie" to a former talukdar helped to explain why many Muslims in a certain area supported the Jan Sangh. This tie was strengthened by the efforts of two Congress Muslims, who were so anxious to defeat Munishwar Dutt Upadhyaya that they campaigned among Muslims on behalf of the Raja. Economic ties were quite important in several instances. It was reported that Brahmins employed by Jan Sangh businessmen supported the Jan Sangh. That several businessmen supported Congress was said, by Congressmen, to be due to the desire for economic advantages flowing from support of Congress. The Congress was in an enviable position in terms of offering material benefits (government jobs, and jobs in private educational institutions) and threatening disadvantages (such as job transfers to "far-off places"). Control of the District Board by Upadhyaya's group enabled the Congress to initiate and complete one small public works project during the campaign itself. Control by this same group over the District Bank and Cooperative Societies provided additional sources of leverage.

The preelection and "normal" Jan Sangh organization has been referred to. For the election a special organization was developed. The constituency was divided into a northern and southern section, each supervised by a "permanent party member" who resided in the town. Each section was successively subdivided into smaller and smaller units. The size of the subdivisions depended on the personnel available.

From the standpoint of garnering support for the candidates, the informal organizational networks were more important. At the heart of the informal organization was a "Raja network" of talukdars and their families, employees, and former employees (including children of former employees) and ex-zamindars with their families, former employees, and so on. The Thakurs might well be placed within this Raja network inasmuch as all talukdars and most of the zamindars were of this caste, and those who were not of zamindar-status tended to support the Thakur cause. Those in the Raja network could be classified as either notables who were prominent in their own right or information agents who were able to transmit data concerning key persons, factions, and local situations.

The Jan Sangh also had a subsidiary "shopkeeper network," primarily of businessmen and moneylenders in the town whose relationship with rural businessmen and moneylenders and their clients could be utilized to advantage. Many of those in this network were "permanent" Jan Sangh members. There was a lawyer network supporting the Jan Sangh (many of them permanent members), their employees, and their clients. A minor network was that of teachers. Both the Jan Sangh and the Congress utilized teachers; the Congress reportedly called on District Board teachers as well as private-school teachers. Some of the District Board teachers were said to support the Jan Sangh, but most of the pro-Jan Sangh teachers were of private schools. These provided mobile manpower for canvassing, as well as influence in rural areas.

The RSS claims a membership of four hundred in the town of Bela Pratapgarh, with few members in rural areas. One informant reported that approximately 20 percent of the RSS members were interested in politics and that these supported Jan Sangh. Many of the RSS members are businessmen or lawyers; some are prominent permanent party members and leaders. These are the people who filled the formal electoral organization posts. Others provided some of the mobile manpower for canvassing. It would be difficult to speak of an "RSS network" in the election, inasmuch as the influence exerted was functionally related to the economic, occupational, or familial categories into which individuals fell.

The detailed election results indicate the extent of the Jan Sangh victory. The party won pluralities in 80 percent of the polling stations—7 of the 9 urban and 59 of the 73 rural polling stations. The Congress won pluralities in two urban areas (both with high Muslim populations), and in 13 rural polling stations scattered through the constituency. The Socialist candidate received a plurality in the rural polling station which included his home village.

The case of Pratapgarh South illustrates several elements in politics. First, in this constituency the Parliamentary contest was by far the most important. The Assembly decision was a by-product of the Parliamentary.

Second, this case illustrates the enormous reserves of power and influence held by former talukdars in the rural areas. Even though (and perhaps because) the Raja had been absent from the district for years, his return and participation was followed by widespread support from various sectors of society. This phenomenon is partly a matter of economics, for the talukdars and zamindars and their fellow Thakurs are still the larger landowners in the rural areas. It is also partly a matter of sentiment and the aura surrounding a Raja.

Third, this case represents friction on a caste basis, between two elite castes. The backward and scheduled castes did not play an active role, although their votes decided the outcome. Both the Congress and the Jan Sangh obtained support from all castes and communities; neither could have won solely by support of the candidates' castes. Yet it was the friction between the Brahmins and Thakurs which set the tone for the election. They were the prime actors. The rivalry between these two castes in Pratapgarh is overlaid by economic rivalry of zamindars versus non-zamindars. The two cleavages coincide here, whereas in other districts this is not always the case. The bitter hostility between the two groups is probably related to this coincidence. This tension has obvious consequences for majority party–minority party relationships on the district and local level.

A fourth feature demonstrates the difficulty of discussing politics in traditional and modern terms. The Thakurs could be said to represent the traditional social order. They had been, before independence, the dominant social, economic, and political group in the district. They had been replaced by Brahmins, non-talukdars, and non-zamindars who had mobilized lower economic classes and lower castes. The landed, rural interest had been displaced by urban, Western-educated, professional, "middle class" interests. They had been overturned in two secular movements: a kisan movement and a nationalist movement, both led by such interests. Yet, could this new group be termed modern? The Brahmins by tradition have the highest ritual status in Indian society. In Pratapgarh the Brahmins suffered from lack of status crystallization in the pre-independence years. Could the political assertion of this group, which led to the establishment of "Shukalgarh," be called modern, or is this basically another traditional group which utilized some modern weapons to assert a traditional status? The weapons included education, an economic movement, a political movement, and participation in party work and elections. In 1962 this group was successfully challenged by the Thakur-talukdar-landed-rural-traditional interests who used modern weapons to reassert their traditional status. The weapons were political: participation in party work and an appeal to the electorate. The appeal involved the talukdar candidate in activities unheard of for the old-time talukdars.

Last, Pratapgarh South illustrates the interaction between social tensions and party building. The Jan Sangh district party leaders were primarily Kayasths and Banias, although some other elite castes were also represented. This group exploited the dominant socioeconomic frictions in the district. They became the spokesmen for, and representatives of, a defensive group. In broader terms, the Jan Sangh performed the function of innovation, organizing voters on other lines than previously and appealing to groups which were excluded from the dominant party. At the same time, the Thakur-talukdar elements exploited the party to serve their own purposes. In this process, the Jan Sangh became a winning party in three Assembly constituencies.

Chapter VI

RISE OF THE MIDDLE
CASTES: BHITAULI
(SOCIALIST PARTY)

BARA BANKI DISTRICT is in central Oudh, adjacent to Lucknow district. This was a talukdari area, but, in contrast with Pratapgarh, no caste or clan had control of extensive tracts of land and the talukdars were of several castes (Muslims and Thakurs being the most prominent). As in Pratapgarh, the nonelite castes are the most numerous. In order of size, the scheduled-caste Pasis, backward-caste Kurmis and Yadavs, and scheduled-caste Chamars are more numerous than the Muslims, Brahmins, and Thakurs. But unlike Pratapgarh, where the lower castes are politically passive and the elite castes dominate political life, Bara Banki is characterized by a self-conscious and politically active Kurmi community which has provided leadership for other nonelite castes. It would not be amiss to say that all the backward and scheduled castes play a more active role than their counterparts in Pratapgarh.

A few variables help to explain the importance of the lower castes, and particularly the Kurmi community. One is their size. Second, the Kurmis are better off economically than Kurmis in many others districts. At the turn of the century many owned their own land and were acquiring proprietary rights in many villages while other caste groups were losing their land to talukdars, zamindars, and moneylenders. Although a few were small zamindars, none were talukdars. Third, according to the 1904 *District Gazetteer,* a fair proportion of Kurmis had acquired some education, and even at that time the caste claimed Kshattriya status.[1]

---

[1] *District Gazetteers of the United Provinces of Agra and Oudh,* XLVIII: *Bara Banki,* by H. R. Nevill (Allahabad, 1904), 71, 82 f. Also *Supplementary Notes and Statistics up to 1931-32,* XLVIII (D): *Bara Banki* (Allahabad: Superintendent, Printing and Stationery, 1935), 14-27; hereafter cited as *Supplementary Notes.*

The Yadavs and the Pasis, although numerous, have lacked in the past the economic and educational position of the Kurmis. Leaders of both castes have allied with the Kurmis.

The Muslim community is larger in Bara Banki than in Pratapgarh and consists of both Sunnis and Shi'as. In addition to traditional religious rivalries between the sects there are some socioeconomic rivalries related to the position of the Shi'as as talukdars. There are also political rivalries. The Raja of Mahmudabad, a Shi'a Muslim with part of his estate in Bara Banki, was the chief financier of the Muslim League. The district was also the home of Rafi Ahmed Kidwai, a Sunni Muslim, and noted Congress leader and foe of the Muslim League. Informants reported that the two sects tend to divide on similar lines.

Bhitauli constituency, in the northwestern part of the district, is rural save for the small town of Fatehpur (less than 10,000 population). Among the larger estates were those of the Raja of Mahmudabad and the Raja of Ramnagar (a Raikwar Rajput).[2] Although many Muslims live in the rural areas, they comprise a fairly high proportion of the town population; most of these are reported to be Sunnis. The Kurmis are concentrated in especially large numbers in this part of the district.[3]

The *Supplementary Gazetteer* of 1935 records the beginning of a kisan movement against the talukdars and zamindars. The latter attempted to raise the already high rents, and Congress workers easily "enlisted the sympathies of the dissatisfied tenantry." [4] As in Pratapgarh, educated Brahmin lawyers of the district town initiated the kisan movement in the rural areas. After mobilizing the kisans (particularly the Kurmis), the Brahmin lawyers returned to the district town. In the Bhitauli area, leadership of the kisan movement and of Congress became lodged with the Kurmis.

Zamindari abolition was reported to have some effect in the Bhitauli area, but the effect appears to have been as much psychological as economic. Informants reported that the zamindars, most

[2] *Supplementary Notes,* pp. li ff.
[3] Bhitauli lies in Fatepur tahsil (district subdivision), where 45 precent of the population is reported to be Kurmi. The Kurmis are concentrated in 22 villages. *Uttar Pradesh District Gazetteers: Bara Banki* (Lucknow: Government of Uttar Pradesh, 1964), p. 56.
[4] *Supplementary Notes,* pp. 27 f.

of whom were of the elite castes, had long lived off the revenue collected and had never worked. With abolition, their income was sharply cut. The kisan movement had already made some impact, as lower castes refused to give free labor or to pay higher rents. Precise data on land transfers are missing, but some zamindars, particularly Thakurs, were reported to have lost land to lower castes. The village settlement pattern was of importance, according to reports. In villages with a sizable Kurmi community, the Thakurs lost land; in Thakur-dominant villages, the Thakurs retained their land. According to Thakur and Muslim Congress leaders, as well as Kurmi Socialist leaders, there was a definite loss of status, position, and economic standing among the Thakurs as a group, with a betterment of conditions among the backward castes generally and among Kurmis in particular. One Kurmi said:

We were scared of Thakurs in zamindar times, but now we have our leaders and have the majority in the area. Why be afraid?

Before independence we were in the same position as the Pasis and Chamars. We were scared of the zamindars: they were the rulers. But we Kurmis are hard workers. At that time we could not prosper because of *begar* [forced labor] under the zamindars. We got little of what we cultivated. Now that is over and Kurmis prosper.

The Yadavs are not quite as well off, but they belong to a fighting class. They are in the majority also and are not afraid of the Thakurs. . . .

The Kurmis began to come on the same level as the Thakurs, and the Thakurs became jealous.

The Kurmis had long claimed Kshattriya (warrior, fighting, ruler *varnashrama dharma*) status; the respondent identifies the Yadavs with this group. The emphasis on present lack of fear due to economic position, leadership, and numbers would seem to indicate that a psychological change did take place. The "jealousy" of Thakurs was mentioned by several respondents of varied castes.

The most important kisan and Congress leader in Bhitauli was a Kurmi, Lala Avadh Saran. He owned some land, was a very small zamindar, had some education, and had been activated by a Congress Brahmin lawyer from the district town. He became a leader of district-level status before independence, and was a member of the Congress Socialist Party. The dawning of independence brought some changes in Congress leadership. Lala

Avadh Saran along with other Kurmi and kisan leaders left Congress with the CSP. Congress leadership rested with representatives of the urban areas, elite castes, Sunni Muslims, and some of the large landowners.

In the first general elections there were three major candidates in Bhitauli. Lala Avadh Saran of the Socialist Party forged an alliance between backward castes and Pasis and was victorious. The Congress leaders considered a Kurmi candidate to be essential not only because of the size of the community, but also because of the kisan movement history. They found a Kurmi to contest —a newcomer to politics and the Congress, not a kisan worker, and not well known. This was Vishal Singh; he lived in the same village as and was a personal enemy of Lala Avadh Saran, and was a slightly larger zamindar than the latter. The third major candidate was a Brahmin of the Uttar Pradesh Praja Party (a zamindar party which opposed Congress policies of zamindari abolition). The Congress and Uttar Pradesh Praja Party candidates split the votes of the talukdars, zamindars, upper castes, and Muslims. As a Kurmi, Vishal Singh obtained some Kurmi support. The division in the electorate reportedly was on a talukdar-versus-kisan basis rather than on a strictly caste basis.

The tension between talukdars and kisans and between Thakurs and Kurmis was not lessened by the victory of Lala Avadh Saran. In 1955 an event occurred which had the effect of emphasizing the caste rather than the economic class distinction. In that year Lala Avadh Saran and another young Kurmi leader organized a mass meeting in a scheduled-caste village to protest activities of the local zamindars (who were Thakurs). The two were warned by certain Thakurs not to hold the meeting, but it was held as planned. A band of Thakurs, some of them ex-zamindars, descended upon the meeting and killed both Lala Avadh Saran and the other Kurmi leader. This incident and the subsequent trial of the Thakurs served to arouse emotions and solidify a caste alignment.

A by-election was held in 1956 to fill the now vacant Assembly seat. The Socialist Party candidate was Lala Avadh Saran's brother, Ram Asrey. By this choice the Socialists capitalized on the intense emotions. Ram Asrey had become interested in politics in the 1930's, but had left political activity to his brother while he devoted himself to agriculture and business. The Congress candidate was again the Kurmi Vishal Singh, who was handicapped by the support of those Thakurs associated with the assassination of the two Kurmi leaders. A third minor candidate was put forward by the Jan Sangh. Ram Asrey won handily with the full support of the backward castes and Pasis. He had also the support of at least two Muslim Shi'a talukdars (the Sunnis supported the Congress).

That this 1956 victory was directly related to the tensions aroused by the assassination cannot be doubted. In the next year the general elections were held. Again Ram Asrey, the Socialist, faced Vishal Singh of the Congress. There was no third candidate of consequence, and Vishal Singh won. He had the support of talukdars, zamindars, Thakurs and others of the elite castes, and Muslim Sunnis (especially the Ansari caste). Also he garnered support from the Kurmi community and received some votes of other backward castes, as he had not in 1956. Congress and Jan Sangh activists reported that the Congress was successful because this was basically a straight fight between the two candidates. A strong third candidate generally tends to draw upper class–elite caste support away from the Congress. This election shows, however, the importance of the backward-caste votes in the constituency. The third candidate in 1956 was not major, but the Congress candidate had received very few backward-caste votes. Respondents also mentioned that Ram Asrey's illness just before the election prevented his campaigning and that the Socialists were overconfident.

In 1962 Vishal Singh again contested, but placed third, winning pluralities in only 7 of 96 polling stations. Ram Asrey, of the Socialist Party, won with pluralities in 56 of 96 polling stations. The second place candidate, who had pluralities in 28 polling stations, was an Independent, the Raja of Ramnagar. This was his first major activity in politics. Although his was the largest talukdari estate in the constituency, he lived in Lucknow city. With his candidacy, once again the talukdar-zamindar-Thakur-elite caste votes were split. Muslim Sunni votes which previously had gone to the Congress were divided because many Sunnis lived in the area which had been part of the Raja's estate. The Raja's strength was geographically concentrated in the portions of the constituency which were formerly in his own or his supporter's talukdari estates. The size of the Raja's vote indicates the reserves of influence that talukdars have when they become candidates. The Raja had no party and little organization; he relied essentially on a "raja network." [5] This was sufficient to give him a larger vote than the Congress candidate.

The Raja helped materially to elect the Socialist Party candidate. Not only did he take votes from the Congress, but his candidacy raised again the Kurmi-Thakur and kisan-talukdar tensions, in an area where the two distinctions tend to coincide with and reinforce each other. Some of the Kurmis and kisans who had supported Vishal Singh in 1957 now shifted ther support to the Socialists. A prominent Congress district leader, a Muslim, summed up the situation:

You see, the Kurmis had been oppressed by the Thakurs, and they resented the Thakurs. They rose against them. Particularly after zamindar abolition when they got certain rights and in many respects became the equals of the Thakurs, they became the bitter foes of the Thakurs.

This caste antagonism will die down after a while, but right now it is thriving. Kurmis and Ahirs are asserting themselves against their former rulers. The Socialist Party has capitalized on this antagonism, and it explains their strength. It is based on social tensions, and not on political principles or ideology. . . . In rural areas the large landholders still have power. There has not been much change. But this is different in Bhitauli and Kursi constituencies because of the Thakur-Kurmi feeling.

Another important factor in the 1962 Socialist victory was the presence of Ram Sevak Yadav on the ticket as the Parliamentary candidate. (See Table 42.) There are no Yadav leaders in Bhitauli constituency although the community is large in size. Ram Sevak Yadav resides in the district town, outside Bhitauli. His candidacy tended to "cement" the Yadav vote to the Socialists. Likewise the Socialist Party MLA candidature of a Pasi in the adjoining reserved constituency served to tie the Pasis to the party in both constituencies. The Kurmi-Pasi alliance has exited for more than a decade, and Kurmi leaders have championed the causes of the Pasis. Constituency borders do not necessarily reflect the borders

[5] A "raja network" refers to political support garnered through the ties of a talukdar and his family to other talukdars and zamindars, former employees and their children, former tenants, and others who lived on their estates.

TABLE 42

CANDIDATES FOR THE ASSEMBLY IN BHITAULI CONSTITUENCY, 1962

Name	Caste	Party	Percent of Vote
Ram Asrey	Kurmi	Socialist	36.8
Amar Krishna Narain Singh (Raja of Ramnagar)......	Thakur	Independent	26.9
Vishal Singh	Kurmi	Congress	19.7
Ram Kumar	Kayasth	Jan Sangh	9.0
Bisesar Prasad	Kurmi	Swatantra	4.3
Jai Shanker	Brahmin	Independent	3.3

SOURCE: *Results of the Third General Election (1962) to the Uttar Pradesh Legislative Assembly* (Allahabad, 1962), p. 36.

of social, political, and economic ties. In these two constituencies both Kurmis and Pasis supported the Socialist Party.

Within the Socialist Party itself there has not been complete absence of friction. There is growing tension between Kurmis and Yadavs. A young Yadav lawyer, Ram Sevak Yadav, had come into contact with Lala Avadh Saran after independence and had joined the Socialist Party. In the sudden leadership vacuum that developed when the two Kurmi leaders were killed, Ram Sevak Yadav rose rapidly. He organized meetings of leaders and workers, took part in the trial of the Thakurs, and became popular among the rank and file. These activities brought him to the attention of state and national Socialist Party leaders. In 1957 and 1962 he was elected to the Lok Sabha from different constituencies, and in 1962 became leader of the Socialist Party in the Lok Sabha. Just as the rise of the Kurmis is associated with the appearance of Lala Avadh Saran as a leader, so the rise of Ram Sevak Yadav was connected with the rise of the Yadavs. "Kurmi-Yadav alliance" became a common term, even though in Bhitauli constituency no respondent of any party and no district-level Yadav could name any Yadav activist.

Some of the Kurmi respondents complained that Ram Sevak Yadav was trying to destroy Kurmi leadership in the party, and expressed concern because Ram Sevak Yadav—a lawyer, urban,

English-educated—has much closer ties to Dr. Lohia and other Socialist leaders than any of the Kurmi leaders. The Kurmi leaders are kisans and small businessmen; none are as highly educated as the Yadav leader. The state and national leaders of the party, by their background, would tend to find greater affinity with the more sophisticated Ram Sevak Yadav than with the Kurmi leaders. Interviews with some of the workers in the party's state organization confirmed the existence of this affinity. Several Kurmi Socialists expressed grave suspicions as to the voting behavior of many Yadavs, although respondents in other parties reported that Yadavs tended by and large to support the Socialist Kurmi. Some Yadavs supported the Jan Sangh candidate in 1962, and some who lived in the former estate of the Raja of Ramnagar voted for the latter. The Kurmis reported, however, that some Yadavs openly advocated a split ticket of Ram Sevak Yadav for MP, and another candidate for MLA. While voicing their suspicions of the Yadavs, the Kurmis glossed over the divisions within the Kurmi community: some Kurmis supported candidates other than Ram Asrey. The Kurmi Socialists also played down the fact that none of the Block Development Committee presidents who were Kurmis supported the Socialist Party—instead, all supported the Congress —and that no lawyers who are Kurmis were Socialist activists. The Kurmi doubts have to be viewed in the light of the admitted Kurmi-Yadav friction.

Shortly after the death of Lala Avadh Saran some of the Kurmi leaders in the eastern part of the district left the Socialist Party and joined the Congress. It is difficult to determine whether these actions followed from the loss of the dominant leader, who had previously been able to reconcile the interests and ambitions of others, or were related to the rise of Ram Sevak Yadav. The latter had contested the MP seat in 1957 in the eastern part of the district where the defections occurred. Most respondents considered the defections to be a result of "Kurmis fighting among themselves."

There may also have been some friction between Kurmis and Pasis, although information on this tension is limited to the case of one Pasi leader who joined the Socialist Party because he thought that in a local election where he pitted himself against a Kurmi the Congress would support the Kurmi. He has allied with

Ram Sevak Yadav within the Socialist Party. Given the importance of a leader of a caste, reflected in the rise of the Kurmis and later the Yadavs, this Pasi's actions may indicate a growing resentment by lower castes of the long-established Kurmi leadership in the party. It may be that Ram Asrey lacks the talents of his brother in representing and mediating among other castes and groups within the party.

One of the difficulties of building a local party emerged in a sidelight concerning the Raja and the Jan Sangh. Before the 1962 election it was reported that Jan Sangh state leaders had tried to persuade the Raja of Ramnagar to take the party ticket and had been unsuccessful. Subsequently the ticket was given to a Kayasth, Ram Kumar, a lawyer in Fatehpur town who was a founder of the Jan Sangh in the district and had sought election in 1956. Then the Raja changed his mind, according to informants, and wanted the Jan Sangh ticket. Although the state leaders were willing to change the candidates, Ram Kumar and some of the local and district party activists were unwilling to make the change. The Jan Sangh is quite weak in Bhitauli area, and while the Raja's candidacy might have temporarily strengthened the party, it might have resulted in the complete disruption of the small permanent party organization which had been built up; the state leaders were not prepared to press the issue and risk splitting the party. Involved in the dispute were political ambitions of local leaders, friction between local "founding fathers" and "new men," friction between state and local leaders, and differing opinions on party-building strategy. Rajas do have influence, but this was a constituency with a long history of kisan-versus-talukdar rivalry. The permanent party workers supporting Ram Kumar had worked hard to gain support from the lower castes, and such support would be diminished if the Raja were the party's candidate. A key question was which element in society was to be utilized to build the party.

In the election, the Jan Sangh won pluralities in five polling stations, three being urban. The Congress won the other three urban stations. The Socialists and the Raja won pluralities only in rural areas. Few villages in Bhitauli were visited to gather details of voting behavior. Party leaders recalled some specific incidents in specific villages which were said to affect voting patterns.

Disputes over land and cattle, personal animosities, and village factions were related to electoral behavior.

Discussion of the politics of Bhitauli would not be complete without mention of what was termed by various respondents the "coalition of criminal and political elements" or the "connection existing between violence and politics." In contrast with Pratapgarh, where financial corruption was a common topic, in Bhitauli the byword was violence and goondaism. The district was noted for these activities before the beginnings of the independence movement and the accompanying socioeconomic movement. The two movements were agitational in nature and sometimes violence entered. Quite a few of the political activists of the present day trace their early political participation to terrorist activities in the 1930's and 1940's. There were frequent displays of physical power by both the kisan and the zamindar elements in the society. In post-independence days, besides the assassination of the two Kurmi leaders in Bhitauli, a Congress MLA in an adjacent constituency met with sudden violent death. Attempts have been reported on the life of the present Bhitauli MLA and also other prominent Kurmi leaders. When asked about the various candidates in elections, some respondents identified each solely according to how many persons each was reputed to have murdered, and his status either as an outright goonda or employer of goondas. Unlike Pratapgarh, where the force and intimidation reported were confined to the election period and consisted largely of keeping people away from the polling booths or removing party flags from worker's bicycles, in Bhitauli the violence was not so confined in time and the preferred tactic has been permanent removal of key individuals from the scene. In Bhitauli the use of physical force was reported on the part of many castes and communities (elite, backward, scheduled, and Muslim). Events in Bhitauli illustrate in a manner different from that in Pratapgarh the intensity of group rivalries. These rivalries have materially aided the building of an opposition party, but the tensions are such that it is difficult to contain them within the limits of a constitutional order. The caste tensions, combined with economic class distinctions and efforts of scheduled castes to improve their lot, have one overriding feature. They illustrate the very basic desires of some groups for upward mobility or recognition of higher status, and the desires of others for maintaining a former status system. Conflict between these groups is found in daily life. It also spills over into political activity. Economic position and social status are not unrelated. We can make a case that in India today, with a representative form of government and universal adult suffrage, political position is not unrelated to both economic position and social status. Achieving an elected political position can lead to the improvement of the economic position of individuals and groups; it can lead to a redress of the gains afforded to certain high-class and high-caste groups through their dominance in appointive administrative positions. The electoral contest becomes part of the struggle to change or maintain the socioeconomic system. These forces are sufficiently strong to lead to the use of violence for trying to achieve or prevent revision of the status structure. The tensions are so basic that it is difficult for groups to accept electoral defeat with equanimity.

Despite the fact that the Socialists have been victorious in Bhitauli and other constituencies in Bara Banki in more than one general election, the party lacks representation on local bodies. There are no Socialists except MLA's and MP's on the District Board, on the governing bodies of the District Cooperative Bank, the District Cooperative Development Federation, or the District Cane Union Cooperative. No Block Development Committee presidents or representatives are Socialists. This poor showing indicates that the party is not so well entrenched as might appear from its general election record. It also indicates that the tensions on which party strength is based can be brought into play primarily in major, direct elections. They cannot be employed with much success on lower levels or in indirect elections where a multiplicity of other factors become important. In the general elections it appears easier for leaders to overcome some of the more parochial considerations and to raise the questions of caste and class to a paramount position.

Bhitauli constituency exhibits an opposition party built upon social forces and groups different from those in our first case. In both instances the opposition parties represent social groups which are not prominent in the Congress. The Jan Sangh in Pratapgarh has been built up on defensive groups, whereas the Socialist Party in Bhitauli has been built on the demand for upward mobility and change in society by groups of fairly recent mobilization. The internal difficulties of the Socialist Party provide some confirmation for the maintenance hypothesis concerning successive mobilization. No longer can the Kurmis, the "founding fathers" of the party, claim sole leadership of all lower castes. There is friction between the founding echelon and the new leaders of other groups.

Chapter VII

A SHOPKEEPER NETWORK: RUDAULI (JAN SANGH)

WHILE THE SOCIALIST PARTY has been victorious in elections to the Assembly in western Bara Banki as has been seen, the Jan Sangh has won seats in the eastern part of the district. An immediate question is whether the two parties have their bases in the same social stratum and utilize the same socioeconomic tensions in the different geographic sectors of this one district. A related question is whether the same factors operate in the western and eastern constituencies. If not, what factors have been important in the east, and why is there a difference?

To investigate these questions Rudauli constituency in the northeast corner of the district was studied. The constituency is similar to the others studied in that it is rural except for the small town of Rudauli. In 1952 the constituency was part of a double-member constituency which elected a Congress candidate, a Thakur. In 1957 and 1962 Rudauli was a single-member constituency and returned a Jan Sanghi. (See Table 43.) That the two opposition parties had different social bases and that different factors were involved as compared with Bhitauli was intimated by identification of the major contestants. The victorious Jan Sangh candidate in the two elections was Mukut Behari Lal, a Bania shopkeeper and moneylender living in the town of Rudauli. The 1957 Congress candidate was Latifur Rehman, a Sunni Muslim who was a long-time Congress and kisan leader and a resident of the same town. The 1962 Congress candidate was Mohammed Ali Zaidi, a Shi'a Muslim and formerly a large talukdar and Muslim Leaguer, who was also a resident of Rudauli town. There were no candidates of the backward castes. Both the 1957 and 1962 elections were extremely close, and election petitions were raised after each.

One of the most important factors in the elections was friction

TABLE 43

CANDIDATES FOR THE ASSEMBLY IN RUDAULI CONSTITUENCY, 1962

Name	Caste	Party	Percent of Vote
Mukut Behari Lal	Bania	Jan Sangh	43.8
Mohammed Ali Zaidi	Muslim Shi'a	Congress	42.8
Pratap Chandra	Bania	Independent	3.8
Bhagwan Bux Singh	Thakur	Swatantra	3.2
Habibul Haq	Muslim Sunni	Socialist	3.0
Salik Ram	Chamar	Independent	2.1
Ibrahim	Muslim Sunni	Praja Socialist	1.3

SOURCE: *Results of the Third General Election (1962) to the Uttar Pradesh Legislative Assembly* (Allahabad, 1962), p. 35.

between Hindus and Muslims. The backward and scheduled castes were passive. Why this difference between Rudauli and Bhitauli constituencies? First, in Rudauli there are comparatively few Kurmis. There are large numbers of Yadavs, but they lack the economic standing and educational position of the Kurmis in western Bara Banki. The kisan movement in pre-independence days was weak in this section of the district. The talukdars and zamindars were Muslims, Thakurs, and Brahmins. The kisan movement was led primarily by Sunni Muslims living in Rudauli town. Of the three most prominent leaders, only one is still alive (the 1957 Congress candidate). The Muslim League was powerful. The town-based, pro-Congress Muslim kisan leaders had difficulties mobilizing both the Hindu kisans, none of whom were as well off as the Kurmi community in Bhitauli, and the Muslim kisans living under talukdars and zamindars supporting the Muslim League.

The Sunni Muslim kisan leaders were also the Congress leaders. It seems, however, that there were only a half-dozen pre-independence Congress workers in the area. Of these only three are still active in Congress. One of them summarized Congress fortunes:

There were no other Congress workers, and after independence we could not produce new, good workers. The older ones were disgruntled and went back to the villages. Big people had come into Congress and had power—they were not good workers.

In Rudauli, Thakurs, Brahmins, and Muslims are dominant. Zamindari
was abolished but the zamindars are still powerful in the villages. Big
talukdars are not powerful; they never lived in the villages; they stayed
in the towns. . . . The zamindars were Brahmins, Thakurs, and Muslims and they stayed in the villages.

We of Congress led the peasant movement against the zamindars and
talukdars, but we did not live in the villages. We had no workers in the
villages. After abolition of zamindari, the zamindars were still living in
the villages and we were not. They had contact daily with people and
therefore had influence. We did not.

There were communal disturbances in the late 1940's. A few
hundred Muslim families departed for Pakistan, but most of the
wealthier Muslims, including talukdars, who had supported the
Muslim League, remained. After independence they entered the
Congress Party. The Jan Sangh picked up support from Hindus
as the Congress became increasingly dominated by Muslims. Both
Congressmen and Jan Sanghis pointed to this background as a
factor in Jan Sangh strength in the constituency.

The Congress was victorious with a Hindu candidate in 1952.
In 1957 a Muslim contested; at the time there was no one else to
give the ticket to. The candidate himself lamented that if only a
Hindu had been put up, the Jan Sangh would not have won.
Given this analysis, we asked respondents why another Muslim—
one with former ties to the Muslim League, no less—was given
the 1962 ticket. Most Congress respondents looked embarrassed,
silently shook their heads, and gave no answer. A few Congressmen
and opponents reported that the wealth of the talukdar was the
decisive factor. Given the organizational and financial weakness
of the Congress, there was perhaps no real alternative.

In the close-fought 1957 election two Muslims and one Hindu
were candidates. Mukut Behari Lal persuaded another Hindu
Bania candidate to withdraw. It was said by some that one induce-
ment to withdrawal was the understanding that in the next election Mukut Behari Lal would not stand and would support the
withdrawing Bania. A Shi'a Muslim ran as an Independent against
the Congress's Sunni Muslim candidate. Friction between Sunnis
and Shi'as was reported to be a factor in the Congress defeat.

There were five candidates in 1962. The race was clearly between Mukut Behari Lal, of the Jan Sangh, and Mohammed Ali

Zaidi, of the Congress. No minor candidate obtained a plurality in any polling station. The Congress won pluralities in all seven urban and 32 rural polling stations. The Jan Sangh had pluralities in 54 polling stations (all rural) out of a total of 93. The Bania who had withdrawn in 1957 ran as an Independent.[1] The Socialist candidate was a Muslim Sunni. Another Muslim Sunni, who reportedly had personal differences with the Congress candidate, ran as an Independent. Sunni-Shi'a friction played a role in the election.

Both Congress and Jan Sangh leaders frankly state that their parties exist only in the town of Rudauli. There is no organization and there are precious few activists in the rural areas. Since Congress organizational weakness is not matched by Jan Sangh strength in the countryside, two questions become important: What is the composition of the activists of the two parties in the town? What kind of information-communication-influence network is brought into play at election time in the rural areas?

District and constituency party leaders of the Jan Sangh and the Congress were asked to identify party activists in Rudauli constituency. Most of these were interviewed and information about those not available was gathered from other workers. Ten activists were named for each of the parties. Eight Jan Sangh activists are residents of Rudauli town. All are Banias who are shopkeepers and some are also moneylenders; all are members of the RSS. Their shops are located on the same street; all grew up together and have been long-time personal friends. Most are in their thirties. Only two rural activists were named—and these with difficulty; both are Thakurs, formerly small zamindars, and both have lived for some time outside the constituency in urban areas.

In contrast, all the Congress activists in the town are Muslims. They have assorted occupations, but many hold local political

[1] The Bania had tried to get the SP ticket, but, even with the help of Ram Sevak Yadav, had failed. Both he and Ram Sevak Yadav are lawyers in Bara Banki. (The Bania's family home is in Rudauli.) Both are "new style" kisan workers who, although able to play an agitational role, can present cases of kisans in the courts and before administrative officials. Local Socialists, led by an ambitious Sunni Muslim, objected to the proposed candidacy. Moreover, Mukut Behari Lal brought morals charges against the Bania. SP state and national leaders gave the ticket to the Muslim.

offices. Two rural activists were named, a Kayasth and a Brahmin (both Hindus). The two striking features are the small number of activists claimed by each party and the dominance of one caste or community in each. In respect to constituency voters and supporters and district-wide activists, both parties are multicaste. But in respect to activists in Rudauli constituency, the two parties could hardly be classified in this manner.

To mobilize support in rural areas in 1962, the Congress candidate relied partly on a "raja network" and partly on a "community network'" of his fellow Muslims. He also tried to develop a "pradhan network" of pradhans, their families, and their village supporters. Many pradhans, however, could logically be placed in other networks. He also tried to gain support of those who had previously supported the Congress.

The Jan Sangh utilized primarily a "shopkeeper network." From wholesalers to both urban and rural retailers to customers (credit or cash), the ties of businessmen were exploited. The shops in Rudauli became centers of communication, information, and persuasion for both urban and rural residents. Through business, shopkeepers become acquainted with hundreds of people. Although party ties to local notables lapse in the interelection period, the business relationship remains, and through this the party leaders gain knowledge of village factions, leaders, events, and problems which is valuable at election time. Congress leaders recognized the effectiveness of this network in party maintenance, pointing out that its importance does not lie so much in the use of economic pressures to gain votes as in the continuous wide contacts with hundreds of people, month after month, year after year. These contacts, they said, are utilized at election time to call on Hindu to vote Hindu. The Congress had no such interelection network. They have few rural activists; the town talukdars and town activists rarely have contact with villagers. Thus rural Congress supporters have no continuing ties to people in the party, whereas Jan Sangh supporters and others have business ties to persons in the Jan Sangh. Thus the Jan Sangh activists have a great advantage in mobilizing notables and voters which the Congress lacks.

Two other groups mobilized by the shopkeepers were a "pradhan network" and an "ex-zamindar network": "People used to look up to the zamindars as gods, and now that those who were zamindars are the pradhans, they look on the pradhans in the same way. They look to the pradhan to help them and to rule them." Respondents spoke in terms of two groups, even though there is some overlapping of membership. The "pradhan group" category illustrates the impingement of the new political order on the older political structure. The shopkeeper-activists also tried to win over other village "influentials," variously described as "respected men," older men, large landowners, rich people, and caste leaders. The activists could also call on those who had previously supported the party, regardless of their status in the society. In Rudauli constituency there was no mention by either party's activists of a "teacher network" or a "lawyer network."

The views of some respondents raise a question regarding the relative political importance of the talukdars as opposed to the zamindars. Earlier in this chapter the statement of one activist was given presenting the view that urban-based talukdars have less influence in rural areas than the rural-based zamindars. Day-to-day proximity carries with it the ability to pressure others before and after an election. Continual influence can be exerted, as opposed to intermittent influence. It will be remembered that only in instances where talukdars and zamindars have been united have "their" candidates been successful (for example, Pratapgarh South in 1962, Bhitauli in 1957). When talukdars and zamindars were not united, "their" candidates lost. The relative position of these two groups deserves further study.

A few issues were mentioned as important in the 1962 election. Jan Sanghiis stressed that they did not "divide caste from caste," but called on "unity of the community." In other words: Hindu vote Hindu. Congress activists and supporters confirmed this approach by the JS workers.[2] Congress urban activists reported another approach used by the JS activists: a vote to Congress is a vote to Muslims who will again partition India. Given the his-

---

[2] Village respondents of the two parties reported that a Jan Sangh activist came to the village and, gesturing with his sacred thread, said: "You are Hindu; I am Hindu. Therefore you should vote Jan Sangh." Congress activists reported that Jan Sangh workers gathered sizable audiences through reading from the religious book of the Hindus, the Gita, and then called for all present to swear on the Gita to support the Jan Sangh. It was said to be difficult for individuals to resist the social pressures of the situation.

torical background and the particular Congress candidate, such an approach might be credible. One Jan Sangh activist mentioned that cow slaughter was an issue. In the few villages visited no one recalled this issue at all. The Muslim urban Congressmen, however, seemed to consider it a major campaign issue. At the same time, their remarks indicated that they had utilized the issue themselves. For example, the Muslim leaders reported that they held a mass Congress meeting-and-demonstration in front of the home of Mukut Behari Lal, the Jan Sangh candidate, in the Hindu section of the town. In speech after speech they demanded that the Jan Sanghi come out and make open charges, but he remained in seclusion. When queried, these Muslim leaders said that the Jan Sangh had held no meetings in the town at all during the campaign. (The town has a high concentration of Muslims.) Further, they reported no communal disturbances of any kind whatsoever. Mobilization of voters along community lines was a feature of the election, but the use of the cow slaughter issue as a focal point is open to question. It is one that would be expected to disturb Muslims. Perhaps they were oversensitive.

Few issues other than community were reported on a constituency-wide basis. Jan Sangh activists reported that the call for reduction of land taxes by half was an issue, but neither Congress activists nor the rural respondents recalled it. Arousal on community lines was by no means complete. Particularly in the sections of the constituency dominated by Hindus and containing few Muslims, "unity of the community" could not be obtained. Village factions became important. Besides such factions, the special relationship to the specific candidates was important. Interaction of these two variables could be spotted in certain instances. For example, in one village a Brahmin village factional leader who had been a tenant under Zaidi supported the Congress. His factional opponent, a Brahmin zamindar, had not been in Zaidi's talukdari and supported the Jan Sangh. In the adjacent village, those who had been in the Brahmin's zamindari also supported the Jan Sangh, such support cutting across the factional lines in the village. Many local events and situations affected voting behavior.

Rudauli constituency illustrates several points about politics in Uttar Pradesh. First is the relationship of long-term socioeconomic structures to the current patterns of politics. Second is the vivid demonstration of how parties are bound by their past identifications with certain groups in the society. It is difficult to cast these aside and attract other groups. Third is the example of the "accidents" by which parties become identified with such groups. Equally important, fourth, is the basically urban nature of all present-day parties in Rudauli. This is a factor which could introduce great fluidity to the political scene. Mobilization and organization in the untapped rural reservoir by any party could materially change the political complexion and political alignments. Very few villagers are "committed" to any party. The fifth point of importance is that it is not always necessary for an opposition party to build a strong organization in order to win. A minimal party framework can suffice to mobilize individuals and groups at election time. This in turn shows the importance of social tensions as the basis of mobilization. For Rudauli we cannot readily identify either Hindus or Muslims as rising groups, threatened groups, or unsatisfied beneficiaries. Religion is the basis of the friction. The cases of Rudauli and Bhitauli, both in the same district, illustrate that quite different situations can and do exist within a relatively small geographic area. Lastly, the Rudauli case pits two types of political organizations against each other: a Raja network versus a shopkeeper network. The latter proved to be the most successful in this instance.

Chapter VIII

TIME MARCHES ON: SAURIKH
(PRAJA SOCIALIST PARTY)

THE PRAJA SOCIALISTS have shown strength in Farrukhabad District. The Congress won the seven Assembly seats in 1952, but in 1957 won three to the Praja Socialist Party's four. In 1962 the PSP again won four seats (retaining three previously won), the Jan Sangh one, and the Congress two. The 1½ Parliamentary seats were held by Congress until the 1963 by-election held after the death of the sitting MP. This "whole" seat was won by Dr. Ram Manohar Lohia of the Socialist Party, who defeated the Congress and PSP candidates.

Formerly a part of the North-West Provinces, Farrukhabad District lies in central-south Uttar Pradesh. This was not a talukdari district; in contrast with Oudh, large percentages of kisans enjoyed occupancy rights. In past decades the land was primarily owned by Thakurs, Brahmins, and Muslims.[1] The zamindars were important, but their position could not be compared to that of the talukdars and zamindars of Oudh.

There are three castes of near-equal strength in the district: Lodhas (backward caste),[2] Chamars (scheduled caste) and the Yadavs (backward caste). These are followed by Muslims, Brahmins, Thakurs, and the backward-caste Kachhis. There are smaller numbers of backward-caste Gadariyas and Kurmis.[3]

[1] District Gazetteers of the United Provinces of Agra and Oudh, IX: Farrukhabad, by E. R. Neave (Allahabad, 1911), 68–88, 264 f.; hereafter cited as Farrukhabad Gazetteer.

[2] In the Farrukhabad Gazetteer (p. 68) these were known by the caste name of "Kisan." Today they prefer to be called "Lodhi-Rajputs," but most respondents referred to them as Lodhas. The older caste name of "Kisan" seems to have been forgotten by most persons. Identification with the broader caste group (Kisan to Lodha) appears to have been a prelude to a more serious effort to raise the status of the caste (Lodha to Lodhi-Rajput).

[3] Census of India, 1931, XVIII: United Provinces of Agra and Oudh (Allahabad, 1933), Pt. II, 499–548.

An official of the state Congress Party organization first drew attention to the dominant social rivalries in Farrukhabad: the rivalry between elite and backward castes. One reason, he said, for the PSP strength was that the PSP represented the backward castes whereas the Congress represented the elite castes. Although many verified this tension, the flat statement must be modified. The consensus among respondents in the district is that the PSP is based on a coalition of Yadavs, Kurmis, and half the Thakurs; the Congress on Brahmins, Muslims, and half the Thakurs; and the Jan Sangh on Brahmins and some backward castes not prominent in the PSP, such as the Lodhas and Kacchis. The castes of candidates put forth by the three parties in the 1962 election tend to support this interpretation. (See Table 44.) For ease of analysis

TABLE 44

CASTE OF CONGRESS, PRAJA SOCIALIST, AND JAN SANGH CANDIDATES,
FARRUKHABAD DISTRICT, GENERAL SEATS, 1962

Constituency	Congress	Praja Socialist	Jan Sangh
Saurikh	Brahmin	*Yadav* (bc)	Lodhi (bc)
Chhibramau	Brahmin	*Thakur*	Brahmin
Bhojpur	*Thakur*	Thakur	Thakur
Farrukhabad [a]	Kurmi (bc)	Muslim	*Kachhi* (bc)
Shamsabad	Thakur	*Yadav* (bc)	—
Kaimganj	Muslim	*Kurmi* (bc)	Brahmin

[a] Farrukhabad is the one urban constituency in the district.

the victorious candidates are italicized and backward-caste candidates identified by the notation "(bc)." In all cases in which an elite-caste candidate was opposed by a backward-caste candidate, the latter won. Backward-caste candidates were defeated only by other backward-caste candidates. Only one Congress candidate was of a backward caste—an elderly, wealthy ex-zamindar with a prominent pro-British, anti-Congress record—and he was chosen in Delhi. It may be that respondents identified the total party composition with that of the district leadership echelon (candidates, district leaders, prominent activists). In the constituency studied, all three parties were multi-caste on the activist level.

The relative mildness of caste-based rivalries as compared to Pratapgarh South or Bhitauli is demonstrated by the coalition of backward and elite castes in the opposition parties. The rivalry can be compared to the lapping of a lake upon a shore rather than the pounding of a surf upon a rocky coast. The absence of a talukdari system and the higher proportion of occupancy tenants help to explain the mildness. Economic differences were not as extreme, and were not sharply reinforced by caste lines.

Saurikh constituency in the southeast of Farrukhabad was chosen for detailed study. It is totally rural, and it lacks a central focal point. The two major roads, running north to south, divide the constituency into an eastern and western portion. There appears to be little east-west travel. Towns often serve as repositories for general historical and political information of the outlying area. In Saurikh there are no towns. Respondents who could discuss the pre-independence kisan and Congress movements, or post-independence politics of the constituency, were hard to come by. Most landholdings were small except for the estate of the Raja of Tirwa.[4] The 1911 *District Gazetteer* indicates that in this area more than 70 percent of the land was held by occupancy tenants, less than 5 percent by proprietors, and the remainder by tenants-at-will.[5]

In 1957, Saurikh was half of a double-member constituency in which two Praja Socialists were elected. When divided in 1962, the general seat was retained by the PSP under Hori Lal Yadav (backward caste). The reserved half, in which the sitting MLA did not contest, was the only 1957 seat lost by the PSP in 1962.

Three major parties contested in Saurikh in 1962: the Praja Socialists, the Congress, and the Jan Sangh. It was a narrow victory (see Table 45). Out of a total of 121 polling stations, the PSP won pluralities in 41, the Congress in 39, the Jan Sangh in 31, and minor candidates in 10. Analysis of this constituency can provide insights into the long-range process of party building and maintenance. Saurikh is the "home base" of Hori Lal Yadav, who has

---

[4] Tirwa is a village of 2,000 inhabitants in the northeast corner of Saurikh constituency. It is the site of a high school and intercollege established in the 1920's by the Raja. The bulk of the Raja's holdings were outside Saurikh. He left Tirwa many years ago, and it was reported that he took no interest in the politics of Saurikh.

[5] *Farrukhabad Gazetteer*, pp. 68–88, 294 f.

TABLE 45

CANDIDATES TO THE ASSEMBLY IN SAURIKH CONSTITUENCY, 1962

Name	Caste	Party	Percent of Vote
Hori Lal Yadav	Yadav	PSP	26.7
Nand Ram	Brahmin	Congress	26.0
Bachchan Lal Verma	Lodhi-Rajput	Jan Sangh	23.6
Latoorey Prasad	(Scheduled)	Republican	6.3
Chandra Bhan	Brahmin	Socialist	5.8
Prem Narain Paliwal	Mahwari	Independent	5.0
Pahlad Singh	(Not ascertained)	Swatantra	3.9
Chhakko Lal	(Not ascertained)	Independent	2.7

SOURCE: *Results of the Third General Election (1962) to the Uttar Pradesh Legislative Assembly* (Allahabad, 1962), p. 76.

been building parties for more than thirty years. Because of him, the PSP has a much longer history than its date of formation would indicate. Since his activities are bound up with the political history of the district, they are presented together.

In the early 1930's the Congress movement, accompanied by a kisan movement—of a milder variety than in Oudh—gained impetus in the district. Hori Lal Yadav became one of the leaders of both movements. By the 1940's he was one of the most prominent district Congress figures; he was the leader of the CSP group. His group controlled the party organization and the District Board. Hori Lal Yadav himself was chairman of the district Congress committee and the District Board when, in 1948, he led part of the CSP out of Congress and formed the Socialist Party. One factor aiding him in Saurikh was his previous leadership status.

Kali Charon Tandon (Khattri, of the Bania group), was a member of the "Hori Lal Yadav group" who chose to remain in Congress. He became the leader of the dominant Congress faction, which group is still dominant. The relationship between Kali Charon Tandon and Hori Lal Yadav has been most amicable. "Hamaaree saath hãi" ("He is with us"), says the Congress leader of his opponent. How different from the "We will smash them"

—uttered with clenched fist—of a Pratapgarh Congress leader about the Jan Sangh opponents! Because of this tie, Hori Lal Yadav had effective access to the leading political and governmental officials and bodies in the district before and after his 1957 electoral victory.

During the independence movement thousands throughout India were engaged in arousing the populace; millions were so aroused. But the land is vast. In a specific area, such as a present-day constituency, only a few were likely to be involved in the task of mobilization. Hori Lal Yadav was one of the three, possibly four, people who were mobilizers on a large scale in this area. Some of those whom he and others mobilized became active on a much more restricted scale. Particularly in rural areas, "activated villagers" were likely to have contacts with extremely few political leaders other than their mobilizer. Such other contacts tended to be infrequent and short. It appears that personal mobilization, reaffirmed over the years by personal contact, creates a tie strong enough in many instances to override competing loyalties such as caste or class.[6] This is not a tie to an abstract entity of "party," but a tie to an individual. So when Hori Lal Yadav left the Congress, most of those he mobilized left with him. Over the years he has built up a considerable personal organization, on an inter-caste basis.

By 1951 seven individuals (besides Hori Lal Yadav) had become pillars of the permanent party. They include one Brahmin, two Thakurs, one Yadav, one Kurmi, one Lodha, and one Gadariya (three elite, four backward). By 1957, the SP having become the PSP, seven new pillars had been added: one Brahmin, two Thakurs, three Yadavs, and one of a small scheduled caste (three elite, three backward, one scheduled). It is significant that all the new backward-caste pillars were exclusively Yadav, whereas

[6] When discussing the caste or intercaste basis of factions and parties it is imperative to recall this pattern of mobilization and contact, and to determine whether it helps to explain factional divisions. Factions can be led by X and Y, of different castes, and the caste tensions may be of utmost importance in explaining the tension between them. Yet both X and Y will have multicaste followings, and the followers will divide not on caste lines, but on the tie to either X or Y. Analyzing the caste composition of each faction will not indicate the degree to which caste friction is involved. The same applies to cleavages related to other factors.

those recruited earlier were of several backward castes. The fourteen pillars are geographically well distributed through the constituency. They form the constituency leadership echelon. Some are prominent persons in their own right, while others have risen in prominence partly because of the tie to Hori Lal Yadav —as he rose, they rose. The pillars are the prime activists who organize electoral campaigns, recruit new members, reactivate former members, make contact with local notables and try to win their support, and find people to staff the electoral organization. Between elections they serve as "contact agents" for the populace and the MLA, and for the populace and government officials. Three pillars operate PSP offices in three market villages in the northeast, northwest, and south. The offices are open and staffed on market days; it is here that villagers make contact with party officials and can arrange to get aid either from the party men or from the MLA. Hori Lal Yadav communicates regularly with those in charge of the offices, and provides advance notice of his visits so that word can be spread. Most of the pillars are active in block politics; several of them have been elected to or have been candidates for block-level positions.

Beneath these pillars are regulars—permanent party members, many of whom have been associated with Hori Lal Yadav personally or with the pillars for many years. At election time, the regulars appear automatically to become part of the electoral organization. They staff the ranks and activate friends, relatives, and acquaintances. Between elections they participate in party agitations or demonstrations, attend party meetings, and provide an additional channel of communication for both the pillars and the MLA. Several of them appear to be touts,[7] assisting individuals with governmental officials and retaining some of the monies involved in the exchange. Becoming a tout is an individual action, but the tie to a party can be an aid. By contrast, the pillars would be classed as brokers. Some of the regulars are more active in the interim period than others, but none are as active as the pillars. These are lesser members, but can be counted on to support the PSP year after year. They identify with the PSP personally.

A third group consists of local notables whose support is gained

---

[7] Bailey, *Politics and Social Change,* p. 149, distinguishes touts from brokers.

at election time. Bailey would term these "vote banks."[8] These notables may officially join the party in an election year, but they do not identify with the party personally, they can shift from one party to another from election to election, and they do not maintain casual membership between elections. They must be approached and persuaded to support the party's candidates before each election, since they cannot be relied upon to stay with the party or its candidates. Although they give their support to a candidate in the election, many consider activities such as canvassing or trying to persuade others also to support the party to be demeaning. Some of these reported that they had told their relatives to join the active electoral organization. Other notables do participate in mass canvassing or try to persuade other "lesser notables" to support the candidate. According to the MLA, the most important notables for him are the pradhans or pradhan contestants, followed (not in order) by the sarpanch of the naiaa panchayat, the sarpanch of the Cooperative Society, the grain dealers, teachers, doctors, large landowners, and village shopkeepers. He added: "I cannot work through moneylenders because I would lose the support of the poorer people. I win through their support." Although the MLA does rely on "poorer people" for his voting strength, much of such support is gathered through the cultivation of those who are not quite so poor. Another group not utilized were sadhus, or religious figures. This was stated to be on the grounds of secularity; however, a contributing factor might well be that many of these would be Brahmins. One of the backward-caste respondents in a village reported widespread displeasure over the attitudes and behavior displayed by some Brahmin priests toward the backward castes.

A fourth group are the people who man the electoral organization. These have their counterparts in the United States: the people who hand out party literature at shopping centers, put bumper stickers on cars, ring doorbells, and so on. In Saurikh the literate workers help make out and distribute slips for individual voters with the registration number of each. Literates or illiterates distribute party printed-matter, shout slogans, mobilize voters for meetings, carry the party flag, wear the red cap of the PSP, and so on. The ties to the party or candidate appear to be slim. Many

[8] *Ibid.,* pp. 109–135.

are young, stirred by the excitement of a campaign. Their activities in turn add to the *tamaasha* ("show") atmosphere. Few of these personally identify with the party, particularly after an election.

One difference between these campaigners and the notables, on the one hand, and the permanent party members, on the other, is that the latter appear to be much more professional in their political role. It is the task of the pillars and regulars to direct the campaign, to discover what groups and what individuals are supporting their candidates, and to try to assess the comparative strength of notables. Their approach appears to be much more analytical than that of the electoral supporters.

These four groups were mobilized by individual personal contact. Each preceding group was to some degree involved in mobilizing the groups or group following. A significant aspect of the organization is that after Hori Lal Yadav's first election, in 1957, expansion of the pillars and regulars almost ceased. He explained the situation in this way:

I have not done much at all to extend the organization since my election in 1957. I don't have time—too busy doing individual and collective works and settling disputes within the public. . . . No, I never have asked a person wanting my help to join the party. I never inquire as to what party he is or whom he supported. I help all who come to me. I have never made joining the party a condition for getting aid. I do not think it is a good thing to combine the two. That is wrong, and a bad thing to do. It is also bad politics. If I made joining the party a condition, then people would not like it and I would lose support. As it is, I can build up some "good will" and make opponents less opposed to me. And if someone is just less opposed to me, or does not work against me, that is to my advantage. I have to impress people by my behavior and my works. I never make a person a member before I help them and do not ask them to join after I help them. Any members I brought in on this basis would not be strong and lasting members.[9]

After winning an election, political wisdom and lack of time make it difficult for many MLA's to strengthen or extend their organizations. In Saurikh, in the 1962 election the MLA relied on the organization built up before 1957.

[9] Interview, Lucknow, February 10, 1964.

In 1962 Hori Lal Yadav also relied on his past works and his general reputation. His reputation is enviable, particularly given his many years in politics. Fellow MLA's, state and district leaders of various parties, defeated opponents, and district and block administrative officials, among others, reacted in one way when his name was mentioned. "Hori Lal Yadav—oh, he's a nice man." "Everybody loves Hori Lal Yadav." Such responses were immediate, and were said with warmth and affection. (This was the only instance in which such a reaction was recorded for any MLA at any time, from any person.) This view was not entirely unanimous, for two or three villagers interviewed seemed to look upon him as a "big man" unconcerned with the problems of poor people. It was reported that in the election there was some feeling among Yadavs that Hori Lal Yadav had become aloof and filled with his own importance. Generally speaking, however, he was highly regarded.

Part of his reputation was built upon his record of services to constituents and his concern with development and education. Somewhat paternalistically, he has advised, encouraged, and pressed village leaders, particularly those of backward castes, to undertake village improvements and to set up schools. In one block, the Block Development Officer reported that Hori Lal Yadav put pressure on block officials to see that loans given were used for the designated purposes: "He wants money spent on proper things, but wants us officials to do the dirty work in the matter. He can't bless people out for using it wrongly because he would lose votes. Hori Lal Yadav knows votes and support will come with improvements and better conditions. Can't get these unless the loan money is used properly." Examples were given of such incidents. Some of these clearly involved supporters of the MLA. These actions appear to be an unusual practice.

In touring villages it was surprising to find how many individuals and villages had been aided by Hori Lal Yadav; it was even more surprising to discover how many knew of other projects the MLA was promoting on the district and state level. The extent of information reflected not only his activities, but also his communication network. In addition to the dissemination of news through organizational channels, mentioned previously, the MLA has traveled through the constituency fairly often. Complaints that an MLA disappeared until election time were heard much less frequently in Saurikh than in other constituencies. It appeared that Hori Lal Yadav has toured the eastern part of the constituency, nearest his home, more often than the western; that he has visited in areas where he had the greatest voting support much more than in the "centers of opposition"; that he has toured the more accessible villages (closer to the main roads) more often than the interior villages. Some of this travel was "just wandering," according to village respondents and the MLA himself. He pointed out that although many constituents do have demands, most constituents do not. It was his belief—and this analysis would certainly be supported by respondents in villages of all the constituencies studied—that most people simply wanted to see and talk with the man elected to the Assembly. By wandering, the MLA maintained this contact.

In contrast, the candidates of the Congress (Brahmin) and Jan Sangh (Lodha) had lived for many years in the district town outside the constituency. Neither had as extensive ties to the people as did the PSP candidate. Neither had as extensive an organization. They were regarded by many as "outsiders" whereas Hori Lal Yadav was regarded as an "insider." They were urban, whereas Hori Lal Yadav was rural. The Congress candidate's behavior was said to antagonize many people, including Congress workers. Congress activists of both factions reported that the displays of temper and air of superiority were important factors since the candidate was not well known. It would seem that particularly in a situation of cross-pressures, the behavior and personality traits of the candidates become variables entering into the voting decision.

The Congress Party is divided into factions in the district, and the factional split extends into constituency units. These divisions were a factor in the PSP victory. In Saurikh, the Congress candidate was a member of the dominant district faction. He had been born in the constituency, but for many years had lived in the district town. The leader of the dissident Congress faction in this constituency, who still lived in his village, had hoped to get the ticket. It was reported that he and the local activists of his faction had not supported the Congress candidate. Some said that these simply "sat on their hands," while others said open support was given to the PSP candidate. Both factions were led by Brahmins.

Another factor of importance in the election was the "ticket balancing" of MP and MLA candidates. Both Congress candidates were Brahmins. The PSP paired its Yadav MLA with a Thakur MP candidate, and the Jan Sangh paired a Lodha MLA candidate and a Brahmin MP candidate. To the extent that some voting decisions are not unrelated to supporting one's own caste fellow, the pairing of candidates of two castes—and of two caste group-ings—benefited the PSP and Jan Sangh. The existence of alterna-tive Brahmin candidates tended to divide Brahmin and other elite-caste votes between Congress and Jan Sangh. (The Socialist MLA candidate was also Brahmin.)

According to block officials in the western part of the constitu-ency, the antagonism between elite and backward castes is more pronounced in block politics than in the general elections. In their opinion, identification with parties mitigate caste tensions in the latter. This raises a question of the interaction of block politics with general election politics. In one part of the con-stituency block politics affected the election. Before the general election, the election was held for president of the Block Develop-ment Committee. There were two candidates, one being a Yadav pillar of the PSP and the other a Thakur Independent "notable" who had in the past supported the PSP. The Thakur requested Hori Lal Yadav to choose which was to become the block presi-dent. After due consideration, Hori Lal Yadav passed the decision to Bharat Singh Rathore, the Thakur MP candidate of the PSP, who decided in favor of the Yadav pillar. Provision was made that in the next election for the block presidency the Yadav would not be a candidate. Yet the choice of the Yadav was reported to have angered the Thakurs in the area, and in the general election many of them did not support the PSP for either MLA or MP. Their votes were divided, but many were said to have supported the Jan Sangh MLA candidate (Lodha) on the grounds that only another backward-caste candidate could defeat Hori Lal Yadav.

This reasoning brings up a significant feature of mobilization over time of different caste groups in Saurikh, and the political consequences of successive mobilization. As is usual, the members of the elite castes were active politically quite long ago. In the 1930's the Yadavs began to become active and assumed leadership of the various backward castes. In the 1950's the Lodhas began to be mobilized; this process is by no means complete. Partly because the Congress appears to be an elite-caste party to many (not related as much to earlier mobilization of elite castes as to withdrawal of the "Hori Lal Yadav group" in 1947) and partly because the PSP is identified with the Yadavs, the Lodhas are gravitating toward the Jan Sangh.

In Saurikh there is not only some tension between elite and backward castes, but also tension is developing among different backward castes. Several backward castes are developing leaders who have political ambitions. With increasing mobilization of the various backward castes, there is a problem for the established parties of attracting or maintaining the support from these rising groups. Neither the Congress nor PSP appears to have been able to solve the problem.

Along with the development of rivalries within the backward castes, there has been division within the elite castes. From these divisions have come coalitions and alliances between some parts of the elite castes with parts of the backward castes. The strength of the backward castes, and the realization of the elite castes that political victotry at the polls is almost impossible without support of the backward castes is shown by the reasoning of some of the Thakurs in the block politics incident. It is seen in the general alliance of Yadavs and Thakurs in the PSP, in the alliance of some Brahmins and Lodhas in the Jan Sangh. Whether this is a case of the elite castes dividing the backward castes, or vice versa, is open to question. At any rate, there has been some modification of the tensions along elite-versus-backward lines. Rivalries still exist, but they have been and are being modified by more recent rivalries.

A perplexing question in Saurikh concerns the differential rate of mobilization of the Yadavs and the Lodhas. Why did the Yadavs become politically active before the Lodhas? Numerically the Lodhas are slightly stronger than the Yadavs. There is no precise information on the economic status of the two castes. In the *District Gazetteer* the Yadavs were considered to be economically worse off than any other backward caste.[10] It does not appear that the Yadavs could be compared to the Kurmis of Bara Banki.

A third index is education. The *District Gazetteer* does not indicate the educational proficiency of any of the backward castes.

[10] *Farrukhabad Gazetteer*, pp. 68 f., 80–88, 264 f.

Since Hori Lal Yadav related his interest in politics to his contact with the faculty of Tirwa Intercollege—the only high school or intercollege in Saurikh—the officials of the Intercollege were interviewed. Specific figures were not available, but the officials reported two impressions: that the number of backward-caste students had increased disproportionately to that of elite-caste students, and that at an earlier date more Lodhas than Yadavs attended the school. The Intercollege is located in an area heavily populated with Lodhas; the Yadavs live beyond this "Lodha circle." School officials also considered the Lodhas to be slightly better off economically than the Yadavs and better able to pay the tuition. If greater numbers havings higher education is a factor in political mobilization, then the Lodhas should have become politically conscious before the Yadavs. No respondent suggested any explanation regarding the development of political leaders within the two castes or the differential mobilization rate. The *District Gazetteer* states that the Ahirs (Yadavs) "have a deep-rooted antipathy toward paying a reasonable rent," which made them undesirable tenants.[11] Does this hint at a caste tradition of protest and articulation of their interests?

In Saurikh, considerable time was spent in field work. Support was found for a host of interpretations of voting behavior. In some places backward-caste respondents clearly had a "chip on the shoulder" attitude toward the elite castes, while members of the elite castes quite definitely looked down upon the backward castes. Village factional alignments occasionally mirrored this antagonism. In other places there was friction between backward castes or between elite castes. In some places, village factional cleavages were intercaste and the factional tie appeared to be of crucial importance. In one village the intercaste factional cleavage was said to be primary, save that a few Yadavs, Lodhas, and Brahmins crossed over to vote for their caste fellows. In some villages divisions were reported on the basis of long-standing factional lines; in others the electoral division was said to be based on recent, transient divisions within factions. In other words, different patterns of caste antagonism and village factional cleavages were observed.

[11] *Ibid.,* p. 85.

Other variables observed included the alignment of respondents with competing leaders of their own caste on a district-wide basis. One Thakur, for example, supported Hori Lal Yadav for MLA, but refused to support his Thakur running-mate because the respondent identified with a district Thakur leader opposed to the PSP MP candidate. In a scheduled-caste village, a respondent referred to the great importance attached to the secret ballot by the self-proclaimed "weak people": "Our village is weak. We do not want to be rivals of anyone. If anyone wants something from us, we give in or back out of a fight. We never fight with anyone. In no case have we ever fought with anyone." Another scheduled-caste respondent said: "We tell everyone who comes, "Yes, yes, we will vote for you. We will vote as you say." We say that to everyone. But this secret ballot is a big help. We vote as we please. The secret ballot is a good thing." The importance of the economic tie or of economic pressure was exemplified by respondents on various occasions. The necessity of obtaining permission to have one's cattle cross another's fields, of working on another's land for one's livelihood, of obtaining a loan or getting an extension of a loan from a moneylender—all were important. Yet there were occasions when such pressure was not successful. These were situations of cross-pressures, where respondents were pulled by opposing loyalties or were pushed by contrary pressures. Such was the case in a small hamlet, separated by fields from the major village of which it was a part. Except for one Chamar family, the hamlet was totally Yadav in composition. The respondents were two brothers plus a half dozen other Yadavs who gathered around and occasionally commented on the account being given. From notes taken, the following account of their 1962 election decision was reconstructed, using their own words as much as possible:

Hori Lal and Bharat Singh came here and we gave our word that we would vote for them, and we did. The moneylender from X———, Mr. ——— [who was a candidate for M.L.A.], came down and said, "I give cash money and grain to you, and you should therefore vote for me." Then he left. But we thought, "We pay him 6 annas per rupee and 1¼ of grain when we repay. Why should we be pressured by him?" So we voted for Hori Lal Yadav.

There was no indication, however, that the moneylender had demanded loan repayment or had threatened no future loans. There was realization that neither money nor grain was "given," and some resentment of the "pressure." In subsequent discussion some other variables were brought forth which may have had some effect. In the major village itself lived a Thakur, a "pillar" of the permanent PSP, who was an influential man in the area. His brother was the head of the village panchayat in which the hamlet was located. The "pillar" was considered to be responsible for having some wells built in the hamlet. Although the Yadavs owned some land, it was not sufficient to cover their needs; all the Yadavs worked on the fields of Thakurs and Kayasths of the major village on a 50 percent basis (they kept half the crop). There were two factions, both headed by Thakurs, in the major village. Many of the Yadavs worked on fields of those in the pillar's faction. The Yadavs, therefore, had a "strong man" in the immediate vicinity supporting them and supporting the PSP as against the moneylender. Of course, the caste tie to Hori Lal Yadav provided an additional incentive.

In Saurikh, priority cannot be easily assigned to any one tension or cleavage. Hori Lal Yadav's greatest strength came from heavily Yadav-populated areas, and the Jan Sangh Lodha's strength came from heavily Lodha-populated areas. Yet voting on caste lines was modified by other ties and other pressures. Priority cannot be assigned to village factional ties, or to the ties to moneylenders, "strong men," or large landowners. A host of influences can be pointed out. Parties have played a role in structuring the situation. Leaders of the various parties appear to have made a conscious effort to construct multicaste organizations. In some places they have bridged factional divisions, whereas in other places they have utilized such cleavages, and so on.

In general terms, Saurikh illustrates a case in the politics of successive mobilization under conditions of only moderate reinforcement of caste by property inequalities. It is particularly revealing because it is entirely rural. The networks must be more specifically and visibly political since the ties of trade, profession, and the like are rudimentary. The time span is sufficient to show successive developments. It may be considered a little case showing one pattern of possible future rural political mobilization. In

Saurikh no single cleavage is sufficient for building a party to winning status. Hori Lal Yadav has combined the use of MLA services to all with an organizational network created over the decades by personal political recruitment. To the extent that his organization is based on caste, the party system gives opportunities to other opposition parties (represented in Saurikh by the Jan Sangh) to champion successively mobilizing groups. To the extent that it is intercaste, the party demonstrates the importance of personal contact for creating new loyalties. By such contact the parties bridge particular cleavages in the society.

Chapter IX

THE SPIRAL OF MOBILIZATION: MORADABAD RURAL (PRAJA SOCIALIST PARTY)

MORADABAD RURAL is a doughnut-shaped constituency; Moradabad city is the "hole." A western district, Moradabad has a high concentration of Muslims—37 percent of the population in 1961.[1] Over the past several decades the district has been a tinderbox of communal tensions between Hindus and Moslems. At partition there were extensive riots; in the mid-1950's riots occurred over several months. Migration of parts of families to Pakistan, and subsequent travel back and forth across the border, when combined with problems of foreign relations between India and Pakistan, have added an element of suspicion and further defensiveness to the situation.[2]

The secular state principle of the Indian constitution, as it has so far been applied, does not resolve the tension. Prescribed textbooks, for example, which seem to the government to present an Indian national perspective seem to Muslims as pro-Hindu and nonsecular. This comes about partly because Islam is not indigenous to India whereas Hinduism is. Some of the most significant events and personalities in Islamic history—important to Muslims —are omitted in studies of Indian history while those significant to Hinduism are included.[3] Second, discussion of the Islamic invasions casts Muslims in the role of outsiders. Little attention, it is said, is given to their contributions to an Indian culture, and

[1] *Census of India,* Paper No. 1 of 1963: *Religion* (Delhi, 1963), pp. 38–39.

[2] Sisir Gupta, "Muslims in Indian Politics," *India Quarterly,* XVIII, No. 4 (October-December, 1962), 355–381. Gupta points out that internal religious tensions are complicated by external tensions.

[3] For example, the fourth Caliph is not discussed, whereas Raam is. The one is important to Muslims, the other to Hindus.

to some, Muslims never become accepted as insiders.[4] The history of the nationalist movement necessarily includes the efforts of Muslims to establish Pakistan, which again emphasizes their separateness. A problem is that there are contradictory desires among Muslims: they want an insider status confirmed while simultaneously wanting their "outside" heritage taught. That neither seems to be accorded is galling. Third, the values underlying many courses offered in secular schools appear to many Muslims to be distinctly Hindu values:

In most of the States—and in Uttar Pradesh, in particular—courses of study were introduced that were literally loaded with the religious beliefs and mythology of the majority community. A curriculum of this kind naturally militates against the very foundations of the Islamic faith, against its concepts of Divinity and monotheism and against the Divine institution of Prophecy and Apostleship.[5]

Promotion, recognition and official use of language provides a further challenge to religious identity. The state language, Hindi, is written in Devanagiri, the script of the Sanskrit classics of Hinduism. The Muslims identify their culture with Urdu, written in the Arabic script, with its equally strong religious significance. Muslims seek to promote Urdu as an official state language, along with Hindi and English. Many Hindus want Sanskrit to be the third language. The MLA representing Moradabad Rural is a Muslim. With two others, he broke precedent in 1962 by taking his legislative oath of office in Urdu.

The village settlement pattern in this constituency is primarily compact or nuclear (not hamleted). There are many totally Hindu or totally Muslim villages. In mixed villages there is a distinct division between the Hindu and Muslim parts, with apparently little communication between the two.

In sum, this is an area with a self-conscious and defensive Muslim minority,[6] and a minority so large and cohesive as compared with the Hindus that it has become a major political force. Among

[4] Abul Hasan Ali Nadwi, *Muslims in India* (Lucknow, n.d.), pp. 128–131. The entire chapter in which this passage occurs is an excellent discussion, by a Muslim, of current Muslim problems and difficulties.

[5] *Ibid.,* p. 128.

[6] The "defensiveness" of the Muslim community was identified as "aggressiveness" by some Hindu respondents.

Hindus, the largest castes are the Chamars, Sainis (who were once known as Malis or Baghbans), Thakurs, and Yadavs.

Several features distinguish the political background of this particular constituency. First, in all three elections different candidates, of different political affiliations, have been elected. In 1952 a Hindu Khattri of Congress, Dau Dayal Khanna, was elected. He was a resident of the city and became a member of the state Ministry. In 1957 he was defeated in a three-cornered contest by Dr. Khamani Singh, an Independent. Dr. Singh was a rural resident, a medical doctor, a former zamindar and large landowner, and Yadav by caste. The third candidate in that race was Riasat Hussain, a Muslim Sheikh, of the Praja Socialist Party. In 1962 Riasat Hussain (PSP) was victorious. He was a rural resident, a social worker, and the son of a small zamindar, who had obtained his education (through Intermediate) in urban areas of Moradabad and Bareilly district and had traveled extensively while in the Air Force during World War II.

Second, the PSP has been built up to "winning party" status in this constituency in a short time. Although there were a few rural activists at independence, the date of activation of the party appears to have been 1956, when Riasat Hussain took the initiative and began building an organization. The relatively short period of time involved enables us to concentrate on specific methods used.

A third feature is the rural-urban interaction. The constituency could be compared to a wheel minus the hub, with the "spokes" of transportation and communication nonetheless running from the missing center. Many villagers commute daily to the city for employment, or for a multitude of other reasons. They return to tell others what has been heard and seen. At election time, this pattern of mobility tends to introduce facets of urban politics and urban tensions into the countryside. One of the most important tensions is the communalism of the city, which is more virulent than in the rural areas.

Another feature concerns the rise of various social groups. Bhitauli and Saurikh constituencies illustrate different aspects of what might be termed the "rise of the backward castes." Moradabad Rural illustrates the "rise and fall of the backward castes." Many of the same factors leading to collapse of cohesion are likely to operate in other areas and among other caste groups.

As was mentioned earlier, the 1952 election was won by the Congressman Dau Dayal Khanna; he had support from all sectors of society. There were essentially no other parties operating in the area, although a few members of the Congress Socialist Party existed. In 1957 the picture changed. One factor was a rural-urban tension. The sitting MLA was a city man. The other two candidates, both rural, exploited a sentiment favoring the election of a rural man in this rural constituency. Closely connected was the "insider-outsider" factor; Dau Dayal Khanna was not of the constituency. His two opponents were "insiders." Further, as an MLA and a member of the state Ministry, Dau Dayal Khanna reportedly was often inaccessible even to rural workers and supporters.

A fourth factor was that the Congress organization was weak in the rural area. District Congress leaders in the city admitted that Congress was an urban phenomenon, with few workers in Moradabad Rural. In 1952, the names of Congress, Gandhi, and Nehru, together with remembrances of independence and the call for Muslims to support Congress for their protection were sufficient to garner a large vote without a strong, extensive rural organization. Once elected, neither the MLA nor other Congressmen seemed to have the desire, incentive, or time to build a rural party. This gave the advantage to other candidates, who worked up a personal network of support and could utilize the first three factors against the Congress candidate.

A fifth factor was the allegiance of the Muslims who had supported Congress in 1952. In 1955–1956 there were communal disturbances in the city of Moradabad. In 1957 there was a Muslim contestant, a rural man and insider. The riots had tended to harden the belief that if one was Muslim, one was in danger. There were two tendencies: to vote for the Congress for protection (except that it was reported that Congress leaders in the city had taken a pro-Hindu stand during the riots) or to "vote Muslim." The majority of Muslims appeared to vote Muslim—or to try to. The loss of extensive Muslim support was a definite factor in Congress defeat.

A sixth factor also involved the Muslims. It might be termed the difficulties of ticket-splitting in an illiterate society. The Praja Socialist Muslim MLA and the Hindu MP candidates ran under the symbol of a hut. A Muslim Independent contesting for

MP was given the symbol of a lion. On the MLA level, Dr. Khamani Singh (Yadav), the Independent candidate, was given a lion symbol. Many Muslims desired to "vote Muslim"—voting "hut" for MLA and "lion" for MP. With both symbols being used in both contests, Muslims in about a dozen polling stations became confused and reversed the symbols. Dr. Singh recognized the mixup as an important factor in giving him the margin of victory.

Another factor in the election was Dr. Khamani Singh's activity between 1952 and 1957 in two caste organizations. In 1954 he played a key role in organizing the Yadav Sabha and trying to activize the Yadavs as a group. He was an active participant in organizing the district Backward Classes Association, in which Yadavs are important leaders. One of the aims of the Backward Classes Association was to pressure the Congress to give tickets to members of the backward castes. Congress gave a few tickets to backward-caste persons in 1957, but not enough to satisfy Dr. Singh. He contested, and, as president of the association, was able to get a resolution passed supporting his candidacy. Yet the resolution divided the organization; some of the caste leaders were important activists in other parties.

There were four other Yadav leaders in Moradabad Rural. Dr. Khamani Singh had the support of only one of the four. Despite the opposition of the other three, Yadavs and backward castes generally rallied about Dr. Singh. The other leaders were unable to exercise control. Such is the magnetism of the caste tie. There was not complete unity of voting within the backward castes, but the cohesion was substantial.

While the bulk of Dr. Singh's vote could be attributed to the backward castes, the margin necessary for victory came from support of other castes. Of importance were Brahmins, Thakurs, and some Muslims. Because voting is not strictly along caste lines, other factors being important, the individuals who were mobilized were able to obtain the support of voters in other castes and communities.

The Congress candidate was reported to have the support of the Jats and Chamars, some Thakurs, and some of all other groups. The PSP Muslim was said to have the support of the Muslims and a few Hindus. It is hard to evaluate such a caste breakdown because other societal units might be more accurate and have greater explanatory value. Perhaps the caste breakdown indicates the support candidates are believed to have obtained from notables of the various caste groups. Thus few Jat notables were considered to have supported Dr. Singh or Riasat Hussain; most gave support to Dau Dayal Khanna. This leaves open the question of whether voting followed village factional lines or class lines. One noncaste group said to have given support to Dr. Singh was the rickshaw wallahs' union in the western part of the constituency.

In the 1962 election there were six candidates (four Hindu and two Muslim). (See Table 46.) Dr. Khamani Singh, the sitting

TABLE 46

CANDIDATES TO THE ASSEMBLY IN MORADABAD RURAL CONSTITUENCY, 1962

Name	Caste	Party	Percent of Vote
Riasat Hussain	Muslim Sheikh	PSP	31.1
Shiv Shanker Trivedi	Brahmin	Congress	23.6
Ganga Ram	Saini	Jan Sangh	20.9
Khamani Singh	Yadav	Swatantra	15.6
Sukha	(Not ascertained)	Independent	4.6
Zakullah Khan	Muslim Turek	Independent	4.2

SOURCE: *Results of the Third General Election (1962) to the Uttar Pradesh Legislative Assembly* (Allahabad, 1962), p. 8.

MLA, contested on the Swatantra Party ticket and lost his deposit.[7] He won pluralities in only 14 of 89 polling stations. Riasat Hussain, defeated in 1957, was elected on the PSP ticket, with pluralities in 35 polling stations. Shiv Shanker Trivedi, Congress, was a new candidate and a Brahmin; he won pluralities in 22 polling stations. The Jan Sangh put up a "new man," of the Saini backward caste who won pluralities in 17 polling stations. A Muslim of a small caste ran as an Independent; some considered him to be a "dummy candidate" put up by the Congress to divide

[7] A security deposit must be paid by each candidate, to be forfeited if he receives less than one-sixth of the vote.

the Muslim votes. An Independent (Hindu) was unknown to the major candidates and their workers.

Reserving matters of organization, we will first take up various factors involved in the election itself. Again, "insider-outsider" and rural-urban questions arose. Riasat Hussain was an "insider," living in the village. Dr. Khamani Singh, during his term as MLA, had moved to the city and divided his time between Lucknow, Moradabad city, and his rural residence. Shiv Shanker Trivedi's family had been zamindars in the area and the family residence lay in the constituency; the candidate himself had lived in the city for years, very infrequently visiting the rural areas. The Jan Sangh candidate was an "outsider," living in the city. A district Congress official recognized the importance of this sentiment, but in a statement clearly illustrating how a party can be bound by its past memberships and leadership, he said: "In the independence movement most of the Congress leaders were urban people —and still are. Yet, most of the constituencies are rural. There is only one urban MLA seat, and then we have to put the other Congress leaders as candidates in rural areas."

This introduces a series of variables concerning the Congress Party. As was mentioned earlier, there was little Congress organization in this constituency before independence, and such was not developed during Dau Dayal Khanna's term of office. After his defeat in 1957, he successfully contested from another constituency. Dau Dayal Khanna took little interest in his former constituency. Neither, apparently, did anyone else. Moradabad Rural remained uncultivated by Congress for another five years. Shiv Shanker Trivedi was given the Congress ticket "at the last moment" before the nomination-filing deadline. He reported that he had not engaged in any organizational work of a party or personal nature up to the actual campaign (a few short weeks). Building a party takes effort; one incentive is the probability of obtaining the party's nomination. In some cases this probability is so remote or so uncertain that there is no incentive.

A hard-to-assess variable is the attitude expressed by some Congress urban district leaders toward villagers. None of the half-dozen activists present objected to or disagreed with one Congress official's statement that before independence "people in rural areas were men only in shape, but really they were just animals." Another, after stating that opposition parties "just want to win a seat and undermine Congress prestige—they are not interested that good men or men of high caliber go to the Assembly," said:

But the problem before Congress is that we are not only wanting to win an election, but we demand that persons be of deserving caliber, be educated, be believers of Congress ideology, because part of our job is to educate the public in our ideology. And people in rural areas are not educated; they are not "Congressmen" in their beliefs. So we can't give them the ticket.

When asked whether the rural educated were supporting Congress, the same respondent (clearly avoiding the question) replied that few rural educated existed, that these few did not know the Congress ideology, and that they "could not be given the Congress ticket." The experiences that some of the rural respondents reported having with the former Congress MLA—still vividly remembered some seven years after his defeat—possibly indicated a reaction to such general attitudes held by urban leaders.

Congressmen reported that there was some difficulty of cohesion in the Congress Party which influenced the election outcome. It was said that a defeated scheduled-caste Congress candidate from another constituency came to Moradabad Rural and worked among the scheduled castes in the last few days before the election, trying to persuade them not to support the Congress. The result, according to respondents, was that many did not vote at all. In the places specifically mentioned, however, there was no noticeable decline in voting participation.

Another factor concerns the process of ticket splitting. The Muslims learned how to split the ticket correctly in 1962 so that their votes were cast for the PSP Muslim MLA and Independent Muslim MP. Not all Muslims "voted Muslim," of course. A few respondents speculated that 80 percent of the Muslims voted for the PSP Muslim candidate, with the other 20 percent being divided among the Congress, Swatantra, and Independent Muslim candidates.

Another factor of importance was the breakdown of cohesion among the backward classes, including the Yadavs. In 1962 Dr. Khamani Singh lost his deposit, which is one measure of the loss of support. One variable was the presence of another backward-caste candidate, a Saini, on the Jan Sangh ticket. It was reported from a non–Jan Sangh source that the Saini was put up to defeat Dr. Khamani Singh after Dr. Singh declined to join the Jan Sangh. (There was no confirmation of this from other sources.) It was widely reported and confirmed that the Saini caste panchayats had supported the candidate and had performed numerous salt ceremonies to promote caste cohesion in voting.[8]

The Yadavs had generally voted for their caste fellow in 1957, even though three caste leaders had supported others. In the interim, some of the enthusiasm of "Yadav for Yadav" seemed to dissipate. Part of this was related to the decline of participation by Dr. Singh in the two caste associations. Constituents—including Yadavs—had difficulties in obtaining specific material advantages. The electoral victory did not give the hoped-for psychological acceptance of "Yadavs are rulers" by others. The Yadavs in this area have definite aspirations of upward mobility. One Yadav villager said, "Lord Khrisna was a Yadav; therefore we ought to be worshiped." There is frank acknowledgement in statements such as "We want power" and "We want to be the rulers." By 1962 the other caste leaders had reestablished their influence in their respective geographic spheres. An additional variable was that the Congress candidate Shiv Shanker Trivedi, one Yadav leader supporting Congress, and Dr. Khamani Singh had their strongest constituency ties in almost adjacent villages. The "friends and neighbors" vote received by Dr. Khamani Singh in 1957, apart from Yadavs, was now divided.

Furthermore, the one Yadav leader who had previously supported Dr. Khamani Singh shifted his influence to the PSP Muslim. There were various reasons given for the change. One was his desire to become president of the block committee. Since the village panchayat pradhans elect the block president, and since there were few Yadav pradhans, supporting Dr. Singh would not have added to his votes in the block election. There were, however, many Muslim pradhans and some Hindu pradhans associated with the PSP. A bargain was struck with the PSP Muslim candidate that the Yadav leader would support the PSP in the

---

[8] Salt is passed to all present, a resolution is made that all will vote for X, and then the salt is placed in a jar. This is a solemn oath that one will abide by his word.

general election in return for Muslim and PSP pradhan support
in the next block election. A second reason lies in the pairing of
MLA and MP candidates. The Praja Socialist MP candidate was a
noted kisan worker and political activist, Buddhi Singh, a Yadav.
There was a caste feature as well as political advancement feature.
Family and friendship ties existed: a cousin of the Yadav leader
was a member of PSP. Also, Riasat Hussain's father had formerly
been the patwari (keeper of land records) in the Yadav's village;
their fathers had been friends. All these factors combined to
encourage a shift to the PSP.

Without the support of any other Yadav leaders, with the increased influence of these leaders over Yadavs in their geographic
spheres, and without support from the Sainis, it became very
difficult for Dr. Singh to mobilize members of other backward
castes. (Details will be discussed in relation to the party-building
activities of the PSP candidate.)

Dr. Singh's support in 1957 had included many Brahmins.
These shifted in their loyalties in 1962 partly because of the
presence of a Brahmin candidate on the Congress ticket. With
the loss of these notables went the loss of support of those in other
castes who were "under the influence" of these Brahmins. Dr.
Singh had the support of Thakurs in 1957, although, according to
him, not a majority. In 1962 this support was diminished because
of the activities of the PSP candidate. It did not appear that Dr.
Singh was able to obtain greater support from other caste groups
such as the Jats and scheduled castes than in 1957. He was unable
to maintain or extend his organization while a legislator.

The Praja Socialist Party in the district is small and weak.
There were a number of activists in Moradabad city, but until
the late 1950's there was only a bare handful in the rural areas.
In Moradabad Rural constituency there were only three persons
identified as activists before the mobilization of Riasat Hussain.
Of these three, one was an "old Socialist," formerly in the Congress Socialist Party. He was concerned with social service, especially education, and it was due to his influence that around
1952–1953 Riasat Hussain became interested in politics and in
the PSP. This was the only political party contact which Riasat
Hussain had during those early years. He entered the party of the
mobilizer. Contacts with other activists of the party were ex-

tremely limited: for example, he did not meet a second activist, although this person lived only three miles away, until 1956, some three to four years after his own mobilization into politics and entry into the PSP. The patterns of mobilization and communication within a party have relevance for understanding the bases of party factions, splits in a party, and "drifting away" from a party. Observers such as Brass, Kothari, and Weiner have pointed out the importance of personal ties in Indian politics and in factions.[9] One reason for the strength of ties to a particular person is that in many cases contact with others is so limited. This would appear to be especially true in rural areas, and less so in towns and cities. Yet in urban areas there is likely to be much more frequent communication among subgroups than between groups.

Sidney Verba's distinction of "wheel" and "circle" communication patterns is useful as an analogy.[10] (In the "circle" system, there is no hub, and all have equal communication with others on the circle. In the "wheel," communications run to and from the hub and the rim.) On the constituency level, a party is likely to consist of a number of different wheels of communication, each with an activist at the hub. Contact between the hubs tends to be limited, and contact between those on the rim of one wheel with those on the rim of another—or to the hub of another wheel—are even more limited.

Although Riasat Hussain was initially recruited in 1952–1953, his interest in candidacy did not begin until 1956. This interest followed very closely on the heels of the communal riots in Moradabad city, and a relationship is suspected even though denied by the respondent. There are a number of variables in the respondent's background which are related to his party-building activities and his 1962 victory. First, he is action-oriented. On returning to his home village after his tour of duty in the Air Force, he was not content to be solely a kisan; he became active in social service work, where he became acquainted with a PSP activist. Second, Riasat Hussain is of a prominent political family

[9] Brass, *Factional Politics in an Indian State,* chap. iii; Rajni Kothari, "Factions in Indian Politics," résumé of a paper presented at the Kothari seminar on "Working of the Party System in India," Centre for the study of Developing Societies, New Delhi, March 13, 1964 (mimeographed); Myron Weiner, *Party Politics in India* (Princeton, 1957), pp. 223–291.

[10] Sidney Verba, *Small Groups and Political Behavior* (Princeton: Princeton University Press, 1961), pp. 235–242.

within a village. His cousin was the hereditary village chief, on whose death in 1949 Riasat Hussain was elected village pradhan. He has been an uncontested pradhan in the three elections. His elder brother was originally a candidate for the Assembly in 1936–1937, but withdrew in favor of another Muslim. This brother held a minor, appointive village position until 1954–1955. His father had been a zamindar and the patwari over several villages. The father thus had contact and ties with many people, both Hindu and Muslim. A third point concerns the ability of individuals to give time and energy to building a party. The earlier activists in this constituency did not have a financial base such as would permit them to forego earning a livelihood while building a party. Riasat Hussain's occupation is agriculture, but since he lives in a joint family, the farming could be left to the other members. From 1956 until his election in 1962 he gave full time to building an organization. Joint-family support of one member in politics may help to explain why so many MLA's record themselves as joint-family members.

Riasat Hussain essentially built up his organization by personal contact. His social service activities had made him known within a specific geographic zone. His religion, caste, and family position could be utilized in making contacts and gaining adherents among Muslims, and among some zamindars and large landowners of various castes and communities. Since many pradhans, pradhan-contestants, cooperative society sarpanches and other local officials fell into one or both of these categories, his contacts gave him some support among these elements. As a pradhan himself, he was in a position to meet other pradhans in block activities. One of his early pre-1962 campaign ventures was to invite pradhans to a meeting in his village where he appealed to the group for support in order to be able to present a "pradhan interest" to the state government. More than a hundred pradhans attended. It was estimated, however, that only about 30 percent of the pradhans supported the PSP. One reason put forth was that the pradhans identify themselves with the Government, and since the district, state, and national governments are controlled by Congress, they consider themselves Congressmen.[11]

[11] It would be interesting to make an intensive study in order to find out whether there is such a psychological identification of village leaders with "Government" on higher levels.

Through the support of large landowners, former zamindars, Muslims, pradhans, and so on, the PSP candidate obtained the voting support of the various socioeconomic groups and village groups under the influence of these individuals. Caste leaders were also approached, whether they had influence in several villages or in one village. Indeed, one pattern is to gain support of a caste leader and to utilize him thenceforth as a source of information about and the "introducer" to leaders of his caste in other villages. This process can be repeated in a chain of contacts.

In the process of building an organization, gaining the support of one person can lead to gaining the support of other persons and groups. We can best illustrate the process with an example. In one village there were two factions, both led by Thakurs. In 1957 both factional leaders supported Dr. Khamani Singh. In the intervening years, it was said, "Khamani Singh did nothing for us." Both groups shifted their support. The majority group leader supported the Congress in 1962, and the minority leader supported Riasat Hussain of the PSP. Personal contact with Riasat Hussain was a key factor in the decision to support the PSP. In this case, contact paid great dividends. The minority leader, a Thakur, had been involved in supporting the cases of backward and scheduled castes against the majority Thakur faction. In the village a Lodhi had recently been murdered. The minority leader offered physical protection to Lodhis against future attacks as well as aid in the court case. At election time he utilized this past aid to get the support of the Lodhis involved in the case. With these Lodhis he visited a number of other villages and obtained the support of Lodhis over quite a wide geographical area. Through the tie of caste, these Lodhis were willing to support a benefactor of another caste, and, through him, support a candidate of yet another caste and community. To many Lodhis, this tie was of greater strength than the tie to their backward-caste fellow, Dr. Khamani Singh. In addition to obtaining Lodhi support, the minority leader gained the support of Chamars and others of scheduled castes. This came about through the expressed demand of the Chamars to be allowed to enter the village temple and participate with the upper castes in the religious ceremonies during a festival. The Thakur majority leaders opposed the demand; the Thakur minority leader supported

the Chamars. The festival and all related events were called off
by the majority group. At election time the Chamars were willing
to support the PSP Muslim through gratitude to the Thakur who
had stood by them. Again through the tie of caste, some Chamars
in other villages were willing to support the PSP. The minority
leader was also active in mobilizing individual Thakurs in other
villages; some of these were village factional leaders, and because
of their support and influence Riasat Hussain again obtained the
votes of persons of varied caste among Hindus as well as Muslims.
This case helps to demonstrate how the interrelationship of village
factions, caste ties, and personal contact can lead to support of a
candidate of caste and community different from that of all
groups involved. It is also an illustration of the way a party
bridges the gap between voluntary and birth-affiliation groups.
Rising above ascriptive ties to join a voluntary association (party),
individuals nonetheless utilize ascriptive ties to strengthen the
party.

Another variable aiding the PSP candidate in his effort to gain
the support of those belonging to different castes and communities
was the existence of party activists of these different groups on
the district and state level. Local Thakur activists recalled a particular party meeting in the constituency which was attended by a
state leader, Chandra Shekar, a Thakur from a far eastern district,
Ballia. By this time, they had already been brought into the PSP,
but contact with Chandra Shekar helped to solidify the tie. It has
already been pointed out that contact with Buddhi Singh (Yadav)
helped to obtain support of Yadavs in the area. The existence of
a multicaste and multicommunity party on higher levels can help
in building a multicaste and multicommunity party on a lower
level.

The PSP candidate tried to utilize block politics to gain support in the general election. A block election was held before the
general election. In one block, an agreement was reached with a
Thakur, Ram Rakshpal Singh, in which Riasat Hussain supported the Thakur in the block pramukh election in return for
the Thakur's support in the general election. Ram Rakshpal Singh
was elected block pramukh. When Riasat Hussain obtained
Buddhi Singh as an MP running mate, however, Dr. Khamani
Singh (Yadav) retaliated by persuading Ram Rakshpal Singh to

take the Swatantra MP ticket. It is difficult to evaluate the impact of Ram Rakshpal Singh's candidacy on the MLA level. According to the PSP leading activists, thousands of Thakur votes were lost. According to the Swatantra MLA candidate, Ram Rakshpal Singh did not work in the campaign for his MLA partner, but only for himself. In many areas there was little evidence of Thakur support for Dr. Khamani Singh. Some of the PSP Thakur respondents noted specifically that many Thakurs supported the PSP candidate for MLA, but shifted to support their caste-fellow Ram Rakshpal Singh for MP.

In this same block, another election was scheduled to be held shortly after the general election. As has been mentioned, a Yadav leader and Riasat Hussain arranged to support each other in their respective elections. The Yadav gave support to the PSP in the general election. When the block election came up, however, Riasat Hussain was unable to keep his end of the bargain. A Muslim ran for pramukh and could not be persuaded to step down, and Muslim pradhans voted for the Muslim candidate. Ram Rakshpal Singh stood for reelection, and the Thakur pradhans who were affiliated with the PSP preferred to support their caste man rather than the PSP-backed candidate. These two cases demonstrate some of the problems involved in bargaining mutual support for elections held on different levels at different times. One of the main problems is that the leaders have little control over and can impose few sanctions on their supporters.

The candidate could also utilize various frictions between Hindus and Muslims. He did not have to talk openly about the tension. It provided a setting in which he was sure to get the support of Muslims. For example, in one village Congress activists (Hindus) reported that Muslims wanted some barren village land on which to build a mosque. The panchayat (Hindu- and Congress-controlled) refused to make the land available, on the grounds that there had never been a mosque in the village and they saw no reason to have one now. In another place a Chamar marriage party came to a village with singers and dancers. The Muslims gathered to watch the *tamaasha*. Then one of the bridegroom's shoes disappeared, and some Chamars said the Muslims had stolen it. The Muslims denied the theft and resisted attempts to search them and their houses. Blows followed. The

Chamars lodged a complaint with the police, and went to the then MLA, Dau Dayal Khanna. Khanna took the side of the Chamars and sent to the village a military truck and subinspector of police who promptly arrested several Muslims. The subsequent investigation showed that a Chamar—a friend of the bridegroom —had taken the shoe as a joke. The Muslims had simply been onlookers. What began as a joke turned into an ugly incident with a definite political aftermath. The Muslims interpreted Dau Dayal Khanna's actions as anti-Muslim and in 1957 supported the PSP's Muslim candidate. The Chamars likewise appreciated the aid of Khanna and supported the Congress. It is quite likely that word of this incident traveled within the Muslim community and possibly entered into the Muslim's evaluation of Dau Dayal Khanna and the Congress Party.

Certainly not all Muslims "voted Muslim." There were other loyalties operating on them. An excellent example was discovered which illustrates one of the pressures that operate against all opposition parties. In this particular village there had never been communal disturbances. The respondent was an elderly Muslim who was a long-time friend of Riasat Hussain's family and whose son was an active Praja Socialist. The respondent himself had campaigned in neighboring villages for the PSP candidate. But on election day he voted for the Congress:

I have begun with Congress, have stayed with Congress and will end with Congress, because Congress is the first party. The flowers that bloom in the field, the crops that grow in the field—they are there because of Congress.

Congress has not taken away our land, or snatched our houses—and no party can say this as long as Congress is here. Congress has ended zamindari and treats all zamindars equally whether big or small. There is no need for the Congress Party to promise anything or say anything in an election, for whatever they have said, they have done. Whatever flowers or roses are on our way today, they were laid by Congress. All that we have is due to Congress. People ask me to leave Congress, but why should I leave when Congress has given me so many comforts and advantages?

This is one way of stating the "Congress myth." It was sufficient to override the ties of family, friendship, community, caste, and actual participation in support of the PSP in the campaign. The

"Congress myth" can be stated in terms of Gandhi, Nehru, and independence. Muslims can point to Nehru and the Congress as "defenders of the Muslims," in contrast with the Jan Sangh. Further, Congress has been and is the Government, on the national, state, and district levels. This example demonstrates one way of describing the aura surrounding the Congress. All opposition parties have problems in overcoming it.

A further tactic utilized by the MLA candidate was to emphasize another kind of sentiment in the constituency. A frequent complaint about MLA's is that, once elected, they disappear for five years. An intrinsic part of Riasat Hussain's campaign was a promise that he would regularly visit each village. Nearly all respondents mentioned this promise. In the course of three elections, many have come to look forward to the "tamaasha" of the campaign and to want it to continue after election. The campaign does provide variety in the daily routine. A promise to "return" seems to imply the return of the tamaasha.[12]

Some public works programs were desired in parts of the constituency. The candidate favored some of these, particularly irrigation works. Most of the respondents interviewed in one section of the constituency wanted a road between an interior market village and a major paved road (a six-mile stretch). They said that the MLA candidate favored the building of the road. The candidate professed his opposition to the proposed road. (The route designated by respondents would have passed near the candidate's village and would facilitate travel to his village.) Voters misperceived the candidate's position. They projected their own wants and desires onto the candidate. Such a misperception could have consequences for future political activity.

In addition to personal contact and utilization of grievances and tensions to gain support, the MLA contestant organized many village meetings and also set up "committees of five" in a number of polling stations. In 34 of the 88 polling stations "committees of five" were established, and in six other polling stations one active worker was listed in the party rolls. These members, by the PSP constitution, are "active members" as opposed to "regular members." Few of these "active members" appear to be either "pillars" or "regulars" as we have defined the term. The ties to the

[12] A show or entertainment.

party appear to be fairly weak, inasmuch as some of those interviewed reported that they were not even members of the party at that time and did not consider themselves to be Praja Socialists. A few noted that since the election no one had asked them to continue their membership. It is significant that after seven years of intensive organization, less than half the polling stations were covered with official committees or workers. Analysis of the community composition of the "active members" on the PSP rolls for this constituency at the time of the 1962 election revealed a breakdown of 50 Hindus and 127 Muslims.[13] A detailed caste analysis of the Hindus listed was not made, but a cursory examination indicated that most were either Thakurs or Yadavs. By the official records the party is not totally Muslim in this constituency, although Muslims are dominant. In the election itself, the Muslim votes provided the bulk of PSP strength; the Hindu votes, however, provided the margin of victory. Geographical analysis of the location of the committees and workers demonstrated that the PSP was not evenly organized throughout the constituency. In the eastern half of the "doughnut" there was greater coverage. One reason was that the MLA candidate and two Yadav leaders supporting the PSP live on this eastern side; another was that larger numbers of Muslims are found on this side. In the western portion, there are more Jats, Sainis, and other Hindus.

In the election, the constituency was roughly divided into three parts, with the northeastern section in the charge of a Yadav leader who had long been in the PSP, the west in the charge of a Muslim worker, and the southeastern portion under the candidate himself. Beneath the MLA in his section were three workers (two Muslims and one Hindu). It appears that these five persons were the "pillars." There are a few workers or notables who seem to be moving up into a "pillar" category.

In sum, this constituency represents a case of a rural organization developed by rural residents. It differs from Saurikh in several respects. First, it is a post-independence party. Second, the PSP has been built to winning status around a Muslim candidate. As compared with Hindus or backward castes, the Muslims appear to be a far more cohesive and a more than usually isolated minor-

---

[13] Taken from the official membership roll of the PSP, made available by Riasat Hussain.

ity. They are on the defensive. Political and social change have posed threats to their cultural identity. The Muslims provide a core of electoral strength larger than would come from any other single group in the society. Whether Muslims would remain Praja Socialist supporters in the absence of a Muslim candidate (particularly if a Muslim contested on another ticket) is highly debatable. One Hindu PSP leader spoke of the hopes of winning Muslim allegiance on a long-term basis by putting up a Muslim candidate. Bringing up the question himself of whether such allegiance had been won, he regretfully expressed the opinion that the PSP was obtaining Muslim support solely because of the Muslim candidate: "They have not become Praja Socialists." The strategy has brought short-term success. But open hostilities between India and Pakistan such as those in 1964 and 1965 raise a perplexing question. To continue with a Muslim candidate might alienate Hindus; to change the candidate to a Hindu could alienate a fearful Muslim community. Even with a Muslim candidate, fear could drive the Muslims to the governing party—the party able to promise protection.

Third, even though the constituency surrounds a large urban center, the extent of political mobilization is not as advanced as in Saurikh. Its very proximity to the city may have retarded mobilization. Urban political workers may have taken the immediate rural vicinity for granted. Rural political workers, as they developed, may have gravitated to the city. Moradabad Rural illustrates a fairly early stage of the spiral of political mobilization. With time and the efforts of political workers, wider and wider segments of the population are mobilized. The first stages of exposure to political movements and "flag wavers' campaigns," wherein people are reached en masse, are followed by campaigns in which contacts with individuals are made in ever increasing numbers. With every election and with the appearance of new candidates the spiraling process continues. Candidates can either try to win the support of the previously mobilized or reach out to tap the nonmobilized strata. Dr. Khamani Singh endeavored to extend the mobilized sector before 1957. The Jan Sangh Saini candidate picked up where he left off, concentrating on the mobilization of a specific backward caste. Riasat Hussain worked from 1956 to 1962 to extend the mobilized sector and tried to win over some of those previously mobilized. We classify the mobilization spiral as being in an early stage inasmuch as several respondents who were village leaders (pradhans, pradhan-contestants, and the like) reported that they were personally approached for the first time in the 1962 election. Others, initially approached by 1957 had contacts with workers of only one party and reported no activity in their respective villages by workers of other parties. As the spiral widens and deepens, there will be fewer such reports.

Like Saurikh, the PSP has been built up by the candidate through personal contact. Both Hori Lal Yadav and Riasat Hussain have played a broker role. They have tried to aid individuals and groups with their problems with various agencies and branches of government. They have offered concrete aid, advice, or, at the least, sympathy. The broker service has been offered across caste and community lines by both men. Riasat Hussain's education, military experience (during which he was stationed in many places throughout India and neighboring countries), family position, and personal characteristics helped to fit him for such a role. By establishing personal ties and by functioning as brokers, both men have been able to obtain support from varied groups in the society.

Chapter X

THE SAINTLY BROKER:
KARCHANA CONSTITUENCY
(PRAJA SOCIALIST PARTY)

LIKE MORADABAD RURAL, Karchana constituency lies immediately south of Allahabad and includes one small part of the city. Many people in the rural area commute daily to the city for employment or for other reasons. But here the similarity ends. Allahabad differs from Moradabad. The confluence of the Ganges and Jumna rivers makes the city a sacred site to Hindus throughout India. The University of Allahabad makes it a center of secular education. As the capital of Uttar Pradesh in the late nineteenth century, it became an important administrative center. As the present site of the High Court, the city continues a secular tradition. As the pre-independence headquarters of the All-India Congress Committee and the residence of such leaders as Tej Bahadur Sapru, Motilal Nehru, Jawaharlal Nehru, K. D. Malaviya, Purosshottamdas Tandon, and Lal Bahadur Shastri, it became a political center for the nationalist movement. In post-independence years, two of the Lok Sabha constituencies in the district repeatedly returned Jawaharlal Nehru and Lal Bahadur Shastri to office. In contrast wth their practice in Moradabad, Congress workers did not neglect the adjacent rural areas.

Given the political background of the district, one would expect it to be a stronghold of the Congress. But in 1962 more than half the Assembly seats were won by opposition candidates: six Praja Socialists, one Jan Sanghi, and one Independent. This phenomenon raises questions of who, why, and how—particularly for the Praja Socialists.

Most of the PSP district leaders are former Congressmen. Some were quite prominent in the pre-independence Congress. For example, Saligram Jaiswal, the dean of the PSP, was secretary of the

District Congress Committee from 1932 to 1942. Factional strife led to his and other's withdrawal. They were Rafiats:

I was in the Kidwai group, and we were against Pant and against Gupta—and Gupta was Pant's man. We did not like the corruption of Congressmen: they were taking bribes and dealing in permits, licenses, and so on. But also they (Gupta and Pant) were engaging in activities to destroy us. We had a majority in Allahabad, but they changed the membership lists, and so on, and changed the voting so that the other group would win. There was nothing we could do. I am bitterly opposed to C. B. Gupta. So one day twenty-six of us crossed the floor [in the Assembly] and formed the opposition. Pant was quite upset over this. He did not think that we would do it since we were old Congressmen. . . . My opponent [in 1962] is a Gupta man, and a bitter opponent.

This group of Rafiats established the Jan Congress in Allahabad. Saligram Jaiswal was one of the state-level leaders. Jan Congress members together with some followers of Acharya Kripalani and other Rafiats formed the KMPP. Subsequently these became the Praja Socialists. Many of the leaders have close personal and even family ties to important Congressmen in the state and nation. Some have long held positions in the District Board, Municipal Board, and District Cooperative Bank; others have held village governmental positions. A few have been or are associated with newspapers, either as editors or directors. Most of the PSP leaders are social-service workers as well as grass-roots political workers. They have set up schools and promoted education among both sexes. Some have entered trade-union activities; some have worked for years for and with kisans. They have been active in religious, caste, and cultural organizations. They tend to be priests, businessmen, lawyers, large landowners, or politicians. It was widely reported from reliable sources that in this district Rafi Ahmed Kidwai financially supported and in other ways aided his followers in the opposition. His backing was said to have made the Allahabad Jan Congress-KMPP-PSP "respectable," making these more than just opposition parties. Despite Kidwai's support and the reputed size of the group, no KMPP candidate was elected in 1952, and only one Praja Socialist (from a city constituency) in 1957. The PSP's rumored strength was confirmed for the first time in 1962.

Brahmins were reported to be the largest Hindu caste in the district and in that area which roughly corresponds to Karchana constituency.[1] Allahabad's being a religious center for Hindus helps to explain the large proportion. Theirs is not a clear numeric dominance, however, for the Muslims are rivals for first place, and shortly behind follow the Chamars, Yadavs, and Kurmis and then the Pasis and Thakurs.[2]

The proprietary tenures of the North-West Provinces applied to the district; there was no talukdari system. The applicability today of the figures given in the 1911 District Gazetteer about the landownership position of various castes can certainly be questioned. At that time the castes holding the largest proportion of the total area were Thakurs, Brahmins, and Muslims, with Banias beginning to show prominence.[3] That Brahmins were the largest Hindu caste numerically, one of the best off economically, and the highest ritually suggests that they would be a politically powerful group.

In the small urban area of Karchana constituency there are three factories (making cotton textiles, glass, and cardboard). During field studies in villages near this urban area it was noted that most of the land was owned by a few persons, while the landless worked regularly in the city.

Politically, Karchana constituency has several distinguishing features. The Congress won the Assembly seat in 1952 and 1957, losing in 1962. In the three elections, three different Congress candidates contested. This is the only constituency studied in which the Congress changed candidates where they were winning. The sitting Congress MLA (1957) was a woman. Many respondents reported dissatisfaction with her performance and cited it as a prime reason for shifting their support to the PSP in 1962. They shifted, even though the 1962 Congress candidate was a man. This suggests that at least some voters regard an election as the time to pass judgment on the past performance of a legislator. What were some of the problems with the sitting MLA? It is difficult for a

---

[1] District Gazetteers of the United Provinces of Agra and Oudh, XXIII: Allahabad, by H. R. Nevill (Allahabad, 1911), 88 f., 258; hereafter cited as Allahabad Gazetteer.

[2] Census of India, 1931 (Allahabad, 1933), XVIII, 499–548.

[3] Allahabad Gazetteer, pp. 102–103.

woman to be an effective rural politician owing to difficulties in travel, communication, and the aiding of supporters. Touring a constituency between elections is arduous and is avoided by many men. The usual reticence of a woman in meeting male constituents is matched by their reluctance to approach her; regardless of her willingness to help those who come to her, she is often regarded as "unavailable." Regardless of her actual ability to help people, she is commonly considered lacking in it. The interaction of these factors resulted in dissatisfaction with her performance and with the Congress Party.

Among the eight contestants in 1962, only two were major. These two candidates had very similar backgrounds. The Congressman, Shitla Din Dwivedi, was a lawyer in Allahabad city. The Praja Socialist, Satya Narain Pandey, was assistant librarian at Allahabad University. Both were Brahmin, urban, English-speaking, and Western-educated. Neither resided in the constituency, although the rural family home of Satya Narain Pandey is there. Furthermore, the Congressman had at one time been a member of the Praja Socialist Party—the only case we have studied of this kind. The similarity of the candidates stands in contrast to the other constituencies studied.

In four of our previous case studies the major candidates represented competing groups in society. In the other, both the Socialist and Congress candidates (Bhitauli) were of the same caste, but each tended to draw his strength from opposing groups. In all the other studies there were tensions operating on a broad scale which could be utilized. Respondents in Allahabad city spoke of a number of rivalries to be found in the district: between Brahmins and Thakurs, elite and backward castes, Hindus and Muslims, upper and middle classes, and labor and management. While all may exist, none appeared dominant in Karchana (Table 47). It may be that the similarity of the major candidates prevented their utilization. Since each was Brahmin, neither could expect to profit by calling on Brahmin-Thakur, elite-backward, or Hindu-Muslim antagonisms. That both would probably be termed members of the same economic class and cultural group tended to work against a class or cultural group distinction. That both lived outside the constituency, in the city, meant that neither could expect to benefit from a rural-versus-urban or insider-versus-outsider sen-

TABLE 47

CANDIDATES OF KARCHANA ASSEMBLY CONSTITUENCY, 1962

Candidates	Caste	Party	Percent of Vote
Satya Narain Pandey	Brahmin	Praja Socialist	39.1
Shitla Din Dwivedi	Brahmin	Congress	37.3
Ajaib Lal	Kurmi (backward)	Independent	13.5
Sant Lal	Pasi (scheduled)	Republican	4.6
Kishori Lal	Chamar (scheduled)	Independent	2.0
Madan Gopal Misra	Brahmin	Independent	1.6
Sharda Prasad	Brahmin	Jan Sangh	1.4
Sri Nivas	Bhumihar	Independent	.4

SOURCE: Names of candidates, party affiliation, and actual vote taken from the *Results of the Third General Elections (1962) for the Uttar Pradesh Legislative Assembly* (Allahabad, 1962), p. 63. Percentages were calculated on the basis of the valid votes polled. Caste of the candidates is from respondents in Allahabad.

timent. What forces, then, could the opposition utilize to achieve victory?

It is probable that had the sitting MLA contested in 1962 she would have been defeated. A man was set up, but in this district as elsewhere it is necessary for a candidate to build his own organization. As one respondent put it: "It is every man for himself. A candidate can get a 'name' from the Congress, but not an organization." Shitla Din Dwivedi had not built up an organization in the constituency. Thus he could not counteract the attrition resulting from the sitting MLA's sex. Beyond this, there were factional difficulties in Karchana constituency. There are numerous Congress factions in the district. The heritage of the varied pre-independence groupings about the great leaders and the development of post-independence leaders on state, district, and city levels make the politics of the Congress exceedingly complex. Fortunately, respondents could explain the Karchana situation by use of the state factional alignments. Shitla Din Dwivedi had been a member of the "Tripathi group" in the district, but in the

District Board elections before the General Election he had supported the local "Gupta group" candidate (a Brahmin). This action won him the enmity of the Tripathi group, whose members worked against him in the General Election.

The margin of victory—or defeat—was only about 700 votes. The defeat was so narrow that any one of these three factors must be considered major: dissatisfaction with the sitting Congress MLA, weakness of organization of the Congress candidate in 1962, and factional strife in the party. The Congress candidate himself reported factional strife as the only factor of importance in the election. That despite these three factors Shitla Din Dwivedi barely lost indicates the real strength of Congress in the constituency.

This strength is further demonstrated by identification of the minor candidates (see Table 47). Three candidates (the one of backward caste and the two of scheduled castes) were reported to have been "dummy candidates" set up to draw votes away from the Congress. Their appeal appeared to be limited largely to a portion of their respective castes. It could not be ascertained whether some or all of these "dummies" had been set up by the PSP or by the dissident Congress faction. The three combined obtained 20 percent of the valid vote cast. Had they not contested, it is highly doubtful that all their votes would have gone to Congress. However, a proportion sufficient to have changed the outcome probably would have been given to Congress.

Field work and interviews with the candidates and their workers gave the overwhelming impression that both major candidates drew on all groups in society for their support. Neither could point to the decided support of any particular group, however defined. The PSP obtained pluralities in 41 polling stations, the Congress in 37, and minor candidates in 3. The Congressman polled a higher percentage of the vote in northern polling stations nearer the city, and the Praja Socialist in the rural polling stations to the south. In many polling stations only a few votes separated the two parties.

Candidates and workers of both parties said they drew support from the lower classes, rural and urban, while simultaneously pointing to the support of notables who were doubtless highly instrumental in mobilizing the lower classes. Said one candidate:

"Personal influence counts for everything. It was a race for influence." Pradhans, pradhan-contestants, Cooperative Society sarpanches, rural court sarpanches, large landowners, moneylenders, small and large businessmen, employers, priests, sadhus, caste leaders on various levels, labor leaders, and wrestlers or "strong men," were approached and mobilized by the candidates. In contrast with some of the previous cases, political mobilization appears to be quite advanced. The influence of notables overlapped to some degree; there were "lesser notables" whose sphere of influence could counteract or reinforce the influence of "greater notables" in the same geographic area or within the same groups.

The consequence of so many cross-cutting relationships was that few activists were able to identify voting groups. Village factions were not considered a base unit of voting behavior, modified by other factors. Neither was caste, class, nor even family. The possibility of a generational division was negated by workers. While activists could easily identify many notables and state their allegiance in the election, they could not determine over whom these had influence. For example, a sadhu supported the PSP. But how did his influence compare with that of village factional leaders, moneylenders, shopkeepers, caste leaders, or others in that area? A businessman supported the Congress. How did his influence with his customers compare with that of the many other notables in the area? The multiple cross-pressures were sufficient, it was reported, to break down the cohesion of all types of groups. Similar reports were given by workers referring to those who lived in or near the city. It is interesting that in Karchana the voting turnout was lower than in the other constituencies studied (see Table 48). Might this be related to the cross-pressures exerted on voters? [4]

Looking more specifically at the PSP candidate and his efforts to win, we first recall that for many years PSP workers had been operating in the area. Saligram Jaiswal, both as a Congressman and in other parties, had actively organized here. Through his

[4] For analysis of the relationship between cross-pressures and nonvoting see: Angus Campbell *et al., The American Voter* (New York: John Wiley & Sons, 1964), pp. 80 ff.; Paul F. Lazarsfeld, B. R. Berelson, and H. Gaudet, *The People's Choice* (New York: Duell, Sloan and Pearce, 1944), pp. 53 ff.; B. R. Berelson, Paul F. Lazarsfeld, and William N. McPhee, *Voting* (Chicago: University of Chicago Press, 1954), pp. 128 ff.

TABLE 48

VOTER TURNOUT IN THE SIX CONSTITUENCIES STUDIED

Constituency	Voter turnout (Percent)
Pratapgarh South	54.1
Bhitauli (Bara Banki)	63.8
Rudauli (Bara Banki)	62.6
Saurikh (Farrukhabad)	57.3
Moradabad Rural	50.4
Karchana (Allahabad)	46.5

SOURCE: *Results of the Third General Elections (1962) for the Uttar Pradesh Legislative Assembly* (Allahabad, 1962), p. 63.

position in Congress he had become acquainted with people mobilized by other Congress workers. He had introduced Satya Narain Pandey to many people. The PSP candidate himself had unsuccessfully run for the Assembly in 1957. Before and after that year he worked to build support. Although a resident of the city, he was described by many respondents of different political affiliation as a "field worker"—essentially a grass-roots political organizer and social-service worker. He toured the constituency frequently, meeting people and trying to help them with their problems. He helped to settle land disputes between individuals; he helped people to get loans; he went with people to the police to register cases and ensure investigation of crimes. He encouraged parents to send their children to school and helped them obtain scholarships. When advice was needed, he gave it; he also offered sympathy in time of trouble. He served as a broker between individuals and government officials, and between disputing individuals or groups. During most of the interelection period he was not "asking for a vote." The image he presented can be expressed in terms of the "saintly idiom": he appeared as a self-sacrificing worker for the people while asking nothing for himself.[5] This image was reported by many respondents, including governmental

[5] W. H. Morris-Jones, "India's Political Idioms," in C. H. Philips (ed.), *Politics and Society in India* (London, 1963), pp. 140–141.

officials; it proved an advantage when he began asking for a vote. His role and image help to explain the kinds of responses given by several in discussing how the PSP candidate obtained their support:

He came and talked very politely and nicely with me. So I decided to support him.

Before 1962 I was in Congress. Then I met Satya Narain Pandey and liked the quiet way he talked, and I changed to PSP.

I met Satya Narain Pandey a few years ago. He is my friend. That is why I support him. What is the basis of friendship?

Many other responses were in a similar vein, stressing the manner of the candidate in asking for support. In probes to determine content of the message, respondents could recall no mention of socialist principles or ideology, of material advantages forthcoming, or the like. The candidate himself emphasized that ideology and principles were not important and that little of these had entered into his message; he did not promise material benefits to obtain support. This was confirmed by respondents in the field, and stands in contrast with Bailey's findings in Orissa.[6] The candidate emphasized that personally meeting people was important; [7] the message was of little consequence. These reports were also confirmed by the Congress candidate who said there were no issues

[6] Bailey, *Politics and Social Change*, pp. 18–68, 138–157. Bailey presents two models to describe the ways politicians persuade voters and recruit workers. In the "machine," voters and workers expect a tangible reward; in the "movement," they are morally convinced of the rightness of the party's policies. Neither model seems appropriate for Karchana constituency.

[7] Other MLA's also reported the importance of personal contact. This may be one explanation for the frequent, puzzling assertion that "people who know a lot of people" are "influential" or "important," irrespective of their social, economic, or political position in society. In a society with a poorly developed system of mass communications, with a more highly developed network of personal transmittal of news, with a relatively decentralized and somewhat autonomous structure of village units, it has become increasingly necessary for political workers to emphasize individual contact rather than to rely on slogan shouting or flag waving in order to build support. Personal visitation from candidates is expected by many. Those who can identify notables in several villages, and who can provide information on factional alignments, are important to a candidate. They are "information agents." They may not have great influence themselves, but they are "influential" in that they can identify those who are important.

in the campaign. The PSP candidate reported one issue (the question of taxing groves, opposed by him), but no one in the field mentioned it.

Such findings suggest that the major candidates tried to draw on one aspect of the Brahmin caste ethic. Brahmins minister to other castes in the rituals and ceremonies of life; they serve other castes in many everyday activities. The function of serving all seems to have been expanded to cover secular activities, including politics. The Brahmin role can be likened to that of lawyer in the United States:

> The attorney is the accepted agent of all politically effective groups of the American people. As the lawyer is habitually the representative of the grasping and the abused in litigation, as he is increasingly the negotiator between businessmen with conflicting interests, as he is more and more the spokesman of individual and corporation in public relations—so is the lawyer today depended upon to represent citizens in the lawmaking body.[8]

The difference is that the lawyer has an acquired status or role, whereas Brahmin status is inherited. What seems to have happened is that the traditional role of priest and teacher has been modified to mean "representative of all groups." This does not seem to be a change limited to Allahabad; Brahmins from other districts explicitly referred to this concept. Both the major candidates in Karchana could try to utilize this caste role of "leaders of others" to gain support of other groups in society. To draw on this role would seem to involve putting little emphasis on particular issues or ideology, because to do the latter would make the candidate appear to appeal to some rather than all groups.

It did not appear that the PSP candidate criticized the Congress to any great extent. This might be related to the Brahmin role. It might also be related to the fact that he had no MP running mate—again, the only case we have studied of this kind. There might be many who would be willing to vote PSP for MLA, but who would vote for the Congress candidate, Lal Bahadur Shastri, for MP. To have severely criticized Congress might have made it difficult for voters to split their tickets; it might have resulted in

[8] Charles S. Hyneman, "Who Makes Our Laws?" in Heinz Eulau and John C. Wahle (eds.), *Legislative Behavior* (Glencoe, Ill.: Free Press, 1959), p. 259.

loss of support. While it did not appear that the Congress MP and MLA campaigns were closely meshed, one cannot help but wonder to what extent the presence of Lal Bahadur Shastri on the ticket aided Shitla Din Dwivedi.

The campaign in Karchana was perplexing. There appeared to be no major issues, no mobilization of deep-rooted tensions. Voting behavior seemed to be more highly atomized than elsewhere. It appeared to be a dull and uninteresting election. Perhaps this helps to explain the low voting turnout.

What does stand out is the building of a party to winning status by performance of a broker function. A party organization existed which had been built up by several workers; there seemed to be a core of activists who identified with the "party" rather than with one man. Yet the party organization had never been sufficient to win an election. The MLA candidate had provided increased support by virtue of an additional personal organization. It had been created by personal contact and the performance of a broker function. Other candidates studied, in many instances, served as brokers, but the relatively strong tensions in operation made it difficult to evaluate the importance of this role. Here the role appeared to be central. Furthermore, Satya Narain Pandey assumed the broker role in a "saintly" manner. He was no tout. The role was established long before the 1962 election. The image was furthered by his caste and his mode of campaigning. In contrast, much of the criticism of the sitting MLA basically involved nonperformance (or insufficient performance) of a broker function. The 1962 Congress candidate had no comparable image and played no comparable role. The two candidates were similar save for this role. It was this role that distinguished Satya Narain Pandey from all other candidates contesting. Whereas several factors helped to explain the decline in the voting support given Congress, they did not explain why the PSP benefited. The "saintly broker" role thus becomes an important explanatory factor. Widespread personal contact must be added to it. It may be that the proximity to Allahabad city, and the apparently higher degree of political mobilization, are factors. This is a fairly sophisticated rural electorate. There was a "felt need" for brokers.

Chapter XI

THOUGHTS ON THE PARTY-BUILDING PROCESS

IN THIS CHAPTER the forces which opposition parties have been able to utilize to build a winning party will be summarized and related to our original hypotheses. Then the candidate-selection process, electoral agreements, and the organization of the parties will be considered.

Review of Tensions

In all six cases, the leadership of the Congress had been set among those groups, and among those leaders, who had become prominent in the party at the time of independence. Not all groups mobilized by that time were included in the Congress leadership echelon, but relatively nonmobilized groups were absent. Groups not well represented in Congress had turned to the opposition, partly because individual leaders of the groups had done so. The importance of one or more persons appearing as leaders of a group cannot be underestimated. For example, while it is difficult to point to any group as definitely mobilized after independence, we can point to postindependence mobilized leaders who were able to change or reconstruct the pattern of voting behavior.

In two totally rural constituencies, tension was evident between rural and urban sectors of society. Many urban dwellers do not recognize this tension, or regard it as "manufactured" rather than "real." Yet the fact that so many active politicians and workers do refer to it tends to indicate that it will possibly become of greater importance in the future. In that event, parties in which urban leaders dominate may have difficulty adjusting to the situation. This may mean that opposition parties will be able to capitalize on rural-urban tension far more than the Congress. The

Congress is organized in all districts and constituencies; Congress leaders in districts, and in most constituencies tend to be urban residents, regardless of birthplace. In some districts and constituencies opposition parties are similarly organized and led. In many districts and constituencies, however, some opposition parties are practically nonexistent. In these the parties are not bound by past identifications and have scope to maneuver. The fact that these opposition parties have won 100 rural to three urban constituencies, combined with the fact that most of their elected legislators are rural residents, tends to suggest that they have already begun utilizing this tension.

Closely connected at times with rural-urban tension is the insider-outsider distinction, connoting those who live in the constituency and those who do not. Some politicians hope their parties can become so well established that any candidate could be put forward and win. That outsiders do not fare well is a source of concern. There are several reasons why an insider has an advantage over an outsider. First, with limited mass media and with most communication by word of mouth, it is difficult for an outsider to become known and trusted. Second, an outsider is often considered as not likely to be available to constituents after an election, or as not concerned with the problems of the constituency. Third, most party organizations are not well established, and an outsider may not have the time to build up an organization of his own; not knowing the situation in detail, he may inadvertently arouse the ire of the existing workers. Some politicians expressed the opinion that the difficulties of outsiders are a reflection of a "politically underdeveloped" society. As the pace of mobilization increases, so the argument goes, voters will become more concerned with electing the "best man" (however that be defined) rather than merely a local man. We can argue in contrary fashion that as political awareness increases, voters will become even more desirous of electing an insider as their representative. If the latter is the case, again opposition parties have a slight advantage over the Congress, because there are so many highly placed political workers in Congress desiring a ticket that some by necessity have to be placed in constituencies other than their own.

Various economic class tensions can be and are utilized. In the former districts of Oudh, tensions between kisans and talukdars or zamindars are an example. We might question whether this is as important as it once was. In three of the constituencies studied the talukdar candidates ran very well, and these were not isolated instances. A few of the opposition MLA's reported friction between small and large kisans apart from caste and talukdar or kisan background. In these cases the MLA's said they had the support of the small kisans. Of course, all rural MLA's can make the same claim. The question is how they got the support of this class.

Another economic friction was reported between labor and employers, such as sugar-mill workers versus the millowners, or textile workers versus employers. The parties have tried to organize labor unions and weld these groups to their party. As was candidly admitted by the opposition party leaders, most of the union membership is on paper and the members do not support the party electorally. More than one state and district party leader pointed out that those activists organizing among labor soon forget the goal of tying the group's loyalty to the party and become concerned with their own status or financial well-being. The Jan Sangh has additional difficulties in organizing workers because of the support given the party by businessmen, including employers.

The parties can also take advantage of groups which are hurt by specific government policies. For example, the Gold Control Act adversely affected many goldsmiths. The Jan Sangh has tried to get the support of this group. In another instance, the Praja Socialists led an attempt to get the support of the small manufacturers of unrefined sugar who were hurt by Congress policies requiring specified amounts of sugar cane to be sold to sugar mills.

Communal tensions between Hindus and Muslims provide another friction about which parties can be built. A party can try to attract Muslims or try to arouse a sense of "Hindu unity." The Jan Sangh is identified solely with the latter appeal, while the other parties utilize appeals to both groups, in different places. To contend that the Jan Sangh wins primarily through exploitation of communal tensions, however, is misleading. It is difficult to unite Hindus unless a major candidate is Muslim. In more than half of the constituencies in which the Jan Sangh was victorious there were no Muslim candidates at all. In eight constituencies the Muslim candidates were minor (as in Pratapgarh South). In 15 constituencies out of the 49 won there were either major Muslim candidates, or important Muslim candidates (if the votes accorded to those Muslims had gone to another major candidate the Jan Sangh would have lost). In more than two-thirds of the seats won the question of Hindu versus Muslim was likely to have been minor. This tension is simply one among many utilized by the party.

In addition to communal tensions there is also friction within the two major communities. Within the Muslims such friction is sometimes on a sect basis, sometimes on a caste basis. The differences between Sunni and Shi'a Muslims can be quite important, particularly in the districts surrounding Lucknow. In Rae Bareli district, for example, the Shi'as tend to support the Congress while the Sunnis tend to support the Jan Sangh. In Bhitauli and Rudauli constituencies, both in Bara Banki, we noted Sunni versus Shi'a conflict. Caste divisions can be important, although it is doubtful whether they are as significant electorally as that among Hindu castes.

Hindu caste distinctions provide easily definable tensions. Several types of rivalries have been noted. First was rivalry within the elite castes, between Brahmins and Thakurs with Banias and Kayasths playing a secondary role. Some respondents interpreted the state's politics as the interaction of these four castes. Part of the rivalry might be related to the caste ethic of Brahmins and Thakurs.[1] The roles of the Thakurs as the ruling class and the Brahmins as advisers to rulers have not characterized recent political history. Many of the great nationalist leaders and "strong men" in Uttar Pradesh have been Brahmins; in a number of districts the Brahmins led the kisan movements and became the Congress leaders; in 1952 there were more than a hundred Brahmin Congress MLA's as opposed to fewer than fifty Thakurs. Thakurs were either displaced or severely challenged by Brahmins. The reassertion of Thakur strength has coincided with an increase in strength of opposition parties. In addition, some of the Kayasth and Bania as well as lower-caste. MLA's had the support of large

[1] A. L. Basham, "Some Fundamental Political Ideas of Ancient India," in C. H. Philips (ed.), *Politics and Society in India* (London, 1963), pp. 11-23.

numbers of Thakurs (for example, Pratapgarh South, Rudauli, Saurikh).

A second type of rivalry is between the elite and backward castes. The demands of the backward castes for higher status are not quickly granted. The elite castes are regarded as the antagonists in many areas. Some, such as the Yadavs, in tracing their history to buttress claims for higher ritual status, have "noted regretfully how the rise of the Rajputs, backed by the support of the Brahmins, marked the beginning of the decline of the Yadavs both in social status and political power." [2] Not only are the elite castes regarded as responsible for past decline; they are also looked upon as present competitors. In elections the backward castes compete directly against members of the elite castes to obtain nominations and to win elections, since they have no reserved seats as do the scheduled castes. Among the most coveted occupations are positions in the governmental administrative services. Unlike the scheduled castes, who have a certain proportion of these positions reserved for them, the backward castes again compete directly against elite caste members. In Uttar Pradesh since 1946 the proportion of gazetted officials from the backward castes has declined in comparison with both the elite and the scheduled castes.[3] Another point of friction lies in the opinions held by each about the other. Many elite-caste MLA's and political activists apparently consider the backward castes to be scheduled (that is, Untouchables).[4] Several spoke of them in derogatory phrases and contemptuous tones. Members of the backward castes are aware of these attitudes. A Yadav MLA commented about his Brahmin opponent, in not a little bitterness, "They are like the white

---

[2] Vithal Krishnaji Khedkar and Dr. Raghunath Vithal Khedkar, *The Divine Heritage of the Yadavs* (Allahabad, 1959), p. xiii. The authors are Yadavs.

[3] Deep Narain Singh, MLA, kindly made available official figures provided him by Home Minister Hargovind Singh. (Interview, February 7, 1964). The 1.1 percent of the gazetted offices held by backward castes in 1946 had dropped to 0.6 percent by 1960. The scheduled castes increased their proportion from 0.5 to 1.0 percent during that period. The elite Hindu castes increased from 38.0 to 88.0 percent, with Muslims holding the remaining offices.

[4] In gathering data on the caste of the 1962 MLA candidates, it was found that elite-caste respondents frequently reported reserved-seat candidates to be of specific backward castes, even when reminded that only members of scheduled castes could contest. Such responses indicated lack of knowledge of the constituency as well as the opinion held of backward castes.

people in your country." In Rae Bareli in 1951–1952 it was reported that members of the backward castes marched through the streets shouting "Blacken the faces of the Brahmans, Thakurs, and Banias!"

The opposition parties are in a favorable position to exploit the rivalry of elite and backward castes because the Congress is dominated by the elite castes. Two Congress leaders, in a position to know, referred to elite-caste supremacy in the Congress district parties and to the efforts of elite-caste leaders to halt the rise of lower-caste leaders as factors important in explaining the growth of opposition parties. Another prominent leader agreed that lower-caste leadership is not desired in Congress, but did not consider this a reason for the rising strength of the opposition. There are important Congress backward-caste leaders in only two out of 54 district parties (Mainpuri and Faizabad). A party with elite-caste leadership could satisfy some backward-caste ambitions by giving MLA tickets to their members while refusing to admit them into the inner circles of leadership. But only 27 tickets were given to backward-caste members, while more than 260 were given to members of elite Hindu castes in 1962. Congress respondents related elite-caste dominance to earlier mobilization in point of time. Their better education, higher economic position, and higher ritual status in a hierarchic society would also have to be taken into account. Since independence, members of the elite castes have maintained and in some districts strengthened their position in Congress.

Opposition parties have four handicaps in exploiting the ambitions of the backward castes. First, opposition parties are also led by members of elite castes. It is difficult for these leaders to divorce themselves from general societal rivalries and attitudes. In the three parties under study, however, the elite caste leaders have been willing to open up state and district leadership positions, both in the organizational and legislative wings, to members of backward castes. The Socialist Party has taken a policy stand favoring the backward castes. Second, there are financial difficulties in building a party based on backward castes. Although some individuals are well off, most are not. Those who finance the party frequently like to exercise some influence over candidate selection and policy determination. Third, the movement of many of these castes into politics is just beginning. The rate of mobilization is not the same for every caste or throughout the state for one caste. Witness the difference of the Yadav community in our six case studies. In some places to try to base a party on backward-versus-elite caste rivalry would be premature.

The fourth handicap is related to the ambitions of the backward castes. A respondent in Allahabad city summed up the problem with much perception:

The backward classes are rising in importance. The Kurmis and Ahirs are middle castes and middle class. They are really upper-middle caste and class, particularly in villages. Not many of them live in urban areas. They are becoming politically conscious all over the state and in this district too.

They want social respectability and to be recognized as Kshattriyas. They want to share in power (ruling power) formerly held by the Brahmins, Thakurs, Kayasths, and Banias. They want to be recognized as equal in this group. They have been handicapped by lack of education and "villagation." But now they are getting educated. In this district they have set up caste schools.

Right now they are going into all parties, but in the last 4–5 years have tended to go to PSP (or SP) rather than Congress. They seem to have realized that they cannot break through into the top Congress leadership ranks. The problem is that they want to share in power and get social respectability—which leads them to Congress. Even if they are only third-level leaders in Congress they get these things because Congress is the ruling party.

In opposition parties they can get leadership positions (the fact that an Ahir is the PSP Assembly party leader is a great fillip to their ambitions) and can get psychological satisfaction of being leaders of their own party. By taking over an opposition party they can get exclusive recognition of their own personality. Nevertheless, in the opposition they can't do much—can't share in ruling. But if any of these opposition parties—particularly PSP or SP— showed an increase in strength, then there might be a massive shift of middle castes to them.

But at present they are vacillating between the desire for a share of power and social respectability (Congress), and, on the other hand, recognition of their own personality and leadership positions (opposition parties).

Other respondents spoke in the same vein, including the editor of *The Yadav,* himself a Congressman, who pointed to the PSP as the party attracting many Yadavs. The vacillation can be seen in the post-election changes of party membership: three of the five Praja Socialists who joined Congress after the 1962 election were Yadav, one was Thakur, and the last of a scheduled caste. In trying to build a party on the backward castes there is a hazard that specific local parties may be reduced to naught as successful backward class leaders are enticed to join Congress. The dominant party does recognize strength—although the strength must be proven at the polls first.[5]

Another tension available for utilization is that between the different backward castes, as seen in Farrukhabad, Bara Banki, and Moradabad districts. Differential mobilization rates appear to play a role. In Saurikh constituency a Lodha said: "The Yadavs have had their MLA. Now it's our turn." It is conceivable, however, that concurrent mobilization of more than one backward caste in any locale could lead to a similar rivalry. A few respondents pointed to the desire of leaders of several backward castes to be leaders of all backward castes. One Kurmi MLA wryly remarked: "Those who have no leaders perish. Those who have many leaders perish." The present and potential lack of unity among backward castes offers an opportunity to many parties and a problem for any one party trying to build on backward-versus-elite caste tensions. Divisions within the backward castes, however, can mitigate tensions based on rivalry between elite and backward castes. Such amelioration of one set of rivalries by another is significant from the standpoint of resolving conflict within the confines of a constitutional order.

It is also possible for friction to exist between the scheduled and elite castes, between scheduled and backward castes and between the different scheduled castes. Two factors operate to limit friction between scheduled and nonscheduled. One is the system

[5] In a one-party-dominant system, a function of opposition parties can be to provide a channel for political participation of newly emerging social groups. In time, the dominant party can broaden its base by including these groups within it. The process is similar to the third parties in the American political system which promoted various programs only to have them taken over by one of the major parties when they became popular. The process has also operated for minority ethnic groups in the United States. Such a process could serve to maintain a one-party-dominant system. The question is whether the Congress elite-caste leaders will react to increasing elite-versus-backward-caste tension by defensively closing their ranks or by opening them.

of reservations for scheduled castes in Assembly seats, governmental positions, and so on. The other is that the scheduled castes tend to support Congress because the dominant party has been responsible for policies giving them advantages. The possibility of future friction between scheduled and higher castes cannot be totally discounted. Should it come, divisions within the scheduled castes would probably alleviate tensions between them and the other caste groupings.

While there are a number of tactics which politicians can utilize to gain votes, and a number of pressures which they and their supporters can utilize, these necessarily operate on a much narrower scale. Personal benefits such as jobs, scholarships, licenses, permits, loan extensions, and gifts such as "gold" (brass) garlands, radios, liquor, drugs, and rupees can be promised or arranged. More general group benefits can also be promised, such as the building of roads, bridges, canals, drainage ditches, and schools. Agreements can be reached regarding mutual support on different political levels. Past or present aid in time of trouble can be utilized to gain support. Ties of community, caste, and caste group can be called upon, within limitations. No candidate could win solely by the support of his own caste, and a caste-bound candidate is a liability to his caste. Yet it is often considered highly desirable, if not mandatory, to be able to carry a large part of one's own caste. The tie of "friends and neighbors" can be employed to gain support. Of utmost importance is the tie established by personal contact. Economic sanctions can be employed, as well as threats against life and property.

In the few situations that were described of candidates' attempting to become the advocate of much lower classes or lower castes, and of getting their support without the mediation of the upper classes or castes, politicians reported using similar tactics. By agitations and incarceration in jails on behalf of such groups, candidates were able to demonstrate their identification with the groups. The sacrifices and extraordinary measures served to make it quickly and visibly clear to rural, illiterate, apathetic, lower-class, and lower-caste groups that a person was "one with them" and their champion. It may be that an important function of agitations is to overcome the barriers of class and caste.

Electoral campaigns and party-building activities have brought about some changes in patterns of behavior which in the long run may have significant effects on the Indian social system. Many politicians have found it necessary to violate the customs of social intercourse in this highly stratified society in order to obtain support. They take tea, water, and both pacca and kachha food from the hands of very low-caste people.[6] They touch the feet of the lower castes, sit at the foot of the charpoy and give the place of honor to men of lower castes, and attach the honorific "sri" prefix and "jii" suffix to the names of lower-caste people. A few follow these practices out of conviction; most, out of political expediency. There are differing degrees of changed behavior patterns among MLA's and activists. In the constituencies studied there appeared, generally speaking, to be a relatively steady gradation toward traditional behavior patterns revolving about two criteria: the position of an individual within the party organization (the more important a position, the more changed the behavior), and rural or urban residence (the more urban, the more changed the behavior).[7] It is possible that different behavior patterns will develop on the lines of strictly party membership. This is illustrated by the remarks of a Kurmi activist:

We will take food from Pasis [scheduled caste]—we will eat food together in the same plate—if they are in our party. We will not take food from those Pasis who are not in our party. And if a Pasi should leave our party, then we will not take food from him. Within the party caste does not matter. In Congress it is the same. . . . No, we do not take food from Congress Pasis, and upper-caste people in Congress do not take food from Pasis of our party.

To get the support of those aspiring to higher status, it is sometimes necessary to grant recognition by changed behavior. But what is done out of expediency by politicians today may be regarded in a different light by affected groups and by the younger generation.

[6] Indians generally accept food and drink from persons of caste status on roughly the same level as their own or on a higher level. The restrictions are slightly relaxed on foods cooked with oil (pacca) and most stringent on those cooked with water (kachha). To take water or water-cooked food from a person of a caste considerably lower in status than one's own is a significant violation.

[7] Interaction of the two criteria gives us four groups, listed here in ascending order as to gradation toward traditional behavior: (1) High party position and urban residence; (2) High party position and rural residence; (3) Low party position and urban residence; (4) Low party position and rural residence.

Candidate-Selection Processes

Manipulation of societal frictions is often related to the identity of the candidates. This brings up the significant question of candidate selection. In some of the case studies, last-minute selection of Congress candidates appeared to aid the opposition. Until the ticket decision was made there was little incentive to organize or mend fences; the lateness of the hour proved a handicap once the decision was made. Do the opposition parties set up candidates at an earlier date? All the opposition parties have an established formal procedure for nominating candidates at approximately the same time as the Congress. As in the Congress, the state and national units of the party approve local candidates and decide among contestants. The informal preliminary procedures vary. Jan Sangh leaders emphasize that the formal procedure is a ritual following decisions made at a much earlier time. Through the organizational wing, and particularly the organizing secretaries, a search for "suitable" candidates is begun years before an election. Individuals are given informal assurance of the ticket and encouraged to organize. The organizing secretary and district leaders quietly promote the candidate within the constituency. By the time of formal announcement the road has been well paved. Dissension, or the effect of dissension, has been minimized. Although the search for candidates begins early, it is not completed for all constituencies until the formal deadline. Thus there are some "last minute" candidacies—and some of the individuals may have a fairly weak and short tie to the party. Immediately after an election, informal assurance of the ticket for the next election is frequently given contestants.

In contrast, informal assurance of a ticket is not usually given in advance in the PSP. A proposal for "permanent candidates"—that is, the selection of candidates two or three years in advance of an expected election—was rejected. Apparently district leaders begin surveying the field for candidates just before the initiation of the formal procedure. Competing applicants informally appeal to competing state leaders and, through a state factional leader, to the national party. In cases of contest, getting the ticket depends on "who one knows" on a higher level and the willingness of that person to back one's claim. When local struggle is transformed to state and national factional competition, the issue becomes one of prestige, "face," as well as the strength of the leaders involved. Dissension on the local level becomes more intense. The final decision is made late, and the disappointed applicants have been known to run as Independents or to fail to work for the chosen candidate. This is not conducive to victory. The PSP procedure is similar to that of Congress. The dominant party can afford to lose several seats through factional infighting, but the consequences for a small opposition party are disastrous. One method of solving the problem of multiple candidacies is to give competitors the ticket in different constituencies. But constituencies available for outside candidates are not likely to be well organized; if they are, there is likely to be internal opposition to an outsider. In addition, if a contestant is given a ticket in a constituency other than his own, he is likely to try and take "his" workers along to help campaign, thus reducing the manpower available to the party in the original constituency.

Of course, in many constituencies there is no contest at all for the PSP nomination. The problem is in finding someone to take the ticket. In other constituencies individuals are aware that they will obtain the ticket with no difficulty. Sitting MLA's and those who have singlehandedly built up a local party are examples. These can, however, be asked to contest the MP seat—for a variety of reasons. The individual may be considered a strong candidate for the MP constituency. But local factionalism can be a factor, as well as an assumption that the seat is "safe" for any party member. Such assumptions in the past have been wildly erroneous.

What types of considerations are taken into account in selecting candidates? A first consideration is who has organized the party in a constituency. Second is the particular characteristics of the constituency. Third is the identity of other candidates, primarily of the Congress. If there is a strong Congress leader who is likely to get or keep the party ticket, an opposition party can attempt to nominate a particular candidate to defeat him. If there is doubt about the identity of the Congress candidate, the opposition must set up a candidate on other considerations. Otherwise the opposition party would be choosing candidates after the Congress, which would probably be an overwhelming obstacle to victory. Although the exact Congress candidate is unknown, opposition party leaders do have an idea of the probable nominees and of those groups in the constituency on which Congress strength is based. Along with these considerations, party leaders report as important such qualifications as: education; the ability to finance one's own campaign and possibly the campaigns of other candidates of the party; a background of social service; and activity in a number of organizations (particularly semiofficial economic organizations).

Electoral Agreements

There are several difficulties in forging electoral agreements with other opposition parties. One is that different opposition parties in the same locale can be led by or draw their strength from rival groups, none of which would be disposed to aid its rivals. Second, an electoral campaign can be viewed as an opportunity to publicize the party and its candidate, symbols, and program, and also to acquire workers for the future, rather than as a contest for immediate victory. Because elections are generally held at five-year intervals, party leaders are often reluctant to pass up any one election. Third, desiring ultimate victory for their own party, leaders are often just as opposed to other opposition parties as they are to the Congress. Indeed, there are instances in which an opposition party's leaders would prefer the Congress to another specific opposition party.

It is rare for state-wide electoral agreements to be reached between opposition parties. Formal or informal agreements are sometimes made on lower levels. This can involve one party's setting up a specific candidate or not setting up a candidate. In the latter case, it is calculated that two candidates would split the same votes and enable some other candidate to win. On the other hand, one effective method of aiding a party is to set up a candidate who will draw votes away from a particular opponent. These are termed dummy candidates.

Dummies can be set up by the major candidates themselves as well as by cooperative parties. Frequently the deposit and campaign funds are provided by those setting up dummies, although occasionally encouragement is sufficient to fire ambitions. One complaint of opposition parties is the lack of funds to set up dummies on a wide scale. This was not the case in one constituency, in which the opposition party candidate set up four dummies to draw votes from the Congress, while the Congress candidate set up one dummy to defeat his prime opponent and the dissident Congress faction set up two dummies to help defeat the Congress candidate. Out of nine candidates, seven were dummies. When several candidates set up dummies, gauging strength becomes more difficult, and uncertainty of outcome is compounded.

Party Organization

No attempt has been made to discuss the formal party organization prescribed by the various parties, for two reasons. First, at the time of the study the formal organization was in the process of modification for the Jan Sangh and the merger of the socialist parties opened the question of what form would be chosen. Secondly, it is doubtful that full-scale organizations on the "old" plan exist anywhere in Uttar Pradesh on the local level. The prescription stood as an ideal. The formal skeleton "paper" organizations which were set up do not appear to have relevance for understanding either the process of party building, electoral victory, or comparison of parties in different constituencies. Local leaders simply do the best they can with what they have, and the resulting edifice in fact rarely resembles the theoretical. For example, in constituencies studied it was common at election time to disregard the formal pattern and set up an organization based on geographic divisions of the constituency. Pratapgarh South was divided into two parts, Moradabad Rural into three, Rudauli into five, and so forth. The divisons were based on personnel available and on geographic features of the area.

Two analytic schemes were developed in the course of the study which appears to have usefulness for studying one party and for comparing parties on the local level. One scheme, set forth in the Introduction, distinguishes the permanent party members (pillars and regulars), from the electoral supporters (notables, campaigners, and voters).

The permanent party members personally identify with the party. They participate in and help organize party activities in between elections as well as at election time. They can be counted on to stay in the party without being wooed in each campaign. A defection within the pillar echelon is a party split. Pillars will take a portion of all other echelons with them. Defections not involving pillars but among regulars seriously weaken the party. The weakening effect may be far out of proportion to the status or numbers of defecting members. One reason is that these people have personally identified with a party in a society in which very few have so identified. Their defection tends to be regarded by others as a symptom of grave troubles and decay within the party, an indicator of party decline.

The electoral supporters are individuals who support and work to further party victory in specific elections, but who do not personally identify with the party. Their support is contingent on a host of factors and they must be approached and won over before every election. The importance of their support—particularly the notables—at election time must not be underestimated, for it is usually required for victory. Defections within the electoral party affect the party's electoral fortunes, but do not have the same repercussions as defections of regulars or pillars. The shift does not jeopardize the continuance of the party itself. This is partly because these supporters do not identify with the party and others do not identify them with it. Furthermore, notables shift both to and from the party in question. The least important of the four groups from the standpoint of electoral victory and continuance of the party are the campaigners.

Political recruitment and socialization are two of the functions performed by these groups. Individuals in each echelon recruit others into that echelon and into the ones below. In the process they participate in the political socialization of the populace. By their own activities they are learning to play new roles.

In elections the four echelons perform an intelligence and communication function. Each collects information on the political predispositions of individuals and groups, and transmits it to regulars and pillars. The pillars, and on a lower level the regulars, collate and analyze information and then make judgments of the political potential of their own supporters vis-à-vis supporters of other parties. Each echelon is similarly involved in eliciting grievances and demands, and transmitting these along with relevant data concerning points of vulnerability of specific individuals and groups to higher echelons. This data can then be utilized by higher echelons to garner support.

In the interelection period it is primarily the permanent party members, especially the pillars, who serve to elicit, articulate, and transmit grievances and demands to party leaders and governmental officials. The pillars and to a lesser extent the regulars perform an essential function of communication within the party, between the party and constituents, between the government and constituents. As such, they frequently perform a broker function.

Although these functions are performed, they are not performed equally well by all parties, nor to the same extent. One factor affecting performance is the number of pillars and regulars. Another factor is the geographic location within the constituency of the pillars and regulars. The functions are less well performed in Pratapgarh South and Rudauli, where the Jan Sangh pillars are concentrated in a town, than in Saurikh, where the PSP pillars are widely dispersed. Another factor is the occupation of permanent party members. Occupations which provide permanent party members with extensive contacts to large numbers of people (shopkeepers, for example), or which allow irregular hours with considerable time off during the year (farmers, for example), give more opportunities to carry on these functions. Other factors include personal characteristics and predispositions.

Another function performed by the structures is the spreading of the prestige of governmental office. The prestige of an MLA is reflected to differing degrees on those in various echelons, with pillars benefiting the most. Through their relationships with others those in the various echelons further diffuse the honor. Personal contact with the MLA in the interelection period contributes to this end.

It is necessary to remember that a political organization operates within a certain context. There are elective offices other than MLA and MP which are also sources of prestige. The political networks surrounding them provide a linkage to government. There are social, economic, and communication networks which exist aside from party. Some of the functions performed by the party structures can be performed by these other structures, networks, and individuals. At the same time, parties can try to make use of these networks and positions to augment their organization.

The sceond scheme of analysis defines various networks of influence utilized by a party. These include a raja network, shopkeeper network, lawyer network, teacher network, caste or community network, and pradhan-group network. Each provides a basis for the establishment of a political relationship. Each provides a certain channel of influence. The raja network describes a relationship between a former raja (talukdar) and other former talukdars, zamindars, employees of former talukdars and zamindars, along with those who lived within talukdari and zamindari estates. By its nature, this network is landed. The shopkeeper network describes a relationship between shopkeepers and their customers or clients. The pradhan-group network describes a relationship between those who occupy or contested certain positions and groups or individuals who have ties of various types to them (factional, economic, social, and so on).

The case studies suggest that there are differences in the "vote-getting" and "notable-acquiring" capabilities of different categories of individuals. For example, one raja has far greater capabilities than one shopkeeper. That lawyer and teacher networks were subsidiary in the constituencies in which they were identified perhaps indicates that the capabilities of these individuals is less than either a raja or shopkeeper. Network analysis can provide information about the party internally, but it has greater usefulness in analyzing the basis of party electoral strength through its concentration on the process of obtaining support. It complements the structural scheme by focusing on the patterns of relationships and influences utilized by parties.

Both schemes are useful for comparing local parties. The structural echelons can be analyzed according to the socioeconomic characteristics and geographical distribution of their members, and to the manner of performing various functions. Networks and their combinations can be identified and compared. The interplay of forces in an election can be better understood. Some perception of the intensity of these forces can be obtained by comparison. For example, the two constituencies with greatest tension were Pratapgarh South and Bhitauli, which were characterized by coincidence of cleavages on the two indices of caste and class for the major protagonists. In each, the two major parties drew their strength from the two major opposing groups in the society. In contrast, the tensions between Hindus and Muslims in Rudauli and Moradabad Rural and between castes in Saurikh were not reinforced by clear-cut coinciding cleavages on other indices. The friction was milder than in the first two constituencies. The tensions were milder still in Karchana, where there were a number of cross-cutting cleavages. That degree of intensity should be related to reinforcing cleavages is to be expected.[8] An important question is whether there are particular combinations of coinciding cleavages which produce greater tensions than others.

The two schemes have relevance for analyzing the party-building process. It appears that a party can become momentarily victorious through the accretion of notables with an extremely small permanent party sector. On the other hand, unless a permanent party is vast in size and quite well developed (much larger than in any constituency studied), adherence of many notables will be necessary for victory. For continuous victories a permanent party must be developed which is capable of activating and winning the support of many notables. Inasmuch as the capability of different kinds of persons varies, the size of the permanent party required for victory will vary also. A party can become momentarily victorious through exploitation of strong socioeconomic tensions. For continuous victories, a strong permanent organization is required in order to reactivate those tensions, and to take advantage of or mitigate the effects of more recent tensions.

[8] David B. Truman, *The Governmental Process* (New York: Alfred A. Knopf, 1959), pp. 505–526.

Part Four

MAINTENANCE OF OPPOSITION PARTIES

ALL PARTIES IN UTTAR PRADESH, including the Congress, have a problem in successfully maintaining a winning local party. In every election old seats are lost and new seats are won. Only 4 of the 25 Socialist seats of 1957 were retained in 1962; only 11 of 44 Praja Socialist seats, and 8 of 17 Jan Sangh seats. Of the 89 new seats won in 1962 by these three parties, 75 had previously been held by the Congress and 14 by other parties. Most of the seats held by the three parties in 1957 but lost in 1962 were won by Congress. All told, only 197 of 430 constituencies remained in control of the same party in both elections, while 233 changed hands.[1] This is reminiscent of a game of "musical chairs." The problems of maintenance are discussed in chapter xii.

The parties also have difficulties with intraparty maintenance. It is not easy to measure the extent of defections and schisms within these three opposition parties. On the district level the press occasionally reports, in a cryptic statement, that a certain number of party workers have resigned to join another party. Not all defections or splits are reported, however, and some of the reported schisms are erroneous. While party splits on the state level are reported, the effects on all the district parties are not. Any numbers given are likely to be "guesstimates" which are inflated or deflated according to the bias of the politician providing the information.

An important factor leading to party disruption can be internal factionalism. The press gives considerable attention to Congress

[1] Of the 233 seats which changed hands, 217 were won by different parties with different candidates, while 16 were won by the same candidate though of a different party. For example, three PSP legislators in 1957 ran and won as Congressmen in 1962; some 1957 Congress MLA's ran and won as Independents in the third general elections. Of the 197 constituencies held by the same party in the two elections, 119 were won by the same candidate and 78 by different candidates.

factions, but it rarely provides information about factions in opposition parties, doing so only when a split is imminent, or when the division is national. Similarly, the press records the winners of state party elections, but does not usually discuss the politics of such elections. While the scant attention given by the press to small opposition parties in a dominant-party system is to be expected, it does make the task of research difficult. Party leaders themselves will generally discuss maintenance problems in specific situations when asked, but are not eager to advertise internal problems. Furthermore, statements and interpretations provided by respondents must be checked against those of others, for respondents are the only real source. It is sometimes difficult to identify "neutral observers."

The different types of problems faced by these three parties in maintaining district and state parties are discussed in chapter xiii.

Chapter XII

MAINTAINING A WINNING LOCAL PARTY

IN THE CONSTITUENCIES STUDIED, it was obvious that the local party had been built to winning status by comparatively few people, and also that it was maintained by few. The key figure is normally the MLA. Others expect him to take the leading role. One problem confronting the MLA is contact and communication with his supporters. His time is divided between the state capital, the district town, his constituency, and, if he resides elsewhere, his home. If his home is outside the constituency, his problems are compounded. He often has to earn a living, generally desires to have some family life, and needs to relax occasionally, but must also maintain the party. His assorted activities necessarily involve a great deal of "wasted" time spent in travel between disparate points. MLA's who can turn over the task of earning a living to others have an advantage over those, such as doctors or lawyers, who try to keep up a practice during their term of office. The latter have precious little time to "keep their fences mended."

Communication Patterns

There appear to be four basic patterns of communication.[1] First, an MLA can thoroughly and repeatedly tour his constituency. This is strenuous, tiring, and time consuming. In addition, those who desire to contact the MLA have difficulty locating him. Extensive touring can make an MLA inaccessible. Very few MLA's appear to follow this pattern.

[1] Some of the Jan Sangh MLA's reported establishing a pattern of contact in neighboring constituencies in which Jan Sangh candidates were defeated in 1962. A few of the Praja Socialist and Socialist MLA's maintain contact with a clientele outside the constituency, such as with labor unions in other districts, with teachers or teachers' associations of other districts, and with kisan group leaders.

Second, an MLA can settle in one place in his constituency, letting the people come to him. This renders him accessible to those needing his services, but it can mean a communications breakdown with those who do not need his aid. The permanent party is not extended; notables can drift away. This pattern seems to be followed by a large number of MLA's.

Third, an MLA can establish his headquarters in one place but occasionally make one-day excursions within the constituency. This combines advantageous features of the first and second patterns, but the location of the headquarters—usually the candidate's home—may present a disadvantage. Unless the locale is in the center of the constituency, daily jaunts may encompass only one geographic segment. Unless the headquarters is readily accessible, supporters may be loath to make the effort of going there. It appears that many MLA's utilize this pattern.

Fourth, an MLA can establish a few centers in different parts of the constituency and make a fairly systematic round of the centers several times a year. Visitation may coincide with customary gatherings, such as a market day. The time spent in each center on any occasion may vary. A fairly definite schedule with advance notification seems to be needed. It is difficult for many to make, much less keep, such a schedule. Some MLA's appear to follow this pattern, though fewer than follow patterns two and three.

It may be that one factor in the defeat of MLA's in subsequent elections is the communication pattern. A recently built party is likely to have few permanent members, either pillars or regulars. To keep the support of notables and others and transform these supporters into permanent members is necessary for continued success at the polls. Basic to such transformation is contact. The two most utilized patterns place the onus of establishing contact on the supporters rather than on the MLA. Many supporters do not take the initiative, either through lack of need,[2] apathy, or the conviction that it is the duty of the MLA to come to them.

---

[2] Lack of need carries two meanings. The supporter may not need the aid of the MLA in getting what he wants. Some notables are or consider themselves to be capable of filling their own needs by their own actions. Or the supporter may not need anything. Some respondents, when asked whether the MLA had ever helped them, replied: "No. Why should he? I don't need anything."

Many of the individuals who do establish contact with the MLA are not notables, nor are they permanent party members; many are "little people" without much influence. Thus even though an MLA talks with and aids hundreds of people, he may derive little political benefit.

There are two subsidiary communication patterns which can be established for a short time. One is based on agitations. Whether it be concerned with a purely local matter (for example, a police case) or with broad public policy, an agitation can be the occasion for mobilizing many people on a basis other than traditional loyalties. Moral indignation, economic interest, or both, can be appealed to. And, as some respondents said, "It gives the workers something to do." It is one thing to exhort party workers to help in maintaining the party by visiting with notables and voters in surrounding villages; it is another thing to ask workers to make such contacts for the purpose of publicizing a grievance and mobilizing people for an agitation. Participation in the agitation itself provides a psychological lift and a renewal of the party tie. A spirit of sacrifice and of accomplishment is present. It is customary for the party to pay transportation costs for those who participate in agitations held in distant towns or the state capital. Demonstrations in these locations, therefore, provide a free trip and a chance to see the sights. A gay holiday spirit often infuses those parading down the streets, protesting a tax increase or the high price of food, or demanding a higher price for sugar cane. These features make the agitation an attractive form of action for party building and maintenance which at the same time puts pressure on the Government. Agitations, however, are not and cannot be a monthly activity of the party. They are supplementary.

A second subsidiary channel of communication is the attendance of the MLA at various celebrations, such as marriages. The major religious celebrations are often a time of visiting one's friends and paying one's respects. Some MLA's prefer to remain at home on such days so as to be accessible to others. Presence not only at the "good times" but also at the "bad times" is enjoined by some. Being available during floods, crop failures, and bad frosts and offering sympathy and trying to relieve distress are considered helpful in building a favorable image.

Material Benefits

Another aspect of maintaining a party is the obtaining of material advantages for constituents. All MLA's gave long lists of the types of assistance they are expected to provide, including: jobs, scholarships, loans of various types, cement permits, gun permits, medical aid, police aid, wells, schools, roads, and transfer of officials.[3] Most MLA's said they helped all who came to them; however, they also reported that important supporters of other parties generally go to their own party leaders for assistance. Thus, his own supporters, together with independents (regardless of whether or how they voted) would seem to account for most of the people approaching an MLA.

Some students of India and Indian politics have expressed the opinion that it is immoral, unethical, or non-Western for an elected politician to aid his caste fellows.[4] What has been apparently overlooked is the relationship between caste and supporter, on the one hand, and between supporter and politician, on the other. To claim that it is non-Western for an elected politician to provide benefits for his supporters is not a tenable position. Many

[3] Practically all of these forms of assistance, obviously, involve governmental agencies. Where a permit is needed, the help of the MLA may be sought in getting the permit from the agency and then in actually getting the agency to act. Cement, for instance, is scarce and the prospective user must first obtain a permit from a governmental agency specifying a legitimate use (there are some checks to prevent cement from reaching the black market). After getting the permit, he may have to wait for months to get the cement, but politicians can help a person, in effect, to "jump to the top of the list" of those waiting. The permit is not a building permit (which may already have been obtained), but a permit to obtain cement.

A highly desired type of well is the "tube well," which is dug deep and fitted out with an electric pump, and has narrow channels leading to the fields. Governmental agencies construct the wells, provide and install the equipment, and connect the pump to the nearest source of electricity (which may be at a great distance). The demand is greater than the supply, and people expect the MLA to persuade the governmental agency to install a tube well near their fields. For other types of wells, they have to get permits to cut down trees (to use in shoring up the well) and to obtain cement (for lining the well), and here also they expect the MLA's assistance.

[4] For two examples see: M. N. Srinivas, "Castes: Can They Exist in the India of Tomorrow?" in Srinivas (ed.), *Caste in Modern India* (Bombay, 1962), p. 72, and C. von Furer-Haimendorf, "Caste and Politics in South Asia," C. H. Philips (ed.), *Politics and Society in India* (London, 1963), pp. 52–70.

would argue that the immoral or unethical nature of such practices is untenable also. It is specious to say that it is all right for a politician to aid supporters as long as they are not members of his caste. If members of his caste have provided support, they have moved into a different category. There could indeed be criticism leveled if a politician aided only his caste fellows among his supporters, but such has not been at issue. By concentrating on the caste aspect, others have neglected the very important question of whom a politician does, in fact, aid—only his caste fellows, only his supporters, constituents generally, or whatever.

Aid is given to individuals and to groups. The bulk of individual aid is in the form of an MLA's signature on an application or a short note to an official, neither of which is customarily followed up by the MLA on his own initiative. If a matter is repeatedly brought to his attention, he may then take further action, such as speaking with an official or asking a question during Question Hour in the Assembly. Many requests are made of an MLA every month. Respondents who were questioned about the procedure uniformly replied that they signed all applications put before them and wrote the short notes requested. For the bulk of routine requests for aid, it would be unusual for an MLA to inquire of the party identification, the voting behavior, or the caste of a supplicant. Even in those cases in which an MLA knows a supplicant has supported another candidate, he gives aid in hope of future electoral support (or, at least, less opposition).

Some of the MLA's pointed out that greater personal attention is given to needs and requests of key individuals in their constituency. These individuals played an important role in their election and thus would fall into our classification of pillars or notables. A few noted that the official's knowledge of important supporters of an MLA was sufficient, without intercession of the MLA at all. For example, one staunch party worker applied for a government job before the 1962 election, but was turned down. After the election he again applied (without the MLA's signature on the form) and got the job. The MLA claimed to have done nothing: "They knew he was my supporter." Another respondent, a teacher, had been transferred to a distant school after the 1957 election, in which he had supported a losing candidate. Requests for transfer were ignored. After the 1962 election, in which his candidate was victorious, he again applied for transfer and got it. According to the respondent and the MLA, no help from the MLA was needed. Besides being known as a supporter, the notables and pillars can work through other individuals than the MLA to satisfy their needs. One respondent pointed out that for certain matters he asked the aid of a district party leader (a lawyer) in the district town; for other matters he approached the MLA. Another noted that for certain wants he worked through the block pramukh. Aid can also be obtained from Block Representatives, chief judges of rural courts, cooperative society presidents, and the like. The giving of aid is not the sole prerogative of the MLA. Nevertheless, being an MLA gives one access to and influence with many officials and agencies—both governmental agencies and those sponsored and encouraged by the Government —from whom benefits, favors, and material advantages can be garnered both for oneself and for one's supporters. In the constituencies studied, aid had been given to supporters who were not of the MLA's caste.[5]

Unlike some systems of government, in Uttar Pradesh the opposition party legislators do not automatically have control of any patronage positions. The need for jobs to hand out to supporters —or to people named by supporters—seems to be one factor in the establishment of private schools by active politicians. Both teaching and administrative positions have to be filled, scholarships can be provided students, and special arrangements about tuition can be made. In addition, building a school presents an image of the MLA as a man who is actively seeking the betterment of the people. In some cases the profits from a school can be utilized for necessary expenditures by the MLA. As can be seen in Table 49, a surprising number of legislators have set up schools.

Material advantages to groups are also provided by MLA's. Roads, schools, wells, canals, and drainage ditches are examples. Supporters can be instrumental in pressuring an MLA for these, but other individuals and groups, many of whom are not supporters (or caste fellows) of the MLA, also benefit. On some occasions the MLA can work through agencies of government to

[5] These details were learned from individuals in the field, not from the MLA. Some names had been given by the MLA's; others had not. Aid to nonsupporters was not taken up.

TABLE 49

SCHOOLS ESTABLISHED BY JAN SANGH, PRAJA SOCIALIST,
AND SOCIALIST MLA's

(by percent and number of party MLA's)

Number of Schools	Jan Sangh		Praja Socialist		Socialist	
None	58.3	(28)	48.5	(16)	50.0	(11)
One to two	25.0	(12)	36.4	(12)	45.5	(10)
Three or more	14.6	(7)	12.1	(4)	4.5	(1)
Not ascertained	2.1	(1)	3.0	(1)	—	—
Total	100.0	(48)	100.0	(33)	100.0	(22)

obtain construction or funds for construction of schools, roads, and so on. On other occasions, an MLA can spur a village panchayat or a group of people to take care of the matter. In part, activities of this nature place the MLA in the role of an educator informing citizens of what they can do and what is available through government agencies.

When a Congress MLA is elected, certain individuals and groups tend to benefit from his aid more than others. When an opposition MLA is elected, different individuals and groups also obtain advantages; if different opposition MLA's are elected, then still different segments of society are benefited. The Congress supporters still obtain some advantages when an opposition MLA is elected because the Congress forms the government at the national, state, and district level in Uttar Pradesh. In general, most of the block leaders are Congressmen, and most of the semiofficial agencies have a majority of members who are Congressmen. Election of an opposition MLA means, then, that a different segment of society joins the ranks of those obtaining advantages.

To obtain advantages the MLA operates in several arenas. One is the district level, with two spheres of action: district administrative officials and the District Board. The effectiveness of MLA's on any level is partially dependent on the interest and activity of the MLA himself. Beyond this, his effectiveness with administrative officials appears to be related to several factors. Most MLA's reported district administrative officials to be receptive rather than resistant (but some qualified their judgment with notes that officials often failed to follow through on promises). Most considered being in the opposition a handicap. In the constituencies studied, however, two factors appeared to be important. One was the relationship—cordial or bitter—between the opposition and Congress leaders in the district. An official has to take some cognizance of political realities. Another is the administrative official's position in relationship to the social tensions generated by the opposition party.

The effectiveness of an opposition party (including the MLA) on the District Board is related in part to the size of the opposition contingent in comparison with the Congress and the Congress factions. Congress divisions can give an opposition party leverage. This is, however, affected by the ability of an opposition party to maintain its cohesion when facing the Congress. If an opposition party is divided into mirror factions of the majority party, it loses some leverage and stands in danger of major defections. A third factor is the personal relationship existing between leaders of the opposition and majority parties, which, again, can be a reflection of the social tensions generated by the two parties. If there is bitter hostility between the two, the opposition can be rendered totally ineffective. Even a fairly large opposition party group can obtain nothing, while in a district with friendly rivalry a relatively small group can obtain more.

On the block level, there are again two spheres of action: block administrative officials and the elected Block Committees. The effectiveness of an opposition MLA with officials is related to the same factors as with district officials, plus one other: the relationship of the block pramukh and the block official, on the one hand, and the relationship of the pramukh and the MLA, on the other. If, for example, a pramukh has ambitions of becoming an MLA himself, and attempts to build a base in the block, he may apply pressures on the block officials which will tend to limit the MLA's influence. If more than one of these factors should operate in the same direction, the MLA's effectiveness would tend to be reduced still further. Of course, basic to the whole question is the MLA's interest in and concern with matters under block jurisdiction.

Faced with the cross-pressures of satisfying constituent demands and maintaining adhesion to the party, several MLA's have "resigned" from Block Committee politics. Technically, parties do not exist in the Block Committee or in the block elections. There are sometimes difficulties in resolving tensions between party and caste affiliation, or between party and some other local affiliation. If an MLA tries to muster support, whether it be for policy or for pramukh, whether it be on party or nonparty lines, he endangers the party. Nonetheless, some MLA's do take part in Block Committee politics. Their effectiveness is related to the numbers of supporters on the committee, whether these be party men, caste fellows, personal friends and neighbors, and the like. It also depends on the political ambitions of the block pramukh. Another factor is the scheduling of Block Committee meetings; some MLA's pointed to conflict between the legislative session and the block meetings. Depending on the strength of the pramukh, the relationship of the MLA with the block administrative officials can be important.

The third political level is the state. Opposition MLA's gave widely divergent responses concerning the receptivity of various Ministers, Deputy Ministers, personal assistants, and so on, with no discernible patterns being revealed for the basis of such receptivity.[6] One difficulty in determining patterns is that many opposition MLA's do not personally approach Ministers, and so on, but ask other MLA's to perform this task. They may rely on one or several MLA's. Sometimes this is dependent on the MLA in question (he may never consider asking more than one MLA to help him) and sometimes on the particular Minister to be approached. Furthermore, both the types and the number of requests made can vary widely. Some MLA's are completely inactive in this sphere. A few respondents reported that the Ministers were helpful in granting requests for individual constituents of an MLA, but not for groups. One purpose of state-level activity of

[6] Some respondents noted greater receptivity on the part of Ministers, Deputy Ministers, and so on, of their home districts; others pointed to the opposite. Some noted that certain Ministers of their own caste (or, for backward and scheduled castes, of their own caste grouping) were more receptive, but most named Ministers, and so on, of various castes. A few said that Ministers of either the Gupta or the Tripathi group were more receptive, while others said that there was no difference. It seems that so many variables are involved for each politician that an attempt to classify with so few respondents would be meaningless.

MLA's (whether it be in approaching Ministers or in formally asking a question on the floor) is to apply pressure on district, block, or other local officials. Sometimes these pressures can mitigate the pressures applied by local Congress leaders.

MLA's also reported that requests are made for the MLA to settle disputes among individuals or groups within his constituency. A few said that 70 percent of requests were of this nature. Although technically a legislator is not an arbitrator or mediator of local quarrels, in Uttar Pradesh this is an informal function. A difficulty is that the MLA stands to lose the support of either one of the parties to a dispute, or both, whether he intercedes or not.

Is the ability to benefit one's supporters materially crucial to party maintenance and reelection? The MLA's interviewed on this point considered it helpful, but not crucial. Some said that if they were not successful in obtaining benefits and someone else was, then a supporter might shift allegiance—but not always. Some said that success in helping people can backfire: if an MLA gets jobs for two people, the one getting a lower salary becomes angry; if an MLA can not get cement for all, cries of favoritism arise.[7] In the case studies of Moradabad Rural and Karchana, one factor in the defeat of candidates was said to be their inability to satisfy demands of supporters, but such charges were not heard in Pratapgarh South or Bhitauli. The original hypothesis that the unsatisfied beneficiaries would turn from a party if it did not carry out promises of specific action is not fully borne out by the study.

Social Configuration

In the course of this study, many MLA's, defeated candidates, and organizational workers singly and in groups were asked this question:

[7] Those who obtain cement permits have their names on a list in the order in which they obtained permits. When a supply of cement arrives, the authorities are supposed to distribute it according to the list. Because of the scarcity, a person may have to wait for months, if not years, before actually getting the cement. Although the MLA can sometimes help to get a person's name placed at the top of the list, the ability to do this for some antagonizes others whom the MLA does not or is unable to help.

One MLA tries to take very good care of his constituents; he tours regularly and tries to help people. And let's say that he is very successful —he is able to get all the things that people ask of him. He can get all the jobs, cement, loans, scholarships, wells, roads, etc. that are wanted.

Then let's take a second MLA. He is not interested in his constituency; rarely goes there; never tours. He doesn't bother most of the time to help people get what they want, but when he does try to get something, he never succeeds. He can't get anything for his constituents.

In the next election, will the first MLA definitely win and the second MLA lose?

The unanimous response was "no." The first MLA, in the opinion of most, would have a better chance, but there was no assurance that he would win or that the other would lose. What was considered to be the key factor? Again, unanimity in the reply: "Who the other candidates are." Many explanations and examples were given by respondents to demonstrate that new or different candidates affect, for better or worse, the electoral fortunes of a sitting MLA. The "social configuration," as one respondent put it, changes as the candidates change. Several pointed out that their election had been won because of the particular candidates running. One Kurmi Jan Sangh MLA pointed out that he eked out a victory over two other Kurmis because in 1962 a Muslim contested as Independent, taking thousands of Muslim votes away from the other two Kurmis. A Bhumihar Praja Socialist explained how he won in 1957 as the only rural candidate in a constituency containing a town and surrounding villages. His vote in the rural area was sufficient to overcome his low urban vote. But in 1962 there was a change in candidates of the Jan Sangh and Congress. In 1957 the Congress had put up a Kayasth and the Jan Sangh a Brahmin. In 1962 the Congress put up a Brahmin and the Jan Sangh a Sonar (goldsmith). Brahmins, particularly in the town, shifted their support to the Congress. The Jan Sangh vote dropped sharply, while the Congress vote rose. The sitting MLA's rural vote was not large enough to overcome the increased vote given to the Congress in the town. This case illustrates that even though a sitting MLA maintains his position among his supporters and increases his actual vote, the shifts of votes among other candidates can bring defeat. This is a consequence of a multiparty system.

There were a number of instances in which new candidates represented a reshuffling of individuals of the same socioeconomic groups, as in the previous case. In other instances the new candidates reflected the processes of social change. In building the party, an MLA mobilizes individuals and groups—up to a point. A difficulty in maintenance is that the processes he has helped set in motion for his victory continue to operate and may both expand in scope and increase in intensity. For a sitting MLA the problem is how to control social change or turn it to his advantage, at a time when he is absent for long periods, while opponents are trying to turn change to their advantage and may be subtly encouraging those changes likely to be detrimental to the MLA's support. A sitting MLA is a "sitting duck." Opponents can take sight on his coalition and try to shoot it to pieces, both by their own organizational activity and by selecting specific candidates.

The smaller the permanent party, the more disastrous are the consequences of new candidatures reflecting social change. The more a permanent party is drawn from a specific socioeconomic group, the more injurious are new candidates reflecting social change. Not just defeat, but overwhelming defeat in which the sitting MLA loses his deposit is likely to ensue. Of the 313 MLA's who ran for reelection in 1962, 40 (12.7 percent) lost their deposits. When candidate changes occur within the same socioeconomic groups, an MLA may lose, but not as badly. Again, the size and characteristics of the permanent party are factors to be considered.

One of the hypotheses for testing was that leadership tended to be frozen among those groups who had achieved leadership positions by the time of victory at the polls. The case studies tend to support this hypothesis. The studies also tend to support a second hypothesis, that an opposition party in a constituency tends to be identified by the populace with those groups represented by the leadership echelon. Thus the Jan Sangh in Pratapgarh South is identified with Thakurs, Kayasths, and Banias (or zamindars, some lawyers, and businessmen). The Socialists in Bhitauli are identified with Kurmis, Yadavs, and Pasis (or kisans). The Jan Sangh in Rudauli is identified with Banias (or businessmen) in particular, along with zamindars. The PSP in Saurikh is identified with backward classes—particularly Kurmis and Yadavs—and

Thakurs. And so on. Because of the similarity of the constituency and district leadership echelons of the parties in the districts studied, it is difficult to gauge the extent to which the group memberships of the district leadership modify those of the constituency leaders in the eyes of the populace.

The case studies also provide some support for the hypothesis that leaders of groups mobilized after victory at the polls of an opposition party tend to seek recognition in other parties. Clear examples are presented by the Lodhi-Rajputs of Saurikh and the Sainis of Moradabad Rural. It is interesting that in both instances the rising groups turned to other opposition parties rather than to the Congress.

A feature that many respondents mentioned as a problem in reelection is the existence of a vague, general dissatisfaction directed against any sitting MLA. Partly this is a reflection of the "revolution of rising expectations." Other parties or candidates can try to heighten this sense of dissatisfaction in order to better their chances.

Thus far, maintenance has been discussed with respect to reelecting a sitting MLA. Basic to the question, however, is the continuance of victories under the party's banner with different candidates. There have been few cases in which a constituency has remained with an opposition party under different MLA's. One was in the district of Deoria where a son followed his father as MLA.[8] A key factor in the problem of passing on party strength intact is the highly personalized method of party building. Loyalty is most often to the individual rather than to an abstract entity. The builders of the party are identified with certain groups and positions in regard to social rivalries. Their successors can never be carbon copies. Another difficulty is that various pillars of the permanent party may seek the mantle of leadership and, upon failing, choose to leave the party or not support it in the next election. The more broadly based the permanent party, the more likely will the maneuvers for succession involve social as well as personal frictions. Through the informal communication system, word spreads of the rivalry and groups related to the unsuccessful become defensive or rebellious. If an outsider is chosen to succeed the sitting MLA, or a nonpermanent party

[8] See Brass, *Factional Politics in an Indian State,* pp. 130–131.

member, it is possible that many of the pillars will rebel. In "losing constituencies," where MLA candidates are changed from one election to the next, the same problems occur.

Review of Six Constituencies

With these factors in mind, the situation can be reviewed in the constituencies studied. In Pratapgarh South there is still extreme bitterness between Brahmins and Thakurs, with the Brahmin Congress leaders resolved to "smash" the Jan Sangh. Congress leaders gleefully (and Jan Sangh leaders woefully) remark that the Jan Sanghiis can "get absolutely nothing" through the District Board. The semiofficial organizations such as the District Bank are controlled by Congress leaders who have the same goal. Of the three blocks within the constituency, only one pramukh is a Jan Sanghi. In another block, despite strenuous efforts by the MP and the MLA, the Thakurs divided and a Congressman was elected. The MLA is not active in block activities in two blocks. He is not active on the state level in trying to get advantages for constituents. He has approached district officials on essentially investigative matters; the district officials are Brahmins. Since the election, the Jan Sangh MLA has divided his time between his law practice and the legislative session in Lucknow. Although he has visited his ancestral home in a village, he has made only infrequent sorties out of the town. He utilizes the second pattern, "letting the people come to him." The Jan Sangh organizing secretary who worked in Pratapgarh South up to 1962, has now turned his attention to organizing party units in other constituencies. Furthermore, the college incident which united the Thakurs has been decided: there are now two Degree Colleges in the district, the Raja's and Munishwar Dutt Upadhyaya's. One Congress leader expressed his belief that a prominent Congress leader in an adjacent district, a Thakur, would persuade the Raja of Pratapgarh to join the Congress. Munishwar Dutt Upadhyaya and other Congress leaders are touring the countryside, trying to rebuild their party. One of these leaders points to a rising backward-caste movement and is working to try to draw backward-caste leaders to the Congress. The Jan Sangh leaders appeared unaware of such a movement. From these signs, it does not seem that the party is being extended, or even maintained. Whether the

Thakurs can be mobilized in the next election and whether they can successfully mobilize other castes are moot questions.

In Bhitauli constituency it does not appear that the friction between Kurmis and Thakurs is declining. On the other hand, tension between Kurmis and Yadavs, both in the Socialist Party, seems to be increasing. The Kurmis were mobilized at an earlier date than the Yadavs. The major consideration in this constituency will probably be "who the other candidates are." In the past, if the Congress and Socialist Party candidates had a straight contest, the Congressman won; with a major third candidate, the Socialist Party candidate won.

In Rudauli constituency, no party is presently trying to build up or extend the party in the countryside. The Jan Sangh is relying on the "shopkeeper network" for communication, which again is the second pattern. There are no Jan Sangh pramukhs, and the MLA is not active in obtaining advantages for his supporters. A major consideration in this constituency will probably be who is put up by the Congress. If a Muslim again contests, the Jan Sangh may again be victorious. If a Hindu runs on the Congress ticket, the outcome is likely to be quite different.

In Saurikh constituency, two of the three blocks are controlled by the PSP. The third was barely lost. The MLA is on very good terms with the Congress district leaders; the PSP contingent on the District Board is large and the MLA has been able to get advantages for his constituents. In the semiofficial agencies there are several PSP members. The MLA has set up a center system of communication and has toured widely (see chapter vi). In communication with constituents and in gaining material advantages, he has an excellent record. Social change, however, continues. Other Yadav leaders and leaders of other backward castes are rising. The Jan Sangh in particular is working among Lodhas. Another complicating factor is the MP by-election which was held in 1963; the combined efforts of the MLA and the MP were not sufficient to prevent most PSP supporters from deserting the party to vote for the Socialist Dr. Lohia. In 1964, when the Praja Socialists split, Hori Lal Yadav (the MLA) was a member of the group that merged with the Lohia Socialists in the new Samyukta Socialist Party.[9] After a few months the new party split, with some former Praja Socialists withdrawing to establish the PSP. Hori Lal

[9] Samyukta means "United."

Yadav remained in the Samyukta Socialist Party, but reconstitution of the PSP may present ambitious constituency leaders formerly under Hori Lal Yadav with a choice of running on their own. Social change and the particular Congress candidate, Jan Sangh candidate, and other candidates set up, as well as educating the public on the change in party symbol, will be problems for the MLA. If Hori Lal Yadav should not run and another candidate is put forward, it is doubtful that the "party" and its support can be transferred intact.

In Moradabad Rural, the PSP controls no blocks, and in one block a pramukh has ambitions of becoming MLA. The present MLA, Riasat Hussain, is active only in one block, which lies partially in and partially outside his constituency, and has "resigned" from politics in the block which was the scene of electoral maneuvering before and after the general election. The PSP is very weak on the District Board and in the semigovernmental agencies. The MLA has been able to obtain some material advantages for many individuals, through officials. He has attempted to follow the third pattern of communication (daily sorties out from a center; in this case both his village and the Moradabad City party office alternate as headquarters) as promised before the election, but in two years had been able to visit only about a third to a half of the villages. He has used village bazaars occasionally for contact, and occasionally asked some of the workers to take petitions around for signing, or to distribute his or the party's literature. Riasat Hussain has also been caught up in the party changes: he joined the new Samyukta Socialist Party and then resigned with others to reconstitute the PSP. This constituency is one in which three different candidates of three different parties have been elected in three elections. "Who the other candidates are" will be an important factor in the next election. A real test of personal influence versus caste influence will come if the Thakur block pramukh does contest.

In Karchana constituency, the MLA is still known as a "field worker" and appears to be in the process of establishing an informal center system of communication. He has been able to obtain some material advantages of an individual nature for his supporters. The MLA is interested in block politics, but there are no Praja Socialist block pramukhs. A key factor in the next election will be who the Congress candidate is. Subsidiary factors will be the extent to which the Congress can be rebuilt, the factions united for the purpose of the campaign, and the identity of other candidates. If the next Congress candidate is not a Brahmin, then it is likely that some existing tensions will be exploited which could not be utilized in a contest between Brahmins.

Summary

In this discussion, two points stand out. First, some of the problems of maintaining a local party are beyond the control of the party. Organizational efforts by other parties, the choice of candidates by other parties, and socioeconomic changes are three imponderables. Second, there are aspects of maintenance which are within the power of a party to control or influence. Contact with supporters is within the purview of the party; the achievement of material benefits for supporters can be influenced by activities of party leaders.

But it seems that many opposition parties lack the resources to do the job. Financially, many local opposition parties can collect sufficient monies to carry on an intensive campaign. In the interelection period, however, substantial contributions are hard to come by. In many instances membership dues seem to cost more to collect than the amount taken in. The funds available in the interelection period set a limit on many activities, including travel. In Uttar Pradesh travel is essential for communication. The party's financial base affects the pattern of communication; it tends to put the burden on the activist's private income. If activists are unable or unwilling to take this burden, the problem of maintaining contact becomes acute. Parties which control the various political and economic organizations use their resources for furthering the party. Opposition parties have not generally been successful in entrenching themselves in these organizations.

There are also problems of personnel resources. In most local parties there are comparatively few permanent party members and, among them, few pillars. Of the six local parties studied, the Saurikh Praja Socialist Party had the largest contingent: after thirty years of effort, fourteen pillars in an electorate of more than 100,000. The fewer the pillars, the greater the burden placed on the MLA and—if there is one—the MP, who lack time and some-times funds for the task of maintenance and extension. Some of the MLA's and MP's show little interest in continuing the arduous task of organization to consolidate their gains after an election. If they are inactive in maintenance efforts, then the pillars tend to become inactive. The Jan Sangh is the only party under study which had official organizing secretaries who work to build the party and which, therefore, could assist an MLA or MP in main-tenance. There are not many organizers in Uttar Pradesh. As shown by Pratapgarh South, the organizer can cease activity in winning constituencies to put effort into losing constituencies. Thus the Jan Sangh appears no better off than the other parties in handling this problem. Lack of sufficient inner party resources compounds the difficulty presented by the imponderables in keep-ing the local party in the winning columns.

Chapter XIII

INTERNAL PARTY MAINTENANCE

IN THIS CHAPTER the focus shifts to the district and state levels of the party. Several party leaders reported that it is more difficult to hold together a district than a state party. Evidently the rivalries in a district are more immediate and damaging to the persons involved. When local leaders meet on the state level, each has a territorial base which is to some extent impermeable to rivals from other districts. Within a district there may be a slightly less territorial impermeability. Furthermore, the kinds of decisions made on the district level are more likely to affect the local position of a leader than those on the state level.

Bases of Conflict

Many of the tensions mentioned in previous chapters have relevance for internal party maintenance. On the district and state levels, some "new" frictions become important. One conflict is usually described in Uttar Pradesh as "lawyers versus workers." Investigation showed, however, that this refers to friction between two kinds of politicians: armchair politicians and grass-roots political workers. Frequently the armchair politicians are lawyers; usually they are urban. Grass-roots political workers can have any occupation or residence. While the latter actively work to build, extend, and repair the party among low-level workers and the electorate, the armchair politicians tend to confine their activities to maneuvering among party leaders. The conflict seems to arise from the impact of a total situation. Since armchair politicians commonly reside in an urban area, they easily become a focal point for transient local leaders. They become the recipient and dispenser of news about their own and other parties. They become a communication hub. Performance of this function frequently leads to a feeling of importance. Although they have not worked to build up the party and have little electoral strength themselves, they often want the glory and power of leadership. They want to hold offices, represent the party in civic celebrations, and be host to visiting state or national leaders. They want to determine party action on the local level, participate in decision making on higher levels, and select candidates—often themselves and their armchair-politician friends—for elections. Although these politicians can perform useful and necessary functions within a party, the grass-roots political workers who have built up the party and have electoral strength tend to resist giving all-encompassing powers of leadership and party direction to them. They want to make decisions and obtain the public recognition that goes with titular leadership. Reports of friction between the two kinds of politicians are most frequently applied to the Praja Socialist and Socialist parties, both of which are stronger electorally in rural than in urban areas.

Friction based on different educational attainments also arises. Those with higher education tend to look down on those with lesser schooling and consider that their education gives them a "right" to party leadership. There are many valid grounds for their position. Full, meaningful participation in governmental and party matters is made easy by education—the more of it, the more ease. We might ask whether a party can long continue without a sizable proportion of educated leaders. But in a society which is largely illiterate and rural, where the educated tend to migrate to cities, a party can hardly be built on simply a highly educated stratum. Nor can the educated reasonably expect the lesser educated to be content with performing menial but essential party functions while all honors and decision-making roles fall to others. What has not been resolved is how to contain and ameliorate the tensions and demands made by those with different levels of education.

Another friction exists between those who finance the party (or are able to obtain contributions) and those who do not. The former have a logical basis for claims to have a large voice in party matters. However, many times it is those in the latter category who have electoral strength and this gives them an equally sound basis for their claims.

A political generation is often considered to be twenty years. We are beginning to see tension between those recruited at different times, in particular between the "independence generation" or the "founding father" leadership echelon and newcomers who are definitely post-independence. Occasionally the conflict coincides with a generational cleavage. The conflict seems to be very mild in places where an opposition party is "losing." But "founding fathers" who have built a party to winning status tend to resist demands of newcomers. Here it is that internal party maintenance and party-electorate maintenance are intertwined. A party cannot continue indefinitely with a set of leaders recruited at a particular time; there must be an infusion of new blood. Newcomers have to be promoted within the party. Many times, however, newcomers or younger people have not developed much electoral strength. They are political neophytes. But with extremely few elective positions and elections at five-year intervals there are not many ways for newcomers to work their way up. Newcomers have to compete directly for the top party and governmental posts. The two socialist parties seem to have a greater problem in this area because so many activists were recruited before independence.

Another maintenance problem is posed by the Congress. Unable to control the District or Municipal Boards in many places, or establish official policy, opposition party leaders have as a prime concern their relationship with the competitive leaders of the dominant party. Decisions on this relationship are a major problem area. Differences within an opposition party are compounded because not only are intraparty questions involved, but the relationships of a number of leaders with a number of Congress leaders as well. Since politicians in an opposition party differ among themselves, since each may have varied experiences with different Congress leaders, and since these politicians have to work through Congress leaders, it is difficult for an opposition party to prevent involvement in Congress factions. Once such involvement occurs, it is difficult to maintain internal cohesion.

A few cases will illustrate these tensions and will show the interrelationship of these with other kinds of cleavages. The first case is the Rae Bareli district Socialist Party, which appeared to be bifactional. The district leadership echelon was divided, with the cleavages on a number of factors tending to cut the same way. The characteristics of the two groups are:

Armchair politicians	versus	Grass-roots workers
Urban		Rural
High education		Little education
Lawyers		Kisans and politicians
Upper-middle class		Lower-middle and lower class
Elite caste (Brahmin especially)		Backward and scheduled caste (Kurmi especially)
Young		Older
Recent recruits		"Founding fathers"

In the 1960's the armchair politicians tried to wrest leadership and party direction from the political workers. Because the former were recruited by a man who is now a state leader, they were able to obtain support from the state party. As a result, all five urban party members are now on the party's district executive committee. Their rise was resisted by the political workers. Electorally the Socialists won three Assembly seats and lost a fourth by a narrow margin in 1962. Their strength is entirely rural and is based on the middle and lower castes. There is a history of elite versus backward caste tension in the district. The conflict between the two groups was in the open over questions of leadership, and it appeared likely to become acute when candidates were selected for the 1967 general elections. The armchair politicians made it clear to us that they intended to replace sitting MLA's and previous candidates with themselves. The grounds given for this decision were (1) that the "founding fathers" had built a caste-based party rather than an ideologically oriented one, and (2) that the founding fathers were barely literate and thus clearly incapable of running a party or representing the party in the Assembly. The highly educated, upper-caste politicians wanted to rectify the situation.

The Socialist Party in Bara Banki also appeared to be bifactional. Both factions were led by political workers; but there were differences between the leaders in education, occupation, residence, caste, style of working (agitational versus institutional) and time of recruitment:

Low education	High education
Kisans, small businessmen, politicians	Lawyers, politicians
Rural, or small town	Medium to large town
Kurmi-led	Yadav-led
Recruited in 1930's	Recruited in late 1940's and 1950's
Political work—agitational only	Political work—institutional and agitational

One area of conflict between the two groups has been candidate selection. In the 1962 general elections the Yadav-led group was successful in replacing a sitting Kurmi MLA with a candidate of the Yadav's group. The Kurmi was placated by giving his sister the MLA ticket in a constituency outside the district—in an area which has few Kurmis. She lost. The Yadav's candidate (a backward-caste Karwal) also lost. This was one incident that led many Kurmis to believe that the Yadav was trying to oust Kurmis from leadership positions in the party. They are resentful. The members of the Yadav-led group whom we interviewed seemed totally unaware of any friction. Granted, their responses may have been related to the desire to present the picture of a unified party to an outsider. If, on the other hand, they do not recognize the cleavage, then it is unlikely that they would take steps to mitigate it.

Differences sometimes become apparent in determining party policy on the District or Municipal Board. For example, a split in the Farrukhabad PSP had for its immediate cause differences as to which Congress factional leader should be supported for chairman of the District Board. The Congress had a majority on the board, and usually Congressmen support the official party candidate. The PSP contingent, however, was sufficiently large to hold the balance between the two Congress factions, and thus it was involved in the informal maneuvers preceding candidate selection. A factional leader assured of PSP support could demand the Congress ticket or threaten an open fight. The PSP was reported to be fairly evenly divided over which Congress faction to support. The group preferring the Congress Gupta group became concerned that they might lose. To prevent this they delayed the meeting of the PSP district executive committee a few hours and changed its meeting place. The other group was notified and attended in full strength. The new location was such as to apply pressure on some of those thought to be favoring the local Tripathi group. When the vote was taken, those favoring the Gupta group had the majority. The leaders of the dissident group thereupon resigned from the PSP and joined the then miniscule Socialist Party. This appeared to be a case for both the PSP and the Congress of old-timers versus newcomers, with a subsidiary east-versus-west cleavage. The PSP "founding father" echelon preferred the Congress faction led by their former associates; the PSP newcomers had developed closer ties to the "new" leaders in the Congress. The old-time PSP and Congress leaders are based in the east, while the newcomers in both parties appear to have a western base; however, the PSP old-timers in the west supported the Congress old-timers too.

In Bareilly city a conflict arose over the Municipal Board. A Congress rebel, a Khattri, was elected mayor as an Independent, with the help of Jan Sangh members. Later a no-confidence motion was successfully raised against him. In the new elections, the Khattri Independent contested against a Congress Bania. In the city there is friction between the Banias on the one hand, and the Khattris and Kayasths on the other. The latter are reported to be lower in economic standing than the Banias, and members of these castes frankly state their resentment of "Bania domination" in the city. The city Jan Sangh leader was a Kayasth and personal friend of the Independent Khattri. The Jan Sangh leader wanted the party councillors to support the Independent, or at least to abstain from voting—not only for reasons of friendship and social friction, but because an Independent was preferred to a Congressman. State Jan Sangh leaders agreed with the latter point and expressed in writing their desire that the councillors should abstain from voting. Two of the four Jan Sanghiis on the Board, however, were Banias; violating the party directive, they voted for the Congress Bania, who was elected. One of the Banias frankly admitted that he and his associate had voted for the Bania because of the caste tie and the friction between Banias and Khattris. State party leaders invoked discipline and suspended the two Banias from holding party office for one year. The Kayasth leader did not approve of this light censure; he resigned from the party with several of his followers.

There have been many cases of opposition leaders joining the Congress. In Ghazipur distrist, prominent PSP leaders joined the Congress immediately before the 1962 election; one was given the Congress ticket for MP and the other the Congress ticket for District Board chairman. Both were successful for the first time in their post-independence political career. Both the Congress and the PSP leaders were identical social groups. The PSP was a "losing party" in the district. A "new man" of a lower and rival social group had just entered the PSP and, as a former MLA (Independent), joined the leadership ranks. He considered one factor in the defection of the two major leaders and their followers to be the background of social tension. While all parties have experienced a drifting movement to the Congress, the PSP has been especially hard hit. Particularly for aging politicians in a place where the opposition party has been unsuccessful at the polls, the Congress appears to be a magnet.

To some extent all the parties have a problem in handling the ambitions of their members. Leadership positions are scarce. Even in districts where an opposition party is small there may be insufficient leadership positions to fill the demand. The Jan Sangh, which boasts of its inculcation of the values of self-sacrifice, devotion to duty, lack of desire for offices, and the like, nonetheless has problems in containing the ambitions of even the core RSS group within the party. A case in point is the Jan Sangh in Agra, doubly interesting because it was initially described as a case of RSS versus non-RSS, and RSS versus Jan Sangh.

The Jan Sangh has won no MLA seats in Agra district and had only six seats in the municipal corporation. Despite its electoral weakness, the party divided after both the first and second general elections. The founder of the Jan Sangh in the district was Ram Babu Verma, an RSS man who was deputed to organize the party and was appointed the party organizing secretary. In 1953, internal party differences caused his resignation or ouster from the party. Involved were differences over the preelection placement and selection of candidates, and over the role of the RSS in the party. The chief protagonist was an ambitious RSS organizing secretary, Baloji Agrawal, who became the new Jan Sangh organizing secretary for the district and later for a zone covering several districts. In 1957 he ran for an Assembly seat and was defeated. The next year Baloji Agrawal wanted the Jan Sangh ticket for a position on the municipal corporation. Some party activists opposed him. State leaders were called down, who dissolved the existing organization and set up an ad hoc committee. Members of the committee reported that this action was necessary because Baloji Agrawal controlled the existing organization. Another Jan Sanghi was given the coveted ticket for the municipal corporation. Baloji Agrawal resigned, or was ousted, from the party. Jan Sangh leaders charged that he was "too ambitious," that he was filled with the "lust for office." One rival, who succeeded him as organizing secretary and was himself an RSS man, amplified the statement: "He always wanted to be the only leader of Jan Sangh—wanted all others to stand behind him. In building a party, you look to find influential people and then contact them. He never wanted [me] or [another Jan Sanghi] to contact these people. Oh, no. Just he himself was to meet these people and get them to support the party. He wanted to be the only prominent person in Jan Sangh." The statement indicates that the respondent and others wanted to share in the glory of leadership.

Members of the "Baloji Agrawal group" mentioned additional factors, some of which were disputed by the Jan Sangh leaders. (1) It was under RSS orders that Baloji Agrawal had moved against Ram Babu Verma, and also it was under RSS orders that Agrawal was removed. (2) According to both ousted members, the RSS "interfered" in the daily working of the Jan Sangh; in particular, RSS leaders chose the party officers and party candidates, and vetoed plans for party organization among specific socioeconomic groups.[1] (3) The state Jan Sangh leaders always supported the local RSS leaders rather than the Jan Sangh local leaders. (4) A

[1] It was reported that plans to organize the party among labor, backward castes, and scheduled castes were vetoed by the local RSS, and that the state Jan Sangh leaders supported the local RSS leaders. It is possible that the dispute was solely within the party, inasmuch as some of the important activists and financiers of the district party are businessmen-employers. Their employees, mainly of the lower castes, are not unionized, and a few of the employers expressed their intention to maintain the status quo. If the RSS did take a stand in this case, very probably it was in support of the business group within the party. Similarly, the stand of the state officials illustrates concern for keeping this group within the party.

party differs from other kinds of organizations; in trying to build a party, leaders develop a "broadened outlook" and place higher value on some considerations than do RSS leaders.

The Jan Sangh leaders reported friction between Baloji Agrawal and the state's organizing secretary. They scoffed at the other charges, stressing that both Babu Ram Verma and Baloji Agrawal had been RSS leaders and that it was resentment at defeat within the party which was behind their charges.

Efforts to untangle the conflicting reports were unsuccessful. Two points do stand out. First, all the key participants were prominent RSS members. This could not realistically be called a conflict between RSS and non-RSS. It is difficult to perceive it as RSS versus Jan Sangh. Second, the key participants were and are ambitious; to rise, each found it necessary to destroy the position of others. That conflict took place around the appointed organizational office as well as the elective office illustrates the importance of the organizational wing in the Jan Sangh.

When asked if district dissension was based on questions of party ideology, specific party policy on an issue, or plans for party activity, prominent leaders of the three parties replied in the negative. Personal differences were viewed as the key factor. Personality clashes, socioeconomic differences, and ambition were involved. Caste also may have been a factor, though to determine its relevance would be difficult. Disputants' being of different castes would not of itself mean that caste was involved. Sometimes caste was relevant when disputants were of the same caste.[2]

Resolving conflict, regardless of kind, is difficult because the type of questions posed on the district level leave little room for maneuver. Opposition parties on this level rarely appear to be concerned with public policy issues; the distance from power is probably a foremost reason. Whom to elect for party offices and choose for party candidates and whom of other parties to support for governmental positions seem to be the prime questions. On these, there is little room for compromise.

---

[2] For example, in many districts and on the state level concern was voiced that different castes and geographic areas should be represented in party candidatures and leadership positions. This can mean that only one position is really open to members of one caste. Intense rivalry results, with caste a very relevant factor. There have been occasions when the losers left the party.

Role of Ideology

Ideology does not appear to become important until the state level is reached. For the Jan Sangh, ideology has tended to be a unifying factor. The emphasis is clearly on nationalism, united India, Bharat culture, and a "return to traditional values." These are vague, general sentiments on which there can be little disagreement, particularly as they are not defined. Several MLA's and district party leaders were asked in a variety of ways to elaborate on the meaning of "return to traditional values" and "building a state on Bharat culture," but not one was able to do so. Respondents several times repeated the general phrases. The principles can be likened to the adage that "politicians are against sin and for motherhood." Under their aegis, groups and individuals with a wide variety of economic and social policy preferences can be drawn together.

Informants reported a growing cleavage within the Jan Sangh regarding economic policy. On the one hand, there are old-timers who place low value on economic policy and wish to avoid discussion of it altogether. On the other hand, some of the newcomers, particularly kisan workers or those with an education in economics, would place economic policy on a par with cultural policy. This latter group is divided on the specifics of economic policy. Some favor a doctrinaire socialism, while others are for a socialism defined in strictly humanitarian terms, and still others are opposed to anything that smacks of socialism. There is probably lack of agreement among those who give economic policy a low rank. Full debate would tend to heighten the differences. Whether the ostrich-like playing down of economic discussion can be long continued is a moot point. Whether the vagueness of "nationalism" and "culture" will be sufficient to bridge the gaps among those with strong feelings on varied economic policies is debatable.

The Praja Socialist Party has lacked a unifying ideology such as the Jan Sangh possesses. "Socialism" has been just as divisive as it has been cohesive, for at least three reasons. First, there are the origins of the PSP in the KMPP–SP. The leaders and activists of the Jan Congress–KMPP were not socialists. After the merger with SP they became socialists in name, but they are not concerned with abstruse doctrines. Some of the former CSP (first Socialist Party) contingent are doctrinaire socialists whereas others tend to view socialism in broad, humanitarian terms. With the emphasis on economics these differences on content tend to be divisive. Second, the gradual adoption by Congress of progressively more socialistic pronouncements has been a disturbing factor. Among those to whom socialism is important the question arises whether to join Congress and "strengthen the socialist forces" or to stand apart on grounds that the Congress has not carried out its official statements and does not intend to do so. For those to whom socialism is not important (particularly the KMPP group who left Congress in factional disputes) rejoining Congress is not acceptable. Oftentimes this group appears puzzled as to why the others are so concerned. Third, since the early 1950's a major issue has been the relationship with Congress. Ashok Mehta's thesis of the "compulsions of a backward economy," [3] which calls for partial support of the majority party, became the catalyst about which advocates of "determined opposition" and "partial [—that is, responsible] opposition" revolved. The declining fortunes of the PSP, combined with the Chinese invasion and the growing strength of rightist parties such as the Swatantra and the Jan Sangh, together with the movement of the Congress toward socialism, presented a dilemma. Groups polarized; personal, geographic, and socioeconomic differences between the leaders of the groups increased. Ideological discussion exacerbated the tensions.

The Lohia Socialist Party's official stand is "total opposition" to the Congress, and there have been no great debates on what sort of relationship to establish toward the Congress or whether to join the Congress. A strict economic emphasis has been modified, however, by increasing stress on social and cultural policies. Calls for Hindi as the national language, special privileges for certain groups, intercaste marriage, the end of caste restrictions,

[3] See Ashok Mehta, "General Secretary's Report," in *Report of the Special Convention of the Praja Socialist Party, Betul (Madhya Pradesh), June 14–18, 1953* (Bombay, 1953), pp. 162–182, and, for debate on the report, pp. 2–78.

and nationalism have become focal points in recent years. Although the principles are a unifying force among the lower castes and social reformers, some elite-caste activists have left the party over the caste issue. Others spoke of their reluctance to join the party because of their distress with and disbelief in party stands. Some have logically accepted the party positions, but still have reservations. The Socialists look upon method as an intrinsic part of their ideology. Overthrow of government by "permanent satyagraha" and similar ideas fall under the rubric of "militant socialism." A "permanent satyagraha" was abandoned a few years ago when enthusiasm waned. A party official remarked on the difficulty of demanding such sacrifices on a permanent basis with no perceivable result. Several informants reported that the SP stands have alienated the party from certain segments of society—the upper castes and classes, a large part of the middle classes, the business and professional element, and urban dwellers.

One by-product of organizing agitations involving a jail sentence appears to be that in jail a party study conference can be held. Small study groups are set up; lectures and discussions on party ideology, policies, and the building of parties occupy the time. Leaders from various parts of the state can get to know one another. One advantage of organizing such activities around a jail term is that board and lodging are free. Most parties and individuals cannot afford to pay for a three-week study conference elsewhere. The Jan Sangh was the only party reported to organize the "jail group" as a parliament, selecting majority party ministers, leaders of the opposition, and so on, who were to present and defend Jan Sangh policy as well as defend jail conditions. The MLA's had been excused from the agitation held during the course of this study because of the budget session. This meant that nonlegislators were introduced to parliamentary routine and practices.

One disadvantage of jail sentences is that minor frictions and disputes can become exascerbated through close, extended contact, which can have far-reaching consequences for party unity. A second disadvantage is the sacrifice of time which could be used to earn a livelihood or to care for a family. Lengthy jail terms can mean an increase in restiveness.

Factional Patterns

Internal maintenance cannot be analyzed without reference to factional divisions and their bases. Two factional divisions were reported in the Jan Sangh, with two subsidiary divisions. The first was rivalry between Brahmins and Thakurs, easily understandable because many were involved in similar rivalries in their respective districts. It is difficult to put aside these tensions. It was widely reported that the change in legislative leadership in October, 1963, in which Yadvendra Dutt Dube (Brahmin) was replaced by Sharda Bhakt Singh (Thakur) was due in part to Thakur resentment of and objections to the Brahmin leader. Another factor was reported to be the defeat of a Jan Sangh leader in an MP by-election in Jaunpur. This was the home base of Yadvendra Dutt Dube, and supposedly victory for the party was ensured. It was also said that Nanajii Deshmukh (organizing secretary for eastern India) was willing to limit the growing power and popularity of Dube within the party. A second major division and a factor in the leadership question was said to be friction between RSS and non-RSS legislators. It will be remembered that no Thakur MLA's mobilized after independence reported the RSS as an agent of mobilization into politics or the party. The two cleavages overlap to some extent. Most of the leaders, however, have RSS ties. The official explanation for the change in legislative leadership was the desire to train as many people as possible in leadership positions. To this end, officials said, the legislative officials would be rotated annually. Yet, well over a year and a half later no new election had been held and no change in officials had taken place.

Friction was reported between the legislative and organizational wings of the party. Jan Sangh leaders have tried to inculcate in their members the idea of the dominance of the organizational wing. The major decisions are made within the organization, and an organizational member has been deputed to watch over and guide the legislative wing. He is called the legislative party-office secretary, but his role far exceeds his title. MLA's reported that he determined who would speak on what and reviewed (and either

accepted or revised) amendments to bills put forward by legislators. Even so, little friction has been generated around this secretary. Tension was reported around decisions made in the organizational branch for the MLA's. One example was the selection
of the Jan Sangh candidate for MLC (indirectly elected by MLA's)
in 1962. The organizational leaders decided whom to support and
then informed the MLA's. Some legislators objected to the procedure. This was adroitly handled by the organizational leaders,
who quickly retreated, explained why they chose the particular
candidate, and asked for legislators' opinions. The MLA's then
agreed to the organization-sponsored candidate. When MLC candidates were chosen in 1964, the organizational leaders called a
meeting of the legislators, presented the names of several candidates, and expressed their opinion as to which should be elected.
The MLA's again supported the organization's preference. In this
way the organizational leaders mitigated friction between the two
wings while still maintaining control. It is possible that future
incidents will be less easily handled.

The other area of friction has already been referred to: the
development of groups about different economic policies. As yet,
the lines do not appear to be clear cut or firmly established. It is
difficult to tell whether the cleavages on this issue will coincide
with other cleavages.

Factional divisions in the PSP are quite complex. A root cleavage within the PSP appears to be based on the members' entry
through either the Jan Congress–KMPP, or the first Socialist Party
(CSP). Triloki Singh, the most prominent leader of one faction,
was a founder of the Jan Congress and subsequently became a
state leader of the KMPP. The two most prominent leaders of the
competitive state faction are Genda Singh and Chandra Shekar,
both of whom had ties to the CSP. Members of the Jan Congress–
KMPP left the Congress in factional struggles. Many were followers of Rafi Ahmed Kidwai, and some of Acharya Kripalani. Like
these two leaders, the prominent figures of the Jan Congress–
KMPP tended to be practical, pragmatic, professional politicians.
In outlook they tended to be humanitarians, Gandhians, and lib-
erals. But they were not and are not now ideologues. The original
foremost leaders of the first Socialist Party—such as Acharya Narendra Dev, Jaya Prakash Narayan, and Ashok Mehta—can be

considered ideologues. For them and other leaders, an ideological commitment was involved in their departure from the Congress. Not all, however, of the followers of these top and middle-level leaders had a similar orientation; in their case there was a personal tie to specific individuals. Continuation of the two groups is predicated partly on the leaders' general orientation toward politics, and partly on long-standing informal communication patterns. Before independence, these individuals did not belong to the same groups in the Congress. After independence it was rare for a district to have strong units of both the Jan Congress–KMPP and the CSP. Informal interdistrict and vertical district-state communications appear to have followed previous group lines. Once the PSP was established, some new lines of communication were developed, but the older patterns persisted.

Besides the new lines of communication, other factors have arisen over the years which have modified the base division. One of these is geography. There is some east-west tension, with Genda Singh and Chandra Skekar (both of northeastern districts) leading the eastern group and Triloki Singh of Lucknow leading the western group. Farrukhabad district lies in the west; although the MLA's of that district were in the CSP, they shifted to support Triloki Singh's group. The reason given by a district leader was that Genda Singh was an eastern regional leader whereas Triloki Singh was a state-wide spokesman.

Another modification is caste. Triloki Singh is a Kayasth. One of the Deoria MLA's with a CSP background is a Kayasth. He had the support of Triloki Singh in getting the MLA ticket in 1962. It is understood that Genda Singh was not particularly keen on his candidacy. The Kayasth MLA shifted to support the Triloki Singh group. The infusion of Yadavs into the legislative party has modified the base division also. One respondent, in a position to know, referred to a "Yadav bloc" operating on legislative leadership questions. Most members of this bloc were either in one or the other of the major factions. Some Yadav MLA's have tried to stay aloof (particularly the recent recruits who had no ties to the parent organizations), but on questions of leadership, they band together. A Yadav was chosen deputy leader in 1962, then twice chosen leader, despite the fact that he had formally joined the PSP just before the 1962 election.

Not only is caste a factor, but also caste in combination with Congress factions. Respondents often referred to Congress factions in caste terms—for instance, a Brahmin-Kayasth alliance (Sampurnand, Gautam, Tripathi) against a Thakur-Bania alliance (Gupta group).[4] Triloki Singh (Kayasth) had a long-standing feud with C. B. Gupta, and it was this friction which led to his withdrawal from the Congress; he was, however, very close to the Congress chief minister, Dr. Sampurnanand (Kayasth). Genda Singh (Bhumihar) and Chandra Shekar (Thakur), on the other hand, have had friendly relationships with C. B. Gupta and his group. C. B. Gupta was once treasurer of the CSP. When Triloki Singh was leader of the legislative party, he was roundly criticized by the Genda Singh group for his ties to the Congress Sampurnanand faction. When Genda Singh became legislative leader, he was equally criticized for his ties to the Gupta group. Such charges may have helped to bring about a slight internal readjustment of factions. One eastern district Brahmin with a CSP history but with ties to the Sampurnanand-Gautam-Tripathi group in the Congress shifted to Triloki Singh's group.

Another point of cleavage appeared at first glance to be an urban versus rural orientation, with Triloki Singh of Lucknow city leading the urban group. Most of the urban MLA's are from Allahabad city; all are in the Triloki Singh group, but these also have a Jan Congress–KMPP background. There are several rural MLA's of various districts in the Triloki Singh group. There were no examples of urban-residence MLA's of the Genda Singh group changing to the Triloki Singh group, or of rural-residence MLA's changing to the Genda Singh group. In the party itself, apart from MLA's there is said to be a more clearly definable urban-rural division.

Informants reported another source of cleavage between armchair politicians (Triloki Singh) and political workers (Genda Singh). Genda Singh is a well-known political worker among sugarcane growers and sugar-mill workers. Triloki Singh is regarded as a "master politician," a "political wizard," and a highly skilled parliamentarian, but not a grass-roots political worker. (Closer

---

[4] Brass's study of Congress factions shows that the matter is not that simple. There is no clear-cut caste division on these lines, although the most prominent leaders of the factions have been of these castes. See Brass, *Factional Politics in an Indian State.*

examination showed, however, that both types of politicians were to be found in both groups and there were no changes in group affiliation which could be related to a division of this nature.) The identification of Genda Singh with sugar interests suggested a cleavage between areas producing sugar cane and areas not producing it. It was reported that Genda Singh had strength in western cane-producing areas (which, however, had produced no MLA's in 1962). There does appear to be some basis for a division on these lines.

Whereas the Triloki Singh group is dominant in the legislative party, the Genda Singh–Chandra Shekar group is dominant in the organizational party. The organizational officers were considered to be in the Genda Singh–Chandra Shekar group, although the state executive includes representatives of the different groups. In contrast with the Jan Sangh, the organizational wing does not dominate the legislative.

In the party split of 1964, national factional alignments were also involved. The Genda Singh–Chandra Shekar group was identified with the Ashok Mehta group on the national level while the Triloki Singh group was affiliated with the S. M. Joshi group. Involved was again the relationships towards the Congress. The crisis began when Jawaharlal Nehru offered and Ashok Mehta accepted a position on the Planning Committee. Ashok Mehta, it might be added, had the year before lost control of the organization and of party tactics to S. M. Joshi. There was widespread discussion over what to do about Ashok Mehta; when the national executive disapproved of his action, the various state parties divided over whether to support the national executive. At this same time the Congress held its annual national session and formally adopted "socialism" as its goal. The usual question arose in the PSP about what to do, but this time a prominent leader (Ashok Mehta) threw his weight toward joining Congress and was in such a position that it seemed advantageous. Entry was delayed by both the Congress and the PSP until Congress organizational elections were held. Then the PSP leaders were essentially "grafted on" to the existing district leadership. Genda Singh (but not Chandra Shekar) joined the Congress along with eleven other MLA's.[5] A

[5] The actual division came after field research was completed; thus no explanation of Chandra Shekar's action can be given. Chandra Shekar did not join the new Samyukta Socialist Party.

few of those eleven had been identified with the Triloki Singh group in recent years; however, they had a CSP history. What are the characteristics of the group joining the Congress and the group joining the Socialist Party?

As expected, the background of party membership is correlated with the action of individuals (see Table 50). No MLA with a

TABLE 50

PAST PARTY BACKGROUND OF PRAJA SOCIALIST PARTY MLA's JOINING
THE CONGRESS OR THE SOCIALIST PARTY, 1964

Past Party Background	Joined Congress	Joined SP	Total
First Socialist Party (CSP)	6	9	15
KMPP	—	7	7
Lohia Socialist to PSP	1	1	2
PSP only	5	3	8
Not ascertained	—	1	1
Total	12	21	33

KMPP history joined the Congress. Many of those with a CSP record preferred the Congress to the Lohia Socialists. Those who had never been members of the parent bodies of the PSP divided, with most going to the Congress.

In caste, proportionately more Thakurs and backward-caste MLA's joined the Congress than others (Table 51). These are the

TABLE 51

CASTE OF PRAJA SOCIALIST MLA's JOINING THE CONGRESS
OR THE SOCIALIST PARTY, 1964

Caste	Joined Congress	Joined SP	Total
Brahmin	1	4	5
Thakur	3	3	6
Other elite	2	7	9
Backward	5	5	10
Scheduled	1	2	3
Total	12	21	33

two groups in the Congress with lesser representation. That the backward-caste MLA's split evenly in the decision of whether to join the majority or join an opposition party offering special policies to favor the backward castes demonstrates the conflict pointed out earlier by an Allahabad respondent.

Looking at the scaled dual occupations, nine of the twelve MLA's who joined the Congress fell into the medium kisan category (eight as primary occupation; one as secondary), whereas only three of the twenty-one MLA's joining the Socialist Party were medium kisans. All the kisans or tenants, businessmen, and white-collar or professional men went to the SP, and most of those reporting politics as their occupation. (See Table 52.)

Those who joined the Congress tended to have less education than those joining the Socialist Party. (See Table 53.) Furthermore, all Praja Socialists falling into the low intergenerational educational mobility category joined the Congress. Not one of the few

TABLE 52

SCALED DUAL OCCUPATIONS OF THE PSP: MLA's JOINING
THE CONGRESS OR THE SOCIALIST PARTY, 1964

Scaled Dual Occupations	Joined Congress	Joined SP	Total
Small kisan or tenant with any secondary occupation	—	6	6
Medium kisan	4	2	6
Medium kisan and business	2	—	2
Medium kisan and politics	2	—	2
White-collar and politics	—	1	1
Business and medium kisan	—	1	1
Professional and small kisan	—	1	1
Politics	1	4	5
Politics and medium kisan	1	—	1
Politics and business	—	1	1
High status (large landowner; priest)	1	2	3
High status and politics	1	3	4
Total	12	21	33

TABLE 53

EDUCATION, EDUCATIONAL MOBILITY, FINANCIAL MOBILITY, STATUS
CRYSTALLIZATION, AND GENERAL SOCIAL MOBILITY OF PRAJA
SOCIALIST MLA's JOINING THE CONGRESS OR THE SP, 1964

Education and Mobility	Joined Congress	Joined SP	Total
Education:			
Low (literate—junior high school)	6	5	11
Medium (high school— intermediate)	4	8	12
High (university and above)	2	8	10
Educational mobility:			
Low	5	—	5
Medium	3	11	14
High	3	9	12
Not ascertained	1	1	2
Financial mobility:			
Better off financially than parents	—	5	5
Same as parents	3	5	8
Worse off financially than parents	7	10	17
Not ascertained	2	1	3
Status crystallization:			
High status consistency	9	9	18
Low status consistency	1	12	13
Not ascertained	2	—	2
General mobility:			
High mobility	—	3	3
Medium mobility	2	9	11
Low mobility	8	8	16
Not ascertained	2	1	3

Praja Socialists reporting themselves better off financially than
their parents joined the Congress; all those "better off" joined the
SP. In status crystallization, however, we see that most who joined
the Congress had high status consistency. Almost all those with
low-status consistency joined the Socialist Party. Again, in the

general social mobility score (combining educational, financial, and agricultural-to-nonagricultural occupational mobility) those joining the Congress tended to have low mobility and those joining SP to have higher mobility.

In chapter iii we asked if the high proportion of Praja Socialists reporting themselves financially worse off than their parents was an indication of lack of self-confidence, and whether this reply helped in understanding why the PSP generally appeared as the supplicant in discussions of merger with the Socialist Party even though the PSP was larger in size. We are now able to base the speculation on more tangible evidence. The question here was whether to join the majority party or to stay in the opposition. Those who elected to give up their status in the opposition tend to have a somewhat "stagnant" background. On several indices they show little advancement as compared with their fathers; in their own lives there is little variation of statuses, as calculated on the indices of caste, education, income, and scaled dual occupations. That this is stagnation and not simply a reflection of status differences is shown by Table 54. Status is not related to

TABLE 54

STATUS RANKING OF PRAJA SOCIALIST PARTY MLA's JOINING
THE CONGRESS OR THE SOCIALIST PARTY, 1964

Status Ranking	Joined Congress	Joined SP	Total
High status score	3	4	7
Medium status score	4	12	16
Low status score	3	5	8
Not ascertained	2	—	2
Total	12	21	33

joining the Congress. What separates these from those joining the Socialist Party is stagnation of mobility. More of those electing to remain in the opposition tend to be upwardly mobile as compared with their parents, and in their own lives show considerable inconsistency of status rankings on the four indices.

During the maneuverings proceeding the split in the PSP there

were numerous reports that while some MLA's might join the
Congress, their workers in the districts would not, or could not.
Several MLA's and a few district party leaders who were considering joining the Congress were asked about this aspect. All confirmed the reports. The reason given as to why workers would not
follow their leaders was that on the local level the workers were
so opposed to local Congressmen that they could not join them
in the same party. Frictions, personal and socioeconomic, were said
to be much more intense for local workers than for elected legislators, most of whom are district or constituency leaders. This
suggests that as activists rise within a party, and become involved
with building a party over a wide area and among different groups,
they tend to gain a broader outlook and learn to work with rather
than against individuals of other socioeconomic groups and per-
suasions. It suggests that some tensions are utilized for electoral
purposes while at the same time the leaders are learning to rise
above such tensions.

These same respondents were asked which party their workers
would be likely to join, should the respondent become a Congressman. After thoughtful reflection, almost all respondents said
in effect that the opposition party which was most strongly organized in their district would probably pick up their workers. Thus,
in Sitapur, where the Jan Sangh is strong and the Socialist Party
and other opposition parties are quite weak, the considered opinion of the PSP district leader was that his workers would probably
join the Jan Sangh. In Azamgarh, where the Communist Party is
the alternative opposition party, the PSP workers whose leaders
joined the Congress would probably join the Communist Party.
In Deoria, where the Socialist Party is well organized, most PSP
workers whose leaders joined the Congress would be picked up by
the Socialists. Such responses indicate that ideological conviction
is not a key factor in the joining of a party, but the proximity
of activists who can establish contact is.

Identification of factions within the Socialist Party was a difficult task, partly because there was no party conference and no
party contest for leadership of either the organizational or the
legislative wing during the course of the study. There is said to
be an east-west division within the party, but this could not be
definitely confirmed. In probing for possible friction on a caste

basis, two prominent party leaders in separate interviews made almost identical observations: there is less Brahmin-versus-Thakur rivalry, but more elite-versus-backward caste rivalry in the Socialist Party. Said one: "In the Socialist Party there is less friction among the elite castes because they have a binding interest as against the backward classes. They have a "back to the wall" feeling against the resurgence of backward and scheduled castes. The backward classes have developed a strong feeling for their own advancement, and are conscious that they have been deliberately kept down." [6]

There was considerable fragmented dissension within the Socialist Party from 1958 to 1962, culminating in the formation of a "Socialist Unity Forum" and its subsequent withdrawal from the party. Its members have since drifted into various parties or have become Independents. Several issues were reported as being involved. One was the "anti-intellectualism" in the party, which was said to have been fostered by Dr. Lohia. It may be that this current was a consequence of the effort to attract the lower castes, who would be presumed to have little interest in or concern with intellectual pursuits. On the other hand, "anti-intellectualism" might have been promoted by Dr. Lohia (an intellectual himself) in an effort to prevent or halt the rise of views which might differ from his own. Another issue arose during the extended satyagraha in 1957–1958. Some activists began to ask why there were making such sacrifices; it was said that the questions aroused the anger of Dr. Lohia. According to a respondent who was a state official in that year, the primary purpose of the satyagraha was to build the party and, as such, there was no intended point of cessation. Connected with this issue was the attempt by some activists to use nonparticipation in satyagrahas as ground for expelling members whom they disliked from the party. Yet another point of friction was the reported attempt of Dr. Lohia to restrict extra-party organizational memberships of activists. This was confirmed by a party official who emphasized that membership solely in the

[6] This respondent also made the interesting observation that the backward-versus-elite caste feeling is stronger in the old districts of Oudh where the backward classes were in poor circumstances under the big talukdars and zamindars, and in the districts bordering on these Oudh districts, such as a Farrukhabad and Fatehpur. The respondent was of an elite caste.

party is desired since memberships in other organizations would weaken loyalty to the party (a fine expression of the effect of multiple group affiliations.) A final factor was the desire for "socialist unity" among many activists, and the firm stand against unity taken by Dr. Lohia. It was under this latter issue that groups and individuals with disparate grievances coalesced. There were, in addition, a number of minor frictions affecting a few individuals. For example, a Socialist MLA was elected deputy speaker of the Assembly. At a later date, the Socialist MLA's withdrew from the Assembly halls and refused to take part in any legislative business. The deputy speaker, however, did not withdraw even when so ordered by Dr. Lohia. He joined the Socialist Unity Forum and subsequently became a member of the Congress.

A common thread running through these assorted frictions is disagreement with Dr. Lohia and an inability to discuss, much less resolve, these differences within the party. Some respondents objected to their party's being called the "Lohia Socialist Party," but by their own statements it seems that the appellation is correct. Dr. Lohia does not brook dissent from his views, policies, or proposed actions. Many activists revere his pronouncements. Personal doubts and misgivings are suppressed on many occasions. But when disagreements become open, there is no way to resolve the question save by apology or withdrawal. It may be that the relationship between dissent, group structure, and expectation of outside conflict posited by Lewis Coser has relevance for this situation. When a group is oriented toward continuous, acute conflict with other groups, says Coser, "every internal dissension appears to endanger the mobilization of concerted energies for the outside conflict . . . No dissent can therefore be tolerated, and the dissenter must be forced to withdraw." [7] He further holds that when "the group defines its structure according to its expectation of outside conflict, its response to inner dissent is no longer a matter of choice, but is determined by this very definition." [8] Socialist respondents pride themselves on their "militancy," their orientation toward active conflict with other groups. This orientation is partially expressed through agitational activities among the populace in the

[7] Lewis Coser, *The Functions of Social Conflict* (Glencoe, Ill.: Free Press, 1956), pp. 99–100.
[8] *Ibid.*, p. 100.

streets, and within Assembly chambers. They regard individuals and groups which are not conflict-oriented as "timid," "weak," "unprincipled," and openly express contempt toward them. Non-violence is given lip service, but leaders frankly state that if such a practice is the only hindrance to obtaining a goal, then violence will be invoked. The party can, it seems, be regarded as a struggle group. In addition, the party is built around the personality and leadership of one man. Disagreement with his views threatens not only his position, but also the entire party. As such, it cannot be tolerated; dissenters must surrender or be forced out of the party.

It was difficult to gather information about the leaders of the Socialist Unity Forum. The caste background was mixed, with apparently more Brahmins being involved than Thakurs. Defections appeared in the eastern and western districts, with few from the old districts of Oudh.

Morale

Morale affects the commitment of individuals to the party and their willingness to work for the party. Party defeat and victory in the state as a whole and in other states can affect morale. Objective measures of growth or decline are modified by subjective considerations. In each election in Uttar Pradesh the Jan Sangh has increased the seats won; there has also been an increase of seats won in other states. Respondents of the Jan Sangh seemed to be delighted with the actual increase and expressed optimism about the party's future. It did not appear that expectations of success were substantially greater than the results. Leaders on state and district levels recognized that building a party is not an overnight endeavor; they tended to view party expansion on a long-term basis and expressed the expectation of eventual majority status. Morale in the party seemed to be high.

Praja Socialist Party respondents reported that when the first Socialist Party and the KMPP were established, leaders and members confidently expected their parties to become major parties in 1951–1952. Although their parties had some success in Uttar Pradesh and other states, the results of the first general elections were a grave disappointment. The merger into the Praja Socialist Party raised high hopes for the future, but the split in 1954 dampened members' spirits. In 1957, although the party registered an increase in strength in Uttar Pradesh and some other states, the results were far lower than had been expected. Disillusionment set in. Activists drifted to other parties or retired. In 1962 the number of seats won by the Praja Socialist Party in Uttar Pradesh declined, and in other states the party did not fare too well. Some Praja Socialists, before the election, hoped for decisive increases in strength; others expected some increase in strength, but recognized that a long-term effort would be necessary for the party to obtain major status. The results were a blow to both groups. Morale within the party seemed to be fairly low. Respondents did not show the enthusiasm of Jan Sangh respondents; they did not refer to the PSP as the "wave of the future."

The low morale, however, seemed not to be explained fully by these factors. An additional element appeared to be the debate over a period of many years as to whether it was worthwhile to continue the party. This debate had various forms. Talks had been held with Congress leaders regarding close cooperation or perhaps reentry; moves had been made to promote merger (including creation of a new party) with the Lohia Socialist Party and other smaller parties. All efforts failed. But the efforts, and the ensuing debates, constantly raised the question as to whether the party would or should continue in existence. The barest minimum of consensus required for an organized group is belief in the value of the organization. When this value is questioned by members, and when members demonstrate willingness to end the organization, then one cannot expect to find high morale within the organization. So it is with the PSP. What began as debate over methods of furthering the PSP cause turned into debate over the party's continuation. But is this questioning of the worth of the party a cause or consequence of low morale? It seems to be both: it reflects the state of morale and at the same time helps to shape it.

The Socialist Party has held its own in Uttar Pradesh, though it has not shown substantial increases in seats won in other states. Some respondents indicated that expectations of success had been higher than the results. Since the election, Dr. Lohia and others have made tentative proposals regarding varying degrees of cooperation with other opposition parties (particularly with the Jan Sangh and the Communists). Within the party in Uttar Pradesh, many middle-level leaders and local workers have expressed desire for unity with the Praja Socialist Party, and as a consequence one might expect morale to be a problem; but morale within the party appears to be fairly high, perhaps owing to the character of the party as a small militant struggle group. Socialists, as mentioned previously, tend to hold high opinions of their party and show contempt for most other parties. They tend to regard themselves as superior to politicians in other parties. The struggle itself seems to have an importance equal to or surpassing that of the obtaining of goals. The value orientation of action for the sake of action, or action without regard for a goal, is enjoined in the Gita and is considered to be a traditional value in the society.

Morale thus seems to be related to three factors: objective success or failure at the polls in the state and other states in any one election or successive elections; subjective success or failure as judged by the comparison of expectations of success at the polls in any one election or successive elections; the nonelectoral or extraelectoral purposes, aims, and values of the party. Thus it appears that morale is related to the ability to attract adherents and engage in the arduous work of building and extending the party, and therefore is involved in providing members both with incentive and the sense of accomplishment.

Chapter XIV

CONCLUSION

ALTHOUGH THE BUILDING AND MAINTENANCE of opposition parties is the focus of the study, it was necessary from the beginning to specify interactions involving the dominant party. In the course of the study, much of importance was learned about the Indian National Congress which may have relevance in studies of other dominant parties.

Vulnerability of the Dominant Party

The Congress was originally classified as a pragmatic, pluralist party; little was found to change the appellation. The Congress has an aura of legitimacy, stemming from its heritage as the national movement seeking independence, from the emotional commitment therein generated, and from its possession of positions of authority, achieved through electoral victories. Congressmen control most of the semipublic economic organizations in Uttar Pradesh, and the party has its own labor unions. Some nonparty social service organizations, such as the Bharat Sevak Samaj, have in effect become Congress fiefdoms. Through its penetration of these institutions, the dominant party can offer many advantages to its supporters in the form of immediate material benefits, broad policies, and psychological satisfactions. Many of its policies have favored large groups in the populace, as well as small. On a statewide basis, all of the major groups in society appear to have some representation in the Congress. It appears to be a broadly based and fairly well-organized party in Uttar Pradesh.

Despite these factors, the Congress has become vulnerable since independence. The five areas of vulnerability must be viewed in the context of the transition from a national movement to a ruling political party. Such a change is common to former colonial revolutionary parties.[1]

[1] Cf. James S. Coleman and Carl G. Rosberg, Jr. (eds.), *Integration in Tropical Africa* (Berkeley and Los Angeles: University of California Press,

First, the Congress has had to find a new rationale and new goals. With the achievement of independence and the establishment of a democratic, representative form of government, major goals were achieved—and thereby lost. Since independence, in the Congress national conventions leaders and activists have searched for an ideology connoting more than "defense of the revolution," "defense of democracy," and the like. Goals of such defense, of economic development, of national integration, of "anti-communalism," "anti-groupism," "anti-casteism," have provided neither the mobilizing power nor the emotional commitment of the clarion call for independence. Congress has accepted the goal of socialism, but it is questionable whether this doctrine can revitalize the party. Over the years the Congress has had to resolve the conflict between two ideological streams. A Western, nationalist, liberal, socialist, secular stream is juxtaposed with an Indian, ostensibly syncretist, but tending-to-be-Hindu stream. Both existed before independence; Gandhi's reconciliation of the two was neither complete nor completely accepted. Before independence the conflict between the two did not emerge; both could be directed toward the goal of independence. After independence the conflict emerged, and it still continues. Although the Congress now officially proclaims "socialism" as a goal, the content of such a doctrine is by no means clear and the practice of the doctrine has yet to be analyzed.

The second area of vulnerability relates to personnel problems in the organization. The transition to a government party meant, on the one hand, that people who previously worked within the party organization had to shift their efforts to the running of the government; as a result, organizational work among the populace suffered. On the other hand, in the post-independence years the party's activities changed, and with such change has come a need for new skills. Agitation against government has changed to support of government. Maximization of grievances has been changed to minimization. Administrators rather than agitators are needed. Yet, not all activists with an agitational background have been able or willing to make the shift. Agitators discovered that their talents could not be used in Congress. Leadership positions, con-

---

1964), pp. 672 ff. Many of these vulnerabilities were also identified in the new states of Africa. See Brass, *Factional Politics in an Indian State,* for a more detailed study of the transition from movement to party.

ferring both power and prestige, have been transferred to those having the requisite skills. The result is that at the very time the Congress needs a substantial increase in personnel to man governmental and party offices, there is reduction of available and skilled personnel from party sources. Disaffection of members, decline of enthusiasm, and weakened commitment to the party come as long-term leaders find themselves passed over and "outsiders" take control.[2] Such changes in leadership personnel are reflected within the populace, in unflattering ways. The loss of leaders with idealism and high goals is moaned; the new leaders are not sanctified by sacrifice, and are considered to have entered politics for strictly personal benefit and with crude motives.[3] Another kind of personnel problem has arisen with the passage of years. The great nationalist leaders such as Gandhi and Nehru have passed on. Many of the early post-independence leaders have died—Pandit Pant, Lal Bahadur Shastri, and Rafi Ahmed Kidwai, to mention only a few from Uttar Pradesh. Others are extremely old; the younger men frequently are not well known. As present-day state leaders move gradually to the national level, new state leaders must be found. To what extent the aura of legitimacy surrounding the Congress is related to specific leaders has not been determined. To what extent cohesion in the Congress is related to the political expertise and prestige of those leaders has not been determined.

A third point of vulnerability relates to the difficulties of governing, and particularly the problems of directing the administrative services. Before independence, Congressmen criticized the administrative services not only for what was being done or not

[2] A transferral or reshuffling of power in Congress around the time of independence (usually from 1945 to 1952) was noted in most of the districts visited and was mentioned by respondents in other districts. The transferral, of course, was a source of "displaced" leaders and groups. Some respondents, in discussing the present high position of Congress leaders in the state, directly related their rise to the possession of administrative skills. One striking example given was that of the young Congress Minister H. N. Bahuguna, whose meteoric rise was said to be due to his trade-union activities and administrative skills (as opposed to agitational). He quickly gained prominence over the former agitational leaders of the trade-union movement.

[3] Such sentiments were frequently mentioned by politicians, lawyers, newspapermen, and villagers throughout UP. Scarcely a month goes by without seeing these criticisms in the public press.

done, but also for the manner in which administrators carried out their duties, and their criticism was directed toward the British. After independence they became aware that most of the administrators were Indian. They have had difficulties in changing the attitudes and behavior of government officials. They have had problems in energizing officials and getting them to undertake new kinds of tasks, and on the part of administrative officials there has been some resistance to control, direction, and redirection by elected officials.[4] Complicating the situation is the fact that since independence the number of government officials in Uttar Pradesh has more than doubled. In the early 1950's the civil service was called the "steel frame." One respondent wryly commented, "but the steel has rusted." When people have troubles or see others having troubles with the local administrators, when they see corruption, favoritism, endless red tape, delays, harassment, and so on, they hold Congress responsible. Identification of the Congress with the Government does not necessarily benefit the party: policies are not always implemented swiftly, completely, or in the manner desired, and more often than not the Congress is criticized for the action or inaction of administrators.

A fourth point of vulnerability is the frustration and popular disenchantment directed toward the Congress as the ruling party. There are several bases for these attitudes. First, expectations of a golden age to dawn with independence were not fulfilled. There was a rude awakening.[5] Second, the personal behavior and attitudes of some Congressmen have tarnished the Congress image. Not only is self-aggrandizement criticized, but also the development of an air of superiority.[6] It is possible to relate present attitudes among the ruling party's members to the models available for emulation, none of which are equalitarian. It is far easier to emulate the old under the pressures of the present than to

[4] Problems with the administration were among the most common topics referred to in the field by politicians of all parties, Independents, and simply chance respondents. In the Assembly a number of problems with administrative officials are taken up daily during Question Hour.

[5] Such expectations were reported by many respondents, including Congress Ministers.

[6] Such criticisms were reported in the case studies of Pratagarh South, Saurikh, and Moradabad Rural in particular. A number of respondents, including Congressmen, noted the existence of such charges and their basis in behavior.

develop different attitudes and modes of behavior. Third, there are some problems which the Government has not been able to solve, or to handle adequately, such as floods, food shortages, the rising cost of living, and population increases. Fourth, some policies that aided large groups in the population have aroused the ire of others, and some policies—tax increases for example—have aroused resentment in those who have and those who have not benefited from other policies. Congressmen remark that some groups who benefited directly from past policies now demonstrate the attitude of "But what have you done for us lately?" Furthermore, Congress policies have tended to accelerate some processes of modernization and not others; the change has been disjointed. Lastly, as the ruling party, the Congress plays a role which has repressive as opposed to liberating aspects. In other words, the policies which Congress has initiated have helped some groups and hurt others. One result has been the creation of defensive groups, beneficiary groups, and what for want of a better term may be called "unsatisfied beneficiary" groups.

A fifth point of vulnerability is the social milieu in which the party operates. The Congress Party on the local level has become identified by the populace with specific groups. It is necessary to clarify what is meant by "identification with," particularly as it applies to Uttar Pradesh. One aspect of identification is the voting support which the party has received from various groups. In a village one party might be identified with a certain faction by the people there and in neighboring villages. Throughout a constituency, district, or state, however, a party can obtain the voting support of a group and not be identified with it. For example, it is widely reported that the Congress obtains the bulk of the scheduled-caste votes in the state. Yet rarely if ever is it described as the party of the scheduled castes. In Uttar Pradesh other indices connote identification. One index is the party leadership. Respondents throughout the state customarily identified district or constituency parties with the socioeconomic groups represented by the district or constituency leadership echelon. A second index is the degree of exertion on behalf of groups by specifically district or local party leaders. If members of the leadership echelon had made extraordinary efforts on behalf of groups of which they were not members, the party was frequently identified with those groups. For example, the Socialist Party of Bara Banki was identified with the Pasis, a scheduled caste, because of the great efforts of Kurmi leaders. The Praja Socialist Party in Jaunpur district was identified by respondents with the lower castes because of the extraordinary efforts of Brahmin leaders. A party on the state or national level can display a statement of principles, policy programs, or legislative record benefiting certain groups. But if local leaders have not exerted themselves for such groups, the party on that level is not likely to be identified with them. Although on the state level the Congress is broadly representative, local identification is what is of import on the local level. In a society with multiple cleavages and strong tensions, overt and latent, between various kinds of groups, there are obvious pressures to restrict the party to a base within a certain segment of society. Although a party can remain open at the voter and low-worker levels, leadership positions can be closed. Leaders have a choice of whether to exert themselves on behalf of subgroups or potential groups. When subgroups and potential groups are considered to be socioeconomic rivals of the leaders and of the groups to which they belong, and when the party is—or is thought to be—clearly dominant, it is not to be expected that party leaders will operate to maximize support within society.[7] Preservation of individual or group status and promotion of the interests of certain groups can be given higher priorities by the dominant party in a one-party-dominant system than in a highly competitive system.

As a national movement, the Congress sought maximization of support. With the achievement of independence and the transition from movement to party, the "size principle" came into operation.[8] Congress leaders permitted and even encouraged the departure of some groups (the Congress Socialist Party, the Rafiats, and Acharya Kripalani's groups, for example). The party did not seek the adherence of new groups. On local levels, the groups with which the Congress is identified tend to be those mobilized

---

[7] See Samuel J. Eldersveld, *Political Parties: A Behavioral Analysis* (Chicago: Rand McNally, 1964), pp. 47 ff.; William H. Riker, *The Theory of Political Coalitions* (New Haven: Yale University Press, 1962), pp. 32–65; and Anthony Downs, *An Economic Theory of Democracy* (New York: Harper, 1957).

[8] Riker, *op. cit.*, pp. 32 ff.

at the time of transition. The operation of the "size principle" in the Congress has made the party vulnerable.

Testing of Hypotheses

The original hypotheses based on expected interactions of social processes, the dominant party, and the opposition parties (see p. 10) can now be reconsidered.

(a) A party of national independence tends to have its leadership frozen in those social groups which were mobilized at that time.

(b) Leaders of more recently mobilized groups will tend to seek recognition and position in opposition parties.

The main hypothesis is supported in all the case studies. Reports from respondents in other districts, and from state Congress leaders, give additional confirmation.

There is some support for the subhypothesis. In Saurikh, the movement of Lodhi-Rajputs toward the Jan Sangh and of some recently mobilized Brahmins toward the Jan Sangh give some confirmation. Reports of respondents concerning the backward castes in Fatehpur, Ghazipur, Azamgarh, and Varanasi add support. It is, of course, easier to illustrate the phenomenon when a recently mobilized group has several identifying characteristics, such as religion, caste, residence, and occupation. The case of Moradabad Rural is important in showing a spiraling down and out of social and political mobilization, with apparently many newly mobilized persons turning to opposition parties.

Field work suggests that amplification of the successive mobilization process is needed. Two situations can be posited. The first concerns conflict deriving solely from the time of mobilization. Leadership positions in the dominant party are held by the previously mobilized. Over time, others are mobilized. The previously mobilized resist entrance of the recently mobilized to leadership positions. The conflict is divorced from cultural group differentiations. Analysis of the socioeconomic origins and cultural-group identifications might reveal little differentiation between the leadership of the parties. The striking difference would be the time of mobilization. A hypothesis could be put forward that the re-cently mobilized will turn to opposition parties. In Uttar Pradesh there were occasional references to such a conflict, with some scat-tered confirmation. The study was not broad enough, however, to explore thoroughly this kind of conflict.

The second situation posits an interaction of cultural cleavages with the time of mobilization. A dominant party has a leadership among a previously mobilized group which is based within par-ticular cultural groups. Over time, others become mobilized. Those belonging to the same cultural groups as the previously mobilized leaders are able to penetrate the leadership echelon of the dominant party. The previously mobilized exert themselves in behalf of the interests of a newly mobilized group sharing its cultural identification (or identifications). On the other hand, those who do not belong to the same cultural groups as the pre-viously mobilized leaders find that dominant-party leadership posi-tions are closed to them, and that the existing party leaders make little effort to promote their interests. In this situation, the newly mobilized belonging to other cultural groups than those of the dominant-party leadership would be expected to turn to opposi-tion parties. This appears to be the much more common pattern in Uttar Pradesh.

There are two factors which tend to modify the process. First, the desire to be identified with the rulers (the governing party) can be sufficiently strong to induce group leaders to remain in the dominant party as activists. It is too early to determine whether there is any time limit operating, and if so, what that time limit might be.

The second factor modifying the process is the operation of the "size principle" in the Congress. If the party loses elections after a recently mobilized group has turned to an opposition party, Congress leaders—to recreate a minimum winning coalition—can open leadership positions to the prime leaders or important lesser leaders of that recently mobilized group. If Congress losses can be attributed to general attrition, factionalism, and so on, Congress leaders might open leadership positions to representatives of newly mobilized groups who have a subordinate status in the party. By doing this, the Congress might weld the group to the party while strengthening its cohesiveness. Defeat and the need for future victory can modify recruitment and promotion practices in the dominant party. It may be that one explanation for the game of "musical chairs" which occurs in each general election lies in the operation of these factors. This is to conceptualize the dominant party as an accordion which, upon defeat, opens to admit recently mobilized groups and then closes.

Our second and third hypotheses (see p. 11) reflect the tensions arising from change in society, which may be the result of policies initiated by the dominant party. Two, or even three groups are created: defensive, potential beneficiary, and unsatisfied beneficiary:

(a) Those who are threatened with loss of status, role, or function by reforms or policies instituted by the dominant party will seek representation in opposition parties

(b) If the dominant party does not carry out policies formulated or justified by its ideology, the unsatisfied beneficiaries of such policies will seek representation in opposition parties

Some confirmation is provided both by analysis of the middle-level leaders and by our case studies. A greater proportion of the MLA's of the three opposition parties than of the Congress are former talukdars or zamindars—a defensive group. The study of Pratapgarh South vividly illustrates the second hypothesis. The third hypothesis is supported by many statements of respondents in the two socialist parties regarding the insufficient scope of social-reform policies or their insufficient implementation as prime reasons for turning to opposition parties.

The study suggests some amplification of these two hypotheses. It is not necessarily state or national policies nor their implementation which can create defensive and unsatisfied beneficiary groups. These groups can arise from the presence and the activities of specific persons in the dominant party on the local level. Cases such as a teacher's reportedly being transferred because of his friendship with a member of the dissident Congress faction; the stopping of the government grant to a school, reportedly by the action of local Congress leaders; respondents' reports of various kinds of harassment by local Congress leaders—these and the like provide examples. Aside from the process of social mobilization and social reform policies, rivalries between individuals and groups can create a defensive situation for some. Many of our examples apply to individuals. By virtue of the social structure and social groupings, however, the defensive mechanism is expanded. Affected individuals seek to relate the conflict to the groups of which they are members. The group is mobilized on a defensive basis.

These same kinds of rivalries can create an unsatisfied beneficiary group. Although some benefits are provided in a policy and received in its implementation, there can be a psychological nonrealization of benefits. The nonrealization is related to the specific persons (rivals) leading the local Congress. Responses that the Congress is the party of the big and the rich, the capitalists, with "no room for kisans," and the party which refuses to give tickets to members of one's group illustrate this kind of situation. Possession of leadership positions in the Congress can provide status for individuals and groups; rivalries which prevent such recognition can easily lead to a sense of deprivation. Furthermore, political decisions made by local Congress leaders in implementing a state or national policy may reduce the benefits expected by specific groups.

The study suggests another tension and its related hypotheses. The tension arises from displacement of a group's leaders in the dominant party. By "displacement," the defection of leaders is not meant, but rather the systematic exclusion of a group's representatives in the local or district leadership echelon. There was a reshuffling in Congress leadership around the time of independence. One factor seemed to be the differing degrees of mobilization among various groups. Representatives of groups with relatively low awareness, interest, and participation in political activities tended to be ousted or passed over in favor of representatives of more highly mobilized groups. Such was the case in Pratapgarh of backward-caste leaders who held positions in the Congress until the transition from movement to party. This case suggests that it is possible for individuals to gain leadership positions in a national movement by their own exertions, even though the cultural groups to which they belong are not highly mobilized. In the transition to party, extent of group mobilization becomes important. Other factors also can play a role in displacement of leaders: the need for personnel with certain kinds of skills, or the sudden entry of new groups who support some leaders but not others. The latter was the case in Rudauli, where former Muslim Leaguers entered the Congress and supported Muslim rather than Hindu leaders. Particularly if new groups were of relatively high socioeconomic status, their leaders gained prominence in the party. (In Rudauli, high-status talukdars led the Muslim Leaguers.) In some places more than one variable was in operation. From our limited observation of such cases, the following new hypothesis and subhypotheses are suggested for future, more extensive testing:

> Leaders belonging to groups not highly mobilized will tend to lose positions held in the national movement during the transition from movement to party

> Leaders having agitational skills who are unable or unwilling to acquire other skills will tend to lose leadership positions during the transition from movement to party

> Leaders who receive no support from large groups led by individuals of high socioeconomic status and entering a party at the time of independence will tend to lose position during the transition from movement to party

> Groups whose leaders are displaced from the leadership echelon of the dominant party during the transition from movement to party will tend to seek representation in opposition parties

There are difficulties in gauging which tensions have been most utilized by the three parties under study. One reason is that parties have taken advantage of differing situations. Our observations and analyses were very limited. A second reason is the existence of multiple cross-cutting cleavages. Recently mobilized, defensive, unsatisfied beneficiary, and displaced groups can be identified. But other lines of cleavage—or, conversely, unifying ties—can be described which cut across them and each other. Through the "expansion mechanism," previously referred to, a core group which can be readily classified as defensive (for example) gathers about it a host of disparate groups. Politicians do have some choice in any constituency as to which cleavages to attempt to intensify and which to attempt to overcome.

Granting the complexities, the Jan Sangh can be described as having support among the more recently mobilized, more recently modernized segment of society, and among the defensive. The characteristics of the MLA's support this description. The two Jan Sangh case studies illustrated a core defensive group. Pratapgarh South showed a coalition between the defensive and the newly mobilized. Lawyers and businessmen, Kayasths and Banias, urban, "middle-class," recently mobilized groups were allied with the defensive talukdar Thakurs. Interviews with other Jan Sangh respondents revealed defensiveness which was related to the presence and activities of personal-factional rival leaders in control of the local Congress. While the Jan Sangh can be identified with these groups, it does have support from some who were early mobilized or were displaced, or were unsatisfied beneficiaries.

The two socialist parties seem to be drawing on those mobilized at an earlier point in time and the displaced. The analysis of the MLA's showed that almost all were politically mobilized before independence, and that many were either displaced from the Congress or associated with those who were displaced. In each party there is a group of unsatisfied beneficiaries—unsatisfied partly because of the displacement. At the same time, while most of the individuals interviewed were mobilized before independence, the groups which they represent are essentially newly mobilizing. The present activation of the backward castes as self-conscious groups, the growing importance of rural-versus-urban distinctions, and the relevance of these identifications for political activity are recalled. To the data already presented in earlier chapters, a note can be added. A number of Praja Socialist and Socialist MLA's of elite castes, mobilized before independence, discussed at some length their efforts to build parties on the middle and lower castes and classes in the rural areas. In classifying the two socialist parties, it is necessary to distinguish between the middle-level leaders and the groups which the leaders represent.

In maintaining successful local parties, the opposition parties confront many of the same problems as the Congress. Frustration and disenchantment seem to be directed against whichever party is victorious on the local level. Some of the basic problems which foster discontent are not and cannot be solved by the election of an opposition candidate. Floods do not cease, prices do not stabilize, food does not become plentiful, and so on. An opposition legislator cannot control local administrators, cannot change their behavior, cannot easily energize them. Nor can he end corruption or red tape. Some respondents said that election of an opposition candidate is a grant of independence to local administrators. Local officials then do not have to pay attention to local Congressmen, because the Congress has lost, and they do not have to pay attention to the elected legislator, because he is in the opposition on the district and state level. Others dispute this interpretation, claiming that administrators are under greater restraints when faced with a legislator who can raise questions about local matters more forcibly in the Assembly than a member of the majority party, who is not obliged to forego agitational activities and who has some ties to higher administrators and politicians. Regardless of which interpretation is favored, there are still going to be difficulties with administrative officials. Disenchantment can also set in if the leaders of the opposition develop an air of superiority or endeavor to enrich themselves through their offices—and some do. The opposition is also rendered vulnerable because of inability to initiate policies or fulfill promises made during the course of a campaign. If a candidate has exploited a deep-rooted desire among groups to become "rulers" or to be accepted as members of the ruling class, he and the party are vulnerable because there is actually very little they can do to satisfy the groups. They have no patronage; they cannot make their supporters "rulers." In other words, no golden age dawns with the election of an opposition candidate.

Another vulnerability shared with the Congress is related to social tensions and the operation of the "size principle." Our original hypothesis and subhypotheses (p. 14) were confirmed by our study:

(a) On the constituency level, an opposition party tends to have its leadership frozen among those groups whose representatives gained leadership positions by or at the time of victory at the polls

(b) Over time, an opposition party on the constituency level tends to be identified with those groups represented by the leadership echelon of the constituency and district

(c) On the constituency level, leaders of groups mobilized after the victory at the polls of an opposition party will tend to seek recognition in other parties

A problem is that information regarding the coalition may be incomplete or inaccurate. Some groups may not be so firmly welded to the party as a victorious candidate believes. Furthermore, there can be inaccurate analysis of the election results. Activists, in many cases, do not seem to be aware that victory was theirs because another party or parties served as a "blocking coalition"—blocking the victory of another candidate. Lack of recognition and failure to take remedial action can partly explain the game of "musical chairs."

It cannot be assumed that the sole goal of opposition party members is success at the polls. Even though a prime aim may be victory, there are likely to be other considerations which restrict the routes by which victory is to be achieved. The orientation toward success is countered by desires to promote or preserve the status of individuals and groups. What is functional for one or a few groups may be dysfunctional for party success. The relative priorities given conflicting aims determines in large measure the adaptability and permeability of a party. Division among the leadership regarding the rank order of the two preferences might easily lead to a party split.

Originally it was thought that the obtaining of material benefits for supporters would be very important in perpetuating a coalition and appealing to potential clienteles. A hypotheses (p. 16) was formulated indicating one variable affecting the ability to obtain benefits. While the main hypothesis was confirmed, to a limited extent, the subhypothesis was not:

(a) On the constituency level, the stronger the tensions between the leaders of a victorious opposition party and those of the dominant party, the less able the opposition party leaders to obtain benefits for their supporters

(b) On the constituency level, if victorious opposition party leaders do not carry out pledges of specific actions made as side-payments to notables in winning their electoral support, the unsatisfied beneficiaries will tend to become apathetic toward or alienated from the party

According to the respondents, the ability to obtain material benefits was not so crucial for maintenance of support within the
electorate as the identity of other candidates. The questions, however, may have lacked the proper specificity. Obtaining material
benefits for constituents generally can be distinguished from obtaining benefits for notables which were promised in return for
support. Furthermore, promises other than material benefits can
be made. More precise testing is necessary.

Any conclusion regarding the question of whether the forces
and interactions postulated are adequate to sustain opposition
parties must be qualified. The forces initially aid the building of
opposition parties, and aid the continuance of opposition as such.
They limit the ability of any one opposition party to maintain
support within the same constituency over time.

Many of the difficulties of intraparty maintenance can be related
to the operation of the same factors which present problems for
party-electorate maintenance. The process of successive mobilization and the appearance over time of new, or at least different,
lines of cleavage are examples. Some kinds of cleavages tend to
become more important in intraparty maintenance, particularly
as wider areas are included. Geographic distinctions, educational
attainment, financial status, and style or type of politician become
critical areas. One basic problem is how to prevent or handle
coinciding cleavages on a number of indices. Prevention may be
out of the question; mitigating the friction is difficult because of
the inability to provide side payments to competitors and because
of the kinds of decisions that are made within the party.

One problem shared by the dominant and opposition parties is
ideology. In all the opposition parties studied there is some conflict between a Western, liberal, socialist, secular stream and an
Indian (syncretic but tending toward Hindu) stream. In choice
of words, the Jan Sangh has emphasized the Indian (Hindu)
stream, but the substantive content of many policy statements is
almost indistinguishable from that of other parties. The Socialist
Party tends to emphasize the Western, liberal, socialist, secular
stream, but a good deal of the substance tends toward the Indian
(Hindu). The Praja Socialist Party tends to lean toward the Western, liberal, socialist, secular stream in both wording and substance more than the other two parties.

Organization and the structure of control is another area of conflict within opposition parties. The Western, liberal, socialist, secular ideology is related to the image of a disciplined and centralized party organization which is part of the British heritage. The Indian, particularly Hindu, ideology is related to a decentralized and not highly disciplined organizational pattern. The concept of "unity in diversity," and the heritage of a loosely organized, decentralized religious structure help to illustrate this point. The Jan Sangh, although leaning toward an Indian (Hindu) ideology, has adapted the Western organization. Its centralization and discipline, and also its evangelism (alien to Hinduism), were criticized by members of other parties and Independents. All were seen as a violation of the Hindu and Indian tradition. The Praja Socialist Party appears to be the most Western-oriented of the three in ideology, but has, in fact, an organization leaning toward the Indian (Hindu) style. Although there are occasional spasmodic attempts at discipline and centralization, they frequently lead to party disruption. The Socialist Party seemingly has tried to establish the Western-style organization and has adopted an evangelical approach. In ideology, however, the Socialists have leaned more toward the Indian (Hindu) stream than have the Praja Socialists. Centralization and discipline are key problems for party leaders. The political, governmental, and socioeconomic structure not only encourages but almost demands decentralization of parties. At first glance, the federal system suggests the probability of the development of strong state parties which vie with the national for internal party control. The absence of any state-wide electoral positions tends to modify the probability. For the dominant party, control of the state governmental apparatus through control of a majority of legislative offices provides the state party leadership with some leverage as against the national party and the local units. But even the state Congress is more realistically viewed as a coalition of strong local parties. For opposition parties there is really no focal point on the state level. The "state party" is an abstraction and an anomaly. The governmental structure does not encourage the development of strong state minority-party units having effective control over local units.

There are few socioeconomic factors which unite Uttar Pradesh as a state while distinguishing it from other states. Hindi is the dominant language, but this does not separate Uttar Pradesh from adjacent states. Questions of language and state boundaries have helped in some parts of India to foster loyalty to a state; language has not so operated here. Furthermore, the dialects within Hindi must be considered. Linguistically, eastern Uttar Pradesh dialects are more closely related to those in western Bihar than to those in western Uttar Pradesh. Agriculturally, the eastern districts are more similar to those across the border than to those in the west; southern districts are more similar to over-the-border districts in Madhya Pradesh; and western districts are more similar to over-the-border districts also. State-wide castes are not limited to this one state; regionally concentrated castes—particularly in border districts—can often look to their caste heartland in another state. All these are factors in the diversity of Uttar Pradesh. Socio-economically, it cannot be defined as a distinct unit. Cross-cutting cleavages on many indices reduce the likelihood of separatist movements. This entire study illustrates the political diversity, which is a consequence of the socioeconomic structure, the governmental structure, and the interaction of social forces.

A state party unit of a minority party can exist as a grouping of local parties, as a center for coordinating policy and action, as a communications center—in short, as a linkage among local parties and between local parties and a national unit. But there are bound to be difficulties in attempting to vest control of local units in the state unit. For the state organization to set itself up as the directive-issuing unit, dictating policy and action to local units—particularly with respect to purely local concerns—and disciplining local units and leaders who do not fall into line, is to invite rebellion and dissolution of the party. Victory at the polls is not demonstrably related to membership in a specific minority party, or to support of prominent state or national party leaders. Most party finances are derived from local sources. Although in campaigns some state and national figures distribute monies to local parties, such distribution rarely if ever is channeled through the state party treasury. The state party unit cannot provide patronage for local units; it cannot provide material benefits. The prime ties binding local units to state and national units are personal loyalty to specific leaders and belief in ideology. There are limits to the sanctions which can be developed about these two factors. Practical considerations encourage decentralization of parties. They also make it difficult to build and maintain disciplined parties. A course of action which is highly functional for the perpetuation, consolidation, or extension of one local unit—whether that unit be defined as a party in one ward of a town, or a city party, or a constituency party, and so on—may be dysfunctional for other units on that same level. Attempts to establish and maintain a strong, centralized, disciplined party on the state level, where so many factors militate against that form, present each party with major problems. Efforts to establish centralized, disciplined parties are perhaps conducive to the promotion of state integration and, ultimately, national integration. Thus far, minority-party state and national leaders seem to have put a higher value on long-term integration than on short-term expansion.[9]

Another problem confronting minority party leaders in their efforts to build and maintain the party is the timing of elections at five-year intervals. The interval gives advantages to the dominant party, especially in regard to party publicity. Minority party resources are something less than ample. It is difficult to keep the name of the party, its leaders, and its policy goals before the public. There has to be a mammoth effort at election time to educate the new entrants and reeducate many former participants to the fact of the party's existence. Changes in candidates require an even greater effort. In addition to the general elections, there are direct elections for village, town, or city governmental positions. Parties do not participate in the former, although they do in the latter. Town and city elections are usually held at five-year intervals, two years after the general elections. The staggered elections and the different constituency size offer opportunities to minority parties for intensive organizational work. The town

[9] The Jan Sangh and the Socialist Party have stressed centralization and discipline. The PSP has theoretically stressed centralization, but in practice has vacillated between it and decentralization. PSP efforts toward centralization and discipline have been hampered by the lack of well-established functioning channels of communication between state and local units. Often the state leaders do not learn what is happening on the local levels until it is too late to take remedial action. Sometimes entry by the state unit into a local dispute has intensified difficulties within the lower unit and has led to schism. The vacillation between centralization and decentralization in practice has resulted in neither state nor local leaders' having a clear idea of their respective powers and responsibilities.

and city elections help to sustain the minority party in urban areas, but not in rural areas.

One feature which has aided minority parties in their efforts is universal adult suffrage. In the process of mobilizing parts of the populace, they have not had to fight for the franchise of these groups. Second, the great proportion of the electorate is not firmly committed to any party. The reservoir of apathetic, uncommitted people having the vote provides both incentives and rewards for minority parties. Third, parties do not have to limit their activities to changing long-established party identifications in the populace; they can mobilize new participants. In other words, there are many "slack resources"[10] available for utilization by the opposition parties.

The same factors that present problems for maintenance of individual opposition parties also tend to limit the ability of opposition parties to merge. Even though the top leadership echelons of different parties are amenable to merger, local situations militate strongly against merger in many places. At times the reverse is the case. Local units may strongly desire merger, but the top leadership echelons of the parties concerned may be so different and the cleavages on so many indices so great that merger is not considered acceptable.

Functions Performed by Opposition Parties

Opposition parties provide channels for political communication both horizontally and vertically. Although these parties cannot be considered the prime communication channels in the political system, they do complement the networks provided by the dominant party and the Government. They extend communications to groups which are outside the Congress network. In so doing, they are helping to bring groups into the political process.

Two of their most important functions are political socialization and recruitment. Given the social milieu, the fact that multiple minor parties exist aids the performance of these two functions. There are several groups which consider as archrivals both the groups identified with the Congress and those identified with one

[10] For a discussion of slack resources and their function in a political system see Robert Dahl, *Who Governs?* (New Haven: Yale University Press, 1961).

or more opposition parties, and the existence of still other minority parties enables these groups to express their own interests. If multiple minority parties did not exist or were not allowed, many groups might not enter the political process at all. They would probably constitute an anomic group. Over time, a substantial portion of the population might become alienated from the system of government. The existence of multiple minority parties enables discontent, divergent interests, and antagonisms between groups to be publicly registered, to be directed against the dominant party and against governmental actions, without being directed against the system. The multiple minority parties compete among themselves as well as with the Congress to mobilize increasingly large numbers of the populace and bring them into the political process as participants. The competition probably has increased both the rate of mobilization and the proportion mobilized. As part of the mobilization process, they encourage the development of different kinds of groups on a broader basis than before—they help to organize and integrate a fragmented society. Within the minority parties both leaders and groups learn by experience to overcome some frictions, and develop some new values. Although the activities of opposition parties in the political and socio-economic systems can be considered divisive, they can on other levels be considered integrative. One of the functions that opposition parties perform is to articulate and integrate different kinds of interests. These interests include desires for status and recognition.

There is debate today concerning whether minority parties are really needed in newly independent, underdeveloped countries engaged in the process of nation building. Usually such a debate is intimately related to democracy, and to the question whether it is possible to have a one-party democratic political system. Some studies indicate that such is possible. The experience in Uttar Pradesh indicates the value of minority parties. Their activities can assist the majority party in the basic task of political socialization, recruitment, interest articulation, and aggregation. It is not clear whether the results of these activities are conducive to economic development. There is little to suggest that the relatively slow economic development of the state is caused by opposition parties. Divisions within the Congress, maladministration, poor planning, corruption, and a host of other factors seem more directly connected with the slowness of economic expansion. The minority parties in Uttar Pradesh have not been separatist, and all have been committed to the idea of India as one state. Of the three parties studied, none can be considered "traditional" in the sense of that might be applied to native chieftains striving to re-establish their former powers or in the sense of being opposed to everything that the Congress stands for. Other kinds of minority parties can exist, however, and as such might not be conducive to the goals of nation building.

It may be that the most important function that opposition parties will play in the long run is as "feeder" organizations to the dominant party. A dominant party is not necessarily an "open accordion." It may be that the dominant party can open its ranks to new groups only when they have become politically significant —which means previous to entry. Opposition parties in Uttar Pradesh could be perennial minority parties, serving to socialize, politicize, recruit, organize, integrate, and articulate the interests of groups only to see them incorporated into the dominant party. Whether this will become their main role would seem to depend on the dominant party. The 1967 election may in the future be considered a "deviating election." The Congress, still the largest party, can open the accordion to groups mobilized by the opposition parties. If it does, the system may revert to one-party dominance. If it does not, the system may become even more competitive. Given the vulnerabilities which tend to limit the expansion of smaller parties, it is unlikely that one of the opposition parties under study will be able to achieve majority status in the state. The governmental instability inherent in coalitions of many parties with divergent policy orientations, combined with differences between the Congress-controlled national government and a non-Congress-controlled state government, could lead to modification, if not downfall, of the parliamentary system. For India as well as Uttar Pradesh, and for the opposition parties as well as the Congress, the succeeding years will be a time of testing.

REFERENCE MATERIAL

BIBLIOGRAPHY

PARTY DOCUMENTS

BHARATIYA JANA SANGH. *Bharatiya Jana Sangh: A Brief Introduction.* Delhi: Bharatiya Jana Sangh, n.d.

———. *Election Manifesto, 1957.* Delhi: Bharatiya Jana Sangh, n.d.

———. *Election Manifesto, 1962.* Delhi: Bharatiya Jana Sangh, n.d.

———. *Important Economic Resolutions, 1952–57.* Delhi: Bharatiya Jana Sangh, n.d.

———. *Manifesto and Programme of the Bharatiya Jana Sangh.* Delhi: Bharatiya Jana Sangh, Central Office, 1956.

———. *Resolutions of the Bharatiya Pratinidhi Sabha.* Delhi: Bharatiya Jana Sangh, 1963.

GHOSH, ACHARYA DEVA PRASAD. *Presidential Address.* Delhi: Bharatiya Jana Sangh, 1963.

MOOKERJEE, DR. SHYAMA PRASAD. *Presidential Address.* Delhi: Bharatiya Jana Sangh, 195.

RAMARAO, A. *Presidential Address.* Lucknow: Bharatiya Jana-Sangh, 1960.

UPADHYAYA, DENNDAYAL. *The Two Plans: Promises, Performance, Prospects.* Lucknow: Rashtradharma Prakasha Ltd., 1958.

———. *Your Vote.* Delhi: Bharatiya Jana Sangh, n.d.

BHASIN, PREM. *Congress and Socialism.* New Delhi: Praja Socialist Party, n.d.

FARIDI, A. J. *Confidential: To Members of the National Executive and PSP Members of the Legislature, Uttar Pradesh.* Lucknow: Privately printed, 1964.

JOSHI, LOK NATH. *The Farce of Discipline.* Lucknow: Uttar Pradesh Socialist Party, 1955.

LOHIA, DR. RAMMANOHAR. *Lohia's Letters.* Bangalore: Socialist Party, Mysore State, n.d.

MEHTA, ASOKA. *Democratic Socialism.* Bombay: Bharatiya Vidya Bhavan, 1959.

———. *The Political Mind of India.* Bombay: Madhu Limaye for the Socialist Party, 1952.

NARAYAN, JAYAPRAKASH. *Political Trends.* Bombay: Madhu Limaye for the Socialist Party, 1951.

PRAJA SOCIALIST PARTY. *Bangalore Resolutions, 1956.* New Delhi: Triloki Singh, General Secretary, Praja Socialist Party, n.d.

———. *Constitution and Rules.* New Delhi: Y. B. R. Murthy, 1959.

———. *Economic Situation in 1957.* New Delhi: Triloki Singh, General Secretary, Praja Socialist Party, 1957.

———. *Election Manifesto, 1957.* New Delhi: Triloki Singh, General Secretary, Praja Socialist Party, n.d.

———. *Election Manifesto, 1962.* Delhi: Praja Socialist Party, n.d.

———. *Facts on Lohia's Attempt at Disrupting the PSP.* New Delhi: Y. B. R. Murthy, 1955.

———. *J.P.–Lohia Talks: A Flashback.* New Delhi: Praja Socialist Party, n.d.

———. *Policy Statement Adopted by the Second National Conference of the Praja Socialist Party held at Gaya, December 26–30, 1955.* New Delhi: Y. B. R. Murthy, 1956.

———. *Political Perspective: Resolutions Adopted by the General Council of the Praja Socialist Party at Delhi, November 2–3, 1957.* New Delhi: Triloki Singh, General Secretary, Praja Socialist Party, 1957.

———. *Praja Socialist Party in Parliament.* New Delhi: The Office of the PSP Group in Parliament, 1962.

———. *PSP General Council Meeting: Background Papers.* New Delhi: Prem Bhasin, Jt. Secretary, Praja Socialist Party, [1962?].

———. *Report of the Special Convention of the Praja Socialist Party, Betul (Madhya Pradesh) June 14–18, 1953.* Bombay: R. P. Parasuram, 1953.

———. *Report of the Second National Conference of the Praja Socialist Party, Gaya, December 26–30, 1955.* New Delhi: Y. B. R. Murthy, n.d.

———. *Report of the Third National Conference of the Praja Socialist Party, Bangalore, November 25–28, 1956.* New Delhi: Y. B. R. Murthy, n.d.

———. *Report of the Fourth National Conference of the Praja Socialist Party, Poona, May 25–28, 1958.* Madras: Commercial Printing and Publishing House, n.d.

———. *Report of the Fifth National Conference of the Praja Socialist Party, Bombay, November 5–9, 1959.* New Delhi: Y. B. R. Murthy, n.d.

———. *Revitalizing the Organization.* New Delhi: Triloki Singh, General Secretary, Praja Socialist Party, 1957.

———. *Socialist Unity: Another Attempt Fails. . . .* New Delhi: Prem Bhasim, Praja Socialist Party, 1963.

SINGH, DAN. *An Appeal to the Chairman and All Members of the Praja Socialist Party*. Naini Tal, Uttar Pradesh: Dan Singh Vakil, [1955].

SINGH, HARI KISHORE. *A History of the Praja Socialist Party*. Lucknow: Narendra Prakashan, 1959.

[CONGRESS] SOCIALIST PARTY. *Report of the Sixth Annual Conference, Nasik, 1948*. Bombay: Suresh Desai, Secretary, Socialist Party, n.d.

————. *Report of the Special Convention of the Socialist Party, Pachmarhi, May 23–27, 1952*. Bombay: Madhu Limaye, n.d.

SOCIALIST PRTY. *Election Manifesto, 1962*. Hyderabad, 1962. Reprinted from *Mankind*, VI (January, 1962), 2–16.

————. *National Committee Resolutions: Hyderabad, Lucknow, Bangalore and Nagpur*. Hyderabad: Socialist Party, 1956.

————. *Statement of Principles*. Hyderabad: Socialist Party, 1956.

————. *Statement of Principles and Programmes*. Hyderabad: Socialist Party, 1956.

PUBLIC DOCUMENTS

GOVERNMENT OF INDIA. *Census of India, 1961*. Vol. XV: *Uttar Pradesh*, by P. P. Bhatnager. *Uttar Pradesh; General Population Tables*. Pt. II-A. Allahadbad: Manager of Publications, 1964.

————. *Census of India, 1951*. Vol. II: *Uttar Pradesh*. Parts A-E. Allahadbad: Superintendent, Printing and Stationery, 1953.

————. *Census of India, 1961. Paper No. 1 of 1962: Final Population Totals*. Delhi: Manager of Publications, 1962.

————. *Census of India. Paper No. 1 of 1963: Religion*. Delhi: Manager, Government of India Press, 1963.

————, Backward Classes Commission. *Report of the Backward Classes Commission*, 3 v. Delhi: Manager of Publications, 1956.

————, Election Commission. *Report on the First General Elections in India, 1951–52*. 2 vols. New Delhi: Government of India Press, 1955.

————, ————. *Report on the Second General Elections in India, 1957*. 2 vols. New Delhi, 1959.

————, Ministry of Information and Broadcasting. *India: A Reference Annual, 1963*. Delhi: Ministry of Information and Broadcasting, Government of India, 1963.

————, ————. *India, 1961: A Reference Annual*. Delhi: Ministry of Information and Broadcasting, Government of India, 1961.

OFFICE OF THE CHIEF ELECTORAL OFFICER, UTTAR PRADESH. *Results of the Third General Elections (1962) to the Uttar Pradesh Legisla-*

tive Assembly. Allahabad: Superintendent, Printing and Stationery, 1962.

INDIA. *Census of India, 1931.* Vol. XVIII, *United Provinces of Agra and Oudh,* by A. C. Turner. Pts. I–II. Allahabad: Superintendent, Printing and Stationery, 1933.

————. *District Gazetteer of the United Provinces of Agra and Oudh.* Allahabad: Government Press, 1900– .

BOOKS

ALI, SADIQ. *The General Elections 1957: A Survey.* New Delhi: All-India Congress Committee, 1959.

ANSARI, GHAUS. *Muslim Caste in Uttar Pradesh.* Lucknow: Ethnographic and Folk Culture Society, UP, 1960.

BAILEY, F. G. *Politics and Social Change: Orissa in 1959.* Berkeley and Los Angeles: University of California Press, 1963.

BAINES, A. *Ethnography of India.* Strasburg: Verlag Karl Trubner, 1912.

BAYLEY, DAVID H. *Preventive Detention in India.* Calcutta: Firma K. L. Mukhopadhyay, 1962.

BLUNT, EDWARD ARTHUR HENRY. *The Caste System of Northern India with Special Reference to the United Provinces of Agra and Oudh.* London: Oxford University Press, 1931.

BRASS, PAUL R. *Factional Politics in an Indian State.* Berkeley and Los Angeles: University of California Press, 1965.

BRECHER, MICHAEL. *Nehru: A Political Biography.* Abridged ed. London: Oxford University Press, 1959.

CROOKE, WILLIAM. *The North-Western Provinces of India, Their History, Ethnology and Administration.* London: Methuen, 1897.

————. *Tribes and Castes of the North-Western Provinces of Agra and Oudh.* 4 vols. Calcutta: Office of the Superintendent of Government Printing, 1906.

CURRAN, JEAN ALONZO, JR. *Militant Hinduism in Indian Politics: A Study of the RSS.* New York: Institute of Pacific Relations, 1951.

DAVIS, KINGSLEY. *The Population of India and Pakistan.* Princeton University Press, 1951.

DUBE, SHYAMA CHARAN. *India's Changing Villages.* London: Routledge and Kegan Paul, Ltd., 1958.

ELLIOT, SIR HENRY MIERS. *Memoirs on the History, Folk-lore, and Distribution of the Races of the North-Western Provinces of India.* London: Trubner, 2 v., 1869.

GUPTA, SHRI VED PRAKASH. *Franchise in India.* Bombay: All-India Institute of Local Self-Government, 1965.

HARRISON, SELIG S. *India: The Most Dangerous Decades.* Princeton: Princeton University Press, 1960.

HUSAIN, S. ABID. *Indian Culture.* Bombay: Asia Publishing House, 1963.

HUTTON, JOHN HENRY. *Caste in India.* Oxford: University Press, 1946.

KABIR, HUMAYUN. *The Indian Heritage.* 3d. ed. Bombay: Asia Publishing House, 1955.

KHEDKAR, VITHAL KRISHNAJI, AND KHEDKAR, RAGHUNATH VITHAL. *The Divine Heritage of the Yadavas.* Allahabad: Parmanand, 1959.

KOGEKAR, S. V., AND PARK, RICHARD L. *Reports on the Indian General Elections, 1951–52.* Bombay: Popular Book Depot, 1956.

MAJUMDAR, D. N. *Caste and Communication in an Indian Village.* Bombay: Asia Publishing House, 1958.

——— (ed.). *Rural Profiles.* Lucknow: Ethnographic and Folk Culture Society, U.P., 1955.

MARRIOTT, MCKIM. *Caste Ranking and Community Structure in Five Regions of India and Pakistan.* Deccan College Monograph Series No. 23. Poona, 1960.

———. "Changing Channels of Cultural Transmission in Indian Civilization," in *Proceedings of the American Ethnological Society, Annual Spring Meeting*, 1959, pp. 66–72.

——— (ed.). *Village India: Studies in the Little Community.* Bombay: Asia Publishing House, 1961.

———. "Western Medicine in Northern India," in Benjamin D. Paul (ed.), *Health, Culture and Community.* New York: Russell Sage Foundation, 1955.

MAYER, ADRIAN C. *Caste and Kinship in Central India.* Berkeley and Los Angeles: University of California Press, 1960.

MAYER, ALBERT. *Pilot Project, India: The Story of Rural Development at Etawah, Uttar Pradesh.* Berkeley and Los Angeles: University of California Press, 1958.

MOORE, FRANK J. *Land Tenure Legislation in Uttar Pradesh.* South Asia Studies, Institute of East Asiatic Studies, University of California. Berkeley, 1959.

MORRIS-JONES, W. H. *Parliament in India.* London: Longmans, Green and Company, 1957.

NADWI, ABUL HASAN ALI. *Muslims in India.* Lucknow: Academy of Islamic Research and Publications, Nadwatul Ulema, n.d.

NANAVATI, MANILAL B., AND VAKIL, C. N. (eds.). *Group Prejudices in India: A Symposium.* Bombay: Vora & Co., Ltd., 1951.

NEALE, WALTER C. *Economic Change in Rural India: Land Tenure and Reform in Uttar Pradesh, 1800–1955.* New Haven: Yale University Press, 1962.

PALMER, NORMAN D. *The Indian Political System.* Boston: Houghton Mifflin Company, 1961.

PHILIPS, C. H. (ed.). *Politics and Society in India.* London: George Allen and Unwin, Ltd., 1963.

POPLAI, SUNDER LAL (ed.). *National Politics and 1957 Elections in India.* Delhi: Metropolitan Book, 1957.

RETZLAFF, RALPH H. *A Case Study of Panchayats in a North Indian Village.* Berkeley: Center for South Asia Studies, University of California, 1959.

SINGER, MILTON. *Traditional India: Structure and Change.* Philadelphia: American Folklore Society, 1959.

SMITH, DONALD EUGENE. *India as a Secular State.* Princeton: Princeton University Press, 1963.

SPATE, OSKAR H. K. *India and Pakistan: A General and Regional Geography.* New York: E. P. Dutton, 1957.

SRINIVAS, M. N. (ed.). *Caste in Modern India.* Bombay: Asia Publishing House, 1962.

—— (ed.). *India's Villages.* Calcutta: West Bengal Government Press, 1955.

SURI, SURINDAR. *1962 Elections: A Political Analysis.* New Delhi: Sudha Publications Pvt. Ltd., 1962.

FISHER, MARGARET W. *The Indian Experience with Democratic Elections.* Indian Press Digests, Monograph Series No. 3, Institute of International Studies, University of California. Berkeley, 1956.

WEINER, MYRON. *Party Politics in India: The Development of a Multi-Party System.* Princeton: Princeton University Press, 1957.

——. *Political Change in South Asia.* Calcutta: Firma K. L. Mukhopadhyay, 1963.

——. *Politics of Scarcity: Public Pressure and Political Response in India.* Chicago: University of Chicago Press, 1962.

WISER, W. H. *The Hindu Jajmani System.* Lucknow: Lucknow Publishing House, 1958.

ARTICLES, PERIODICALS, AND UNPUBLISHED MATERIALS

AHMAD, ENAYAT. "Rural Settlement Types in the Uttar Pradesh," *Annals of the Association of American Geographers,* XLII (June, 1952), 223–246.

Asian Recorder. Vols. I–IX (1955–1964).

BAILEY, F. G. "Politics in Orissa," *Economic Weekly* (Bombay), Vol. XI. Series of nine articles in consecutive issues: August 29, September 12, 19, 26; October 3, 10, 17, 24; November 7, 1959; pp. 1203–8, 1271–76, 1297–1302, 1331–38, 1369–75, 1403–8, 1433–40, 1469–76, 1503–10.

BHATT, G. S. "The Chamar of Lucknow," *Eastern Anthropologist,* Vol. VIII (September, 1954).

BRASS, PAUL R. "An Industrial Labor Constituency: Kanpur," *Economic Weekly* (Bombay), special number, July, 1962, pp. 1111–18.

CHAUHAN, D. S. "Caste and Occupation in Agra City," *Economic Weekly,* XII (July 23, 1960), 1147–49.

COHN, BERNARD S. "Madhopur Revisited," *Economic Weekly,* XI (1959), 963–966.

————. "The Initial British Impact on India: A Case Study of the Banaras Region," *Journal of Asian Studies,* Vol. XIX (August, 1960).

————. "Political Systems in Eighteenth Century India: The Banaras Region." Paper presented at meeting of the Association for Asian Studies, Chicago, March 29, 1961. (Mimeographed.)

————. "Some Notes on Law and Change in North India," *Economic Development and Cultural Change,* Vol. VIII (October, 1959).

DUBE, S. C. "Cultural Factors in Rural Community Development," *Journal of Asian Studies,* Vol. XVI (January, 1956).

GOULD, HAROLD A. "Sanskritization and Westernization," *Economic Weekly,* XIII (1961), 945–950.

————. "The Peasant Village: Centrifugal or Centripetal?" *Eastern Anthropologist,* XIII (1959), 3–16.

————. "Studies in Voting Behavior. Traditionalism and Modernism in UP: Faizabad Constituency," *Economic Weekly,* XIV (1962), 1343–50.

GUPTA, SISIR. "The Political Mind of Uttar Pradesh," *Indian Affairs Record,* II (May, 1956), 5–8.

————. "Islam as a Factor in Pakistani Foreign Relations," *India Quarterly,* XVIII (1962), 230–253.

————. "Moslems in Indian Politics," *India Quarterly,* XVIII (1962), 355–381.

HART, HENRY C. "Urban Politics in Bombay: The Meaning of Community," *Economic Weekly,* special number, June, 1960, pp. 983–988.

Hindustan Times. Daily. Lucknow. 1962–1964.

"India's Second General Election: Congress Receives a Warning," *The World Today,* XIII (June, 1957), 232–241.

Janata. Weekly. Bombay. Vols. XII–XX (1957–1965).

KHARE, R. S. "The Kanya-Kubja Brahmins and Their Caste Organization," *Southwestern Journal of Anthropology*, XVI (1960), 348–367.

KOTHARI, RAJNI. "India's Political Take-off," *Economic Weekly*, XIV (February, 1962), 149–153.

MAHAR, PAULINE MOLLER. "Changing Caste Ideology in a North Indian Village," *Journal of Social Issues*, XIV (1958), 51–65.

————. "Changing Religious Practices of an Untouchable Caste," *Economic Development and Cultural Change*, VIII (April, 1960), 279–287.

MARRIOTT, McKIM. "Interactional and Attributional Theories of Caste Ranking," *Man in India*, XXXIX (April–June, 1956), 92–107.

————. "Social Structure and Change in a UP Village," *Economic Weekly*, IV (1952), 869–874.

————. "Technological Change in Overdeveloped Rural Areas," *Economic Development and Cultural Change*, I (1952), 261–272.

MAYER, ADRIAN C. "Some Hierarchical Aspects of Caste," *Southwestern Journal of Anthropology*, XII (1956), 117–144.

————. "The Dominant Caste in a Region of Central India," *Southwestern Journal of Anthropology*, XIV (1958), 407–427.

MEYER, RALPH C. "Socio-economic Background of Uttar Pradesh Legislators." (Unpublished data, collected 1963–1964.)

MORRIS-JONES, W. H. "Indian Elections," *Political Quarterly*, XXIII (1952), 235–249.

National Herald. Daily. Lucknow. 1956–1964.

OPLER, MORRIS EDWARD. "Economic, Political and Social Change in a Village of North Central India," *Human Organization*, XI (1952), 5–12.

————. "The Extensions of an Indian Village," *Journal of Asian Studies*. XVI (1956), 5–10.

————, AND SINGH, R. D. "Two Villages of Eastern UP: An Analysis of Similarities and Differences," *American Anthropologist*, LIV (1952), 179–90.

Organizer. Weekly. Delhi. 1960–1965.

PARK, RICHARD LEONARD. "Indian Democracy and the General Election," *Pacific Affairs*, XXV (1952), 130–139.

————. "Indian Election Results," *Far Eastern Survey*, XXI (1952), 61–70.

————. "India's General Elections," *Far Eastern Survey*, XXI (1952), 1–8.

PATEL, TARA. "Caste as a Factor in Social Tensions," *Journal of Social Sciences*, supplement, 1961, pp. 73–80.

Pioneer. Daily. Lucknow. 1963–1964.

PRADHAN, MAHESH CHANDRA. "Socio-political Organization of the Jats of Meerut Division." (Unpublished doctoral dissertation, School of Oriental and African Studies, University of London, 1961).

"Profiles of the Third General Election," *Political Science Review,* II (October, 1963), i–lxii.

RUDOLPH, LLOYD I., AND RUDOLPH, SUZANNE H. "Political Role of India's Caste Associations," *Pacific Affairs,* Vol. XXXIII (January, 1960).

RUDOLPH, SUZANNE H. "Consensus and Conflict in Indian Politics," *World Politics,* XIII (April, 1961), 388–399.

SARAN, A. K. "Emotional Integration of India," *Journal of Social Sciences,* supplement, 1961, pp. 23–43.

SCHWARTZBERG, JOSEPH E. "The Geography of Caste in the North Indian Plain." Paper presented at the University of Chicago Conference on Social Structure and Social Change in India, June 3–5, 1965. (Mimeographed.)

SHARMA, K. N. "Occupational Mobility of Castes in a North Indian Village," *Southwestern Journal of Anthropology,* XVII (1961), 146–164.

SILVERBERG, JAMES. "Caste-Ascribed 'Status' Versus Caste-Irrelevant Roles," *Man in India,* XXXIX (1959), 148–162.

SINGER, MILTON B. "Cultural Pattern of Indian Civilization," *Journal of Asian Studies,* XV (1956), 23–36.

SINGH, R. D. "Unity of a North Indian Village," *Journal of Asian Studies,* XV (1956), 10–19.

SINHA, D. P. "Caste Dynamics: A Case from Uttar Pradesh," *Man in India,* XL (January–March, 1960), 19–29.

SRINIVAS, M. N. "Changing Institutions and Values in Modern India," *Economic Weekly,* XIV (1962), 131–137.

————. "The Dominant Caste in Rampura," *American Anthropologist,* LXI (February, 1959), 1–16.

SRINIVASAN, N. "Village Government in India," *Journal of Asian Studies,* XV (1956), 201–213.

SRIVASTAVA, S. K. "Cultural Integration and Indian National Character," *Journal of Social Sciences* (Supplement, 1961), pp. 115–140.

Statesman. Daily. New Delhi. 1962–1964.

STEVENSON, H. N. C. "Status Evaluation in the Hindu Caste System," *Journal of the Royal Anthropological Institute,* LXXXIV (1954), 45–65.

Thought. Weekly. Delhi. Vols. XIV–XVI (1962–1964).

TINKER, HUGH RUSSELL. "Authority and Community in Village India," *Pacific Affairs,* XXXII (December, 1959), 354–375.

INDEX

Activists: political mobilization, 88, 95; party mobilization, 97, 100, 101, 102; in Pratapgarh, 118-120, 126-128; in Bhitauli, 130-141 *passim*, 143-144; in Rudauli, 145-146; in Farrukhabad, 151, 154-155; in Saurikh, 154-157, 159; in Moradabad Rural, 170, 175-177, 179, 184-185; in Karchana, 192-194, 196; types of, 193-194, 237-238, 240-241, 252-253, 274; in agitations, 221, 248; in Rae Bareli, 239-240; in Agra Jan Sangh, 244-245; in PSP split, 258

Agitations: Lohia Socialists, 41-42, 248, 259; in political mobilization, 87, 89; in building process, 109-110, 205, 221, 248; in Bhitauli, 139-140; in Saurikh, 155; communications, 221

Agra, city, 22, 243-245 *passim*

Agrawal, Baloji, 243-245

Ahar. *See* Yadav

Ahir. *See* Yadav

AJGAR, 27

Aligarh Muslim University, 31

Allahabad, city, 22, 30, 51, 186, 189, 252

Ambition, 243-245

Ansari caste, 28, 134. *See also* Julaha

Arya Samaj, 8, 80, 93-94

Asrey, Ram, 133-141 *passim*

Bania caste: described, 27; MLA's, 56, 105; in Pratapgarh Jan Sangh, 118, 129, 275; in Rudauli Jan Sangh, 142-147 *passim*; in Allahabad, 188; caste rivalries, 200, 242-243; in Bareilly city, 242-243. *See also* Caste, elite

Bara Banki. *See* Districts

Bareilly (city), 242-243

Bharatiya Jan Sangh: history, 31, 34-36; program, 35; characteristics, 35-36, 199-200; MLA's, 49-100 *passim*; in Pratapgarh, 117-129, 232-233; in Bhitauli, 138; in Rudauli, 142-149, 223; in Saurikh, 151-154, 159, 160, 233-234; in Moradabad Rural, 171, 174; in Bareilly city, 242-243; in Agra, 243-245. *See also* Caste; Factionalism, Identification; Ideology

Bhitauli. *See* Constituencies

Bhumihar caste, 28, 229, 252

Block Development Committee, 116, 137, 140, 160, 226-227 232-234 *passim*

Block politics, 155, 160, 174-175, 179-180, 226-227, 232-234 *passim*

Brahmin caste: described, 27, 29, 195; MLA's 55-56, 105, 254; political mobilization, 90, 202, 270; rivalries, 91, 125, 200-204, 249, 258-259; in Pratapgarh (Congress), 117-129 *passim*, 232; in Bhitauli (Congress), 130, 132, 133; in Rudauli, 143, 144, 146, 148; in Farrukhabad (Congress, Jan Sangh), 150, 151, 154; in Saurikh (Congress, Jan Sangh), 156, 159-160, 162, in Moradabad, 170, 171, 175; in Allahabad, 188, 189; in Karchana (Congress, Praja Socialist Party), 195, 235; in Rae Bareli (Lohia Socialists), 240; in Jaunpur (Praja Socialists), 269. *See also* Caste, elite

British policies, 23-24

Broker role, 45, 52, 155, 185, 193-196, 212

Building process: defined, 3; hypotheses, 9-12, 15-16, 197-206, 270-276